"安徽大学211工程"教材建设与出版资助项目

实用英语技能训练教程（上）

（第二版）

主　编　张同乐　胡学文
副主编　曹杰旺　郝涂根　高玉兰
编写人员　张同乐　王蒙　张虹
　　　　　程鹏　李琳　张颖

北京大学出版社
PEKING UNIVERSITY PRESS

图书在版编目(CIP)数据

实用英语技能训练教程.上/张同乐,胡学文主编. —2版. —北京:北京大学出版社,2014.5
(大学英语立体化网络化创新系列教材)
ISBN 978-7-301-24198-1

Ⅰ.实… Ⅱ.①张…②胡… Ⅲ.英语—高等学校—教材 Ⅳ.H31

中国版本图书馆CIP数据核字(2014)第086774号

书　　　　名:	实用英语技能训练教程(上)(第二版)
著作责任者:	张同乐　胡学文　主编
责 任 编 辑:	黄瑞明
标 准 书 号:	ISBN 978-7-301-24198-1 / H·3514
出 版 发 行:	北京大学出版社
地　　　　址:	北京市海淀区成府路205号　100871
网　　　　址:	http://www.pup.cn　新浪官方微博:@北京大学出版社
电　　　　话:	邮购部 62752015　发行部 62750672　编辑部 62754382　出版部 62754962
电 子 信 箱:	zbing@pup.pku.edu.cn
印　　刷　　者:	北京大学印刷厂
经　　销　　者:	新华书店
	787毫米×1092毫米　16开本　14.75印张　380千字
	2010年3月第1版
	2014年5月第2版　2015年7月第2次印刷
定　　　　价:	36.00元(配有光盘)

未经许可,不得以任何方式复制或抄袭本书之部分或全部内容。
版权所有,侵权必究
举报电话:010-62752024　电子信箱:fd@pup.pku.edu.cn

序

　　安徽大学外语学院张同乐教授的新作《实用英语技能训练教程》即将出版,谨在此表示衷心祝贺。

　　张同乐教授热爱国家外语教育事业,在第一线长期从事大学英语和研究生英语教学,曾数次获得安徽大学优秀教师奖,2009年获该校和安徽省教学名师称号,这是我们应当向他学习的,但张同乐教授更可贵之处在于他能做到教学科研两不误。他不仅编写了十余部有关英语听说读写技能和测试的教材和参考书籍,而且写了三十余篇论文。值得注意的是他的论文除结合常规的英语教学外,不少论文涉及语言学、语法学、翻译学、跨文化学,以至文学题材。显然,这要求张同乐教授要有扎实的外语功底,更需要有在繁忙教学之余挤出时间,埋头案桌的毅力。对比之下,有的老师甘当教书匠,却缺乏干一番事业的雄心壮志;有的老师心有余而力不足,知其然而不知其所以然。在这个意义上,榜样的力量是无穷的,张同乐老师以自己的行动表明对高校大学英语教师的这个要求是可以实现的,当然这也是对英语专业教师的友谊挑战。

　　那么,拿在我们手中的《教程》究竟有哪些特色呢?首先,《教程》融听说读写译于一体,这体现了当代对语言的全面认识,弥补了外语教学中过度地把听说与读写分家,把语言技能和语言知识分家的缺陷,这就是说,外语教学中,有的地方、有的学校出现了不是读写妨碍了听说,导致了聋哑病,就是听说挤走了读写,培养的会是文盲。第二,从《教程》可以看到,作者高瞻远瞩,注意到理论知识与技能训练的互补,这反映了当代先进的体验学习理论,我们既要强调学生的实际参与和亲身体验,也要引导学生对所学内容结合语境进行理解、分析和比较,进入初步的感悟阶段,最后升华为知识。例如,作者希望读者阅后能举一反三,实现对所学英语的真正感悟。最后,作者告诫我们学习外语既要讲究实效,也要持之以恒。相信读者会领悟作者这一番肺腑之言。

胡壮麟

北京大学蓝旗营

2010年元月末

前　言

　　本教程非应景之作,而是融听、说、读、写、译之理论知识与技能训练的小百科。

　　作为国际交流的通用语言——英语,近30年来受到教育主管部门的高度重视并在国人间掀起阵阵学习热潮。但纵观其学习成效,事倍功半者甚多。究其因,除学习环境因素外,学习策略、学习内容、理论指导、技能训练等不足则是学习者通往成功之路的几大障碍。

　　本书正是为解决上述问题而编,希望能为英语学习者提供一种学习方法,送上必需的营养食粮。

　　本教程以大学非英语专业本科生及研究生为对象,以讲解理论、传播文化为主线,辅以翔实的语言素材,经典的句法表达,力求使读者阅后能举一反三,收事半功倍之效。

　　本教程分上下两册,内容覆盖听、说、读、写、译五项。为拓宽学生的知识面,编者特意编排了实用英语表达900句篇、口译技能篇和实用词汇篇等,使本教程更具实用性和可操作性。

　　本教程自2010年问世以来,深受读者好评。本次修订对教程结构进行了微调,篇幅上亦增添部分针对性较强或删减部分不甚实用的内容,旨在使教程日臻完善。但因编者学识有限,绠短汲深,不当之处在所难免,恳请同行专家及读者不吝指正。

　　古人云:"骐骥一跃,不能十步,驽马十驾,功在不舍。"学习英语的成功秘诀不在一蹴即致,而在你持之以恒。希望本教程成为阅读者坚持不懈学习过程中的良师益友。

张同乐
2014年3月10日

目 录

实用英语900句 …………………………………………………………… 1

常用句型100例 …………………………………………………………… 37

阅读技能与训练 ………………………………………………………… 99
  一、阅读意义/99
  二、阅读技巧/100
    1. 设定积极的目标主动阅读(Setting up a positive goal to read initiatively)/100
    2. 测试阅读速度和理解力(Measuring reading rate and comprehension)/102
    3. 不良的阅读习惯(Bad reading habits)/105
    4. 训练眼睛的移动(Training eye movement)/106
    5. 协调的注视节奏(Harmonious fixation)/108
    6. 确定文章的体裁 (Types of writing)/109
    7. 体裁：确定阅读的重点(The focus of reading of different types)/113
    8. 区分事实和看法 (Distinguishing facts and opinions)/125
  三、图式理论在阅读理解中的应用/139
  四、全国大学英语四、六级考试新题型简介/142

听力技能与训练 165
  一、语音/165
  二、听力习惯及文化背景/168
  三、听力主要内容及技巧/168

实用英语900句

（常用语、警句、名句、谚语、名诗等）

1. How are you (doing)? /How is it going? / How are you getting along? / How is everything with you? /How is the world treating you? / How is your life? 您好吗？/近来如何？

2. Pretty good! /Couldn't be better. /Can't complain. / In good shape. / So far so good. /Not so bad. / I'm doing all right./I'm getting by. / Nothing much.
很好。/ 还不错/ 凑合着。到目前都还好/ 没什么。

3. It's nice (a pleasure) to see you. /I'm glad (pleased, happy) to meet you. /What a pleasant surprise to meet you here. / This is a nice surprise. 见到你真高兴/ 见到你真令人惊喜。

4. What's up? You've got stars in your eyes. 怎么了？你看起来满面春风。

5. Fancy meeting you here! / It's realy a surprise to meet you here. 真没想到在这儿遇见你。

6. I ran into him. /I bumped into him. 我偶然碰到了他。

7. Time is really flying by! /How the time has flown by! 时间过得真快呀！

8. It's really an honor/a pleasure for me to meet him. 我很荣幸能认识他。

9. I've heard so much about you. 久仰，久仰。

10. You can say that again. 我同意你的建议。/我赞同。

11. Would you do me a favor? / May I ask a favor of you? 你能帮我个忙吗？

12. Would you like me to give you a hand? / Can I be of any help? 我能为你效劳吗？

13. I appreciate all you did very much. / I'm very grateful to you for your kindness. / I don't know how to express my thanks. 万分感谢！

14. Thank you ever so much for your hospitality. 十分感谢你的盛情款待。

15. I feel I'm in your debt. 我觉得我欠了你的人情。

16. No skin off my back. 举手之劳。

17. Would you please accept my apology? 你能原谅我吗？

18. If you feel really sorry, I'll accept your apology. /I'll give you a break.
如果你能认识到错误，我原谅你。

19. A flood of emotion has flowed through my mind. 我是百感交集。

20. To me, that's the last straw at that time. 对我来说，那时我已是忍无可忍了。

21. It left me with a lot of hard feelings. 因为这件事我有了心结。

22. You are getting on my nerves. Stop it. / Don't bother me. 你别再来烦我了。

23. It's none of your business. 你别多管闲事。

24. Did you get up on the wrong side of the bed? 你心情不好吗？

25. It made my hair stand up on end. 那使我毛骨悚然。

26. Maybe he went too far. / Maybe he went overboard. 他好像太过分了。
27. I've got butterflies in my stomach. 我紧张得很。
28. In my opinion, that's much ado about nothing. 我认为,那是小题大做了。
29. Don't let me down. 不要让我失望。
30. I wish you wouldn't split hairs. 你别这么斤斤计较。
31. If I follow you rightly, then... 如果我没领会错的话……
32. We can't live up to his expectation. 我们无法满足他的期望。
33. What's meant to be will be. / Whatever will be, will be. 一切顺其自然。
34. That's driving me crazy. Who told you that? 这可把我逼疯了。谁告诉你的?
35. There are no extensions of time in life. 生命短暂,不能延长。
36. The world is a lot tougher than you think. 世事无常,不是我们想象的那么容易。
37. Life is too short to do things you'll regret. 人生苦短,别做后悔之事。
38. You know everything has its price. 天生我材必有用。
39. Take it easy. / Hold your horses. / Stay cool. / Keep your shirt on. / Calm down. 别紧张。
40. You'd better mind your p's and q's. / Mind your manners. 注意你的言行举止。
41. Don't say one thing and do another. 别言行不一。
42. Don't wear out your welcome. 别在别人家待得太久招人烦。
43. He is doing well with the work and environment. / He got into the swing of things. 他已适应了这里的工作氛围。
44. Nobody can make heads or tails of it. 谁也无法理出头绪来。
45. We have good chemistry. 我们心意相通。
46. We know what each other's thinking. / We are speaking the same language. / We are always connected. / Great minds run in the same channels. 我们心有灵犀。
47. You look as if you just won the jackpot. 你看上去好像中了头彩。
48. How does this idea strike you? 这个主意怎样?
49. You are kidding me. / You are teasing me. / You are pulling my leg. 你在开我的玩笑。
50. He told me a white lie. 他撒了一个善意的谎。
51. How many lies did you tell? / How long was your nose? 你撒了多少次谎?
52. Never make, but break. 成事不足,败事有余。
53. Life is not all roses. 生活并不都是鲜花美酒。
54. We'll certainly have some ups and downs. 我们肯定会遇到各种艰难险阻。
55. Complaints are always negative numbers in human life. 抱怨对人生永远是个负数。
56. Every tide has its ebb. 兴盛之日必有衰退之时。
57. Stretch your imagination. 发挥你的想象吧。
58. Don't beat around the bush! 说话别绕圈子。
59. What I am trying to say here is that ... / The main point I'm trying to make is... 我想要说的就是……
60. Books and friends should be few but good. 读书如交友,应求少而精。
61. The pros outweigh the cons. 正面理由超过反面理由。

62. As to whether it is a blessing or a curse, however, people take different attitudes.
至于它是祝福还是诅咒，人们持有不同的态度。

63. Lately I have been burning the candle at both ends. 最近我总是熬到半夜。

64. It seems to me, both views are lop-sided. 依我看，双方的观点似乎都有片面性。

65. There is probably some truth on both sides. 也许双方都有一定的道理。

66. You have to be full-hearted for it. There is a light at the end of the tunnel after all.
你得有信心，否极泰来嘛。

67. The longest night will have an end. 否极泰来。

68. How about going to the cinema with me? 一起看电影怎么样？

69. I'm tied up. /I wouldn't be able to make it. 我有事走不开。

70. I'd like to say yes, but that's just impossible. 我是心有余而力不足。

71. Do you feel like going to that new restaurant this evening?
今晚去那个新开的饭店吃饭如何？

72. I'd be very happy to accept your invitation. / It would give me the greatest pleasure to accept your invitation. 我非常高兴接受你的邀请。

73. Great! /Fantastic! /Marvelous! /Incredible! /Terrific! /Superb! /Good! 太好了！

74. Could you make it another time? 下次如何？

75. Gee, thanks. You made my day. 你这么说我真高兴。

76. You're sharp. /You're smart. 你很聪明。

77. Your presentation is smashing. 你的表现十分出色。

78. I think you deserve the highest praise. 我认为你应该得到最高的赞赏。

79. You're a superb teacher. /You're a smashing teacher. 你是个很棒的老师。

80. He thinks highly of you. / He has a high opinion of you. 他对你评价很高。

81. You're really capable and have good taste. 你真能干，也有很好的鉴赏力。

82. All the credit goes to you. 这得归功于您呀！

83. Cheer up! /Pull yourself together! /Get a hold of yourself! /Be of good cheer!
打起精神来！

84. You're nearly there. /You're halfway there. 你就要成功了！

85. You have our backing. /We support you. 我们支持你。

86. The sea has fish for everyone. 人人都有机会。

87. Every man is the architect of his own fortune. 每个人都是他自己命运的建筑师。

88. Come on. Be a man. /Be a good sport and have a try. 拿出点勇气来。

89. Don't be a chicken. 不要畏惧。

90. There's no reason to feel discouraged at all. / There's no reason to lose confidence in you.
根本没有理由感到气馁。

91. Time is life, time is speed, and time is strength.
时间就是生命，时间就是速度，时间就是力量。

92. Lose an hour in the morning, and you will spend all day looking for it. 一日之计在于晨。

93. Men talk of killing time, while time quietly kills them.
人们谈论着消磨时间，与此同时，时间也在悄悄地消蚀人们的生命。

94. If you want to succeed in your career, you must value the time and make full use of it.
想成就事业就必须珍惜时间,充分利用时间。

95. Age is a matter of feeling, not of years. 年龄只是感觉问题,而不是岁月问题。

96. Seize now and here the hour that is, nor trust some later day! 只争朝夕,勿待明日。

97. At that time we were all dying of curiosity. 当时我们都好奇得很。

98. If someone tried to blackmail me, I would tell the police.
如果有人企图敲诈我,我就向警方告发。

99. Shakespeare says, "Neither a borrower nor a lender be."
莎士比亚说:"既不要向人借钱,也不要借钱给人。"

100. Money is not everything, but without money we are nothing.
金钱不是万能的,但没有金钱是万万不能的。

101. He is a chronic complainer. 他老是牢骚满腹。

102. He is Jack of all trades and master of none. 他样样都会一点,可又样样都不精通。

103. It is no use doing what you like; you have got to like what you do.
不能爱哪行干哪行,要干哪行爱哪行。

104. Things will work out in the end. /Everything will work itself out. / Everything will fall into place. 事情最终都会解决的。

105. Living without an aim is like sailing without a compass. 生活无目标,犹如航海无指南针。

106. The important thing in life is to have a great aim, and the determination to attain.
人生要事在于确立伟大的目标与实现这目标的决心。

107. Art is long, but life is short. 人生有涯,而学无涯。

108. Working without a plan is like building a house without a blueprint.
工作没有计划就像建房子没有蓝图。

109. That suits me all right. 这正合我的胃口。

110. Maybe you can give me some feedback on this problem. 或许你能给点儿建议。

111. It's a good idea, but I'm afraid it's impracticable. 这个主意是好,但恐怕行不通。

112. Don't be so mean (unkind). /Don't be so bitchy. 别这么刻薄(令人讨厌)

113. Don't be so stuck-up. /Don't be self-important. /Don't be so arrogant. 不要那么自大。

114. We shouldn't speak ill of others. /Don't speak bad things about other people.
不应背后说别人的坏话。

115. Make up your mind after thinking it over carefully. /Make up your decision after thinking again and again. 三思后而行。

116. Don't go back on your word. /Don't break your promise. 不要言而无信。

117. There isn't much merit in doing things like this. 这样做也得不到太多的好处。

118. Don't attempt more than you are capable of. /Don't do what is beyond you. /Don't bite off more than you can chew. 做力所能及的事。

119. He is all brawn and no brain. (Full belies makes empty skulls.) 他四肢发达,头脑简单。

120. We shouldn't judge a book by its cover. 人不可貌相。

121. Don't count your chickens before they are hatched. 不要高兴得太早。

122. Don't give way to feelings. 不要感情用事。

123. I'm ready to accept the failure. /I'm ready to throw in the towel. 我已准备承认失败。

124. Do what you can, with what you have, where you are. 直面现实,凭你所有,尽力而为。

125. Try and look on the bright side. 尽量朝好的方面看吧。

126. We were filled with admiration to his courage. 我们对他的勇敢充满崇敬之心。

127. If you don't follow my advice, you will be sorry. / You'll suffer a great loss.
    如果你不听我的建议,你会后悔的。/你会损失很大的。

128. Let bygones be bygones. 过去的事就让它过去吧!

129. You are really potato-headed. 你真是个傻瓜。

130. Does rock 'n' roll grab you? 摇滚乐对你有吸引力吗?

131. This tape serves my purpose. 这盘磁带正合我意。

132. I advised him not to copy other's homework. But he said I am meddlesome.
    我劝他别抄他人的作业,他反而怪我多事。

133. You should give him a dose of his own medicine. 你应该以其人之道还治其人之身。

134. So he mistakes your kindness as ill intentions. 那他真是把你的好心当做驴肝肺了。

135. I didn't mean to blame you. I was only to take the matter as it stands. If I hurt you, please beg your pardon. 我并不是故意指责你,我只是就事论事,如果我伤害了你,请你原谅。

136. This is for your ears only. 我只讲给你一人听。

137. Keep it under your hat. 不要告诉别人。

138. This is just between you and me. 这事是天知、地知、你知、我知。

139. You can't keep it a secret. Your eyes will give you away.
    你无法藏住这个秘密。你的眼睛会泄密的。

140. I have to work against the clock to get my report done. 我得争分夺秒完成这份报告。

141. Surfing is what turns me on. 我觉得冲浪很刺激。

142. I have moonlighting jobs sometimes. 我晚上有时做兼职。

143. We were really under the gun with that task. / We had a hard time due to being pressed by that work. 那事把我们忙死了。

144. It pays not to put off work. 多亏没有往后推迟。

145. Stress is called the silent killer. Be careful. 压力是无形的杀手,小心啊!

146. If we keep on like this, it's going to be neither here nor there.
    如果我们继续这样做,早晚会出问题。

147. He plays multiple roles in our office. / He wears many hats in our office.
    他在办公室一个人做几个人的活。

148. A person's value (self-worth) is determined by how much he values himself.
    一个人的价值在于他是如何评价自己的。

149. He survived the trouble. 他闯过了难关。

150. He is always painstakingly at his books. 他总是埋头苦读。

151. Independent thinking is an absolute necessity in study. 独立思考在学习中是绝对必要的。

152. I am very sorry that the pressure of other occupations has prevented me from sending an earlier reply to your letter. 近来忙于各种事务,未能早些复信,深感抱歉。

153. My conscience told me that I deserved no extraordinary politeness.
凭良心讲,你待我礼貌有加,我却受之有愧。

154. It is said that a person needs just three things to be truly happy in the world: someone to love, something to do and something to hope for.
据说,人活在世上真正的幸福只需三条:有所爱、有所为、有所盼。

155. There are only three types of people: those who make things happen, those who watch things happen and those who say, "What happened?"
世上只有三种人:实干者、旁观者、打探者。

156. Nothing is more deceitful than the appearance of humility. 谦卑的外表是最易使人上当的。

157. A man of learning is not always a man of wisdom. 有学问的人并非都是有智慧的人。

158. The good and the beautiful do not always go together. 善和美未必总是兼备。

159. You ought to know better than to do such things. 你不该做这种事。

160. It is not seldom that the unexpected happens. 出乎意料的事时常发生。

161. I know but too well to hold my tongue. 我深知少说为妙。

162. We cannot recommend this book too strongly. 这本书很好,无论如何推荐,也不过分。

163. Justice must not be denied to anyone. 无论对谁都要公道。

164. Health is not valued till sickness comes. 病后方知健康之可贵。

165. Variety is the spice of life. 生活的趣味就在于丰富多彩。

166. Happiness often comes in small grains. 幸福总是以点点滴滴的形式出现。

167. It not seldom happens that what seems to be impossible is made possible.
似乎不可能的事变得可能,并非少见。

168. Let's escape from the hustle and bustle of the city.
让我们暂时摆脱都市生活的嘈杂和喧闹吧。

169. I can't keep up with the fashion. /I can't keep track of the fashion. 我落伍了。

170. Behavior is a mirror in which every one shows his image.
行为是面镜子,映射出每个人的形象。

171. I didn't make an all-out effort to do that. /I didn't stand in the line of fire to do that.
我没有尽全力去做那件事。

172. It's entirely at your disposal. / You are at liberty to use this as you please.
你想怎么做,就怎么做。

173. This project is pressing, but the other one can wait. 这件事要紧,那件事不用那么急。

174. I have to cut down on expenses. /I have to tighten my belt. 我必须勒紧腰带。

175. He made it by the skin of his teeth. 他勉强合格了。

176. I have a better idea. Let's do rock, scissors, paper.
我有个更好的主意,我们来用石头、剪刀、布来决定。

177. Let's decide it by flipping (tossing) a coin. 我们用抛硬币来决定。

178. They clapped their hands yelling, "Encore!" 他们鼓掌并大喊:"再来一个!"

179. This time he missed the boat. 这一回他坐失良机了。

180. How can we live on such a small salary? /How can I live on this shoestring budget?
这么少的钱怎么生活?

181. It's just one of those days. You'll be yourself tomorrow.
今天算你倒霉。明天你就会好的。

182. After the verb to love, to help is the most beautiful verb in the world.
除了"爱"之外,"帮助"是世界上最美的动词。

183. Swimming is my favorite sport. I can get more exercise, a better appetite and a better figure by swimming. 我喜欢游泳。它使我得到充分锻炼,增强食欲并拥有强健的体魄。

184. Playing computer games and playing bridge are my two great hobbies.
玩电子游戏和打桥牌是我的两大嗜好。

185. I like photography very much. I was awarded second prize in a photography contest at our university. 我很喜欢摄影,我曾经在学校举办的摄影大赛中获得二等奖。

186. I'm a photography enthusiast, outdoor camping enthusiast.
我是摄影爱好者、户外露营爱好者。

187. The trouble with photography is that it's an expensive hobby.
摄影爱好的缺点是它是一种昂贵的爱好。

188. 8 centimeter single-lens is the best seller at present.
8厘米单眼摄影机是目前最畅销的货品。

189. Can you tell me where the secret is? 你能告诉我秘密何在吗?

190. There's no secret at all. The only thing for you to do is to practice more. Remember, "Sweat never drips in vain."
说来并无秘密,你唯一要做的就是多练。记住"汗水不会白流"。

191. Sow an act, and you reap a habit. Sow a habit, and you reap a character. Sow a character, and you reap a destiny. 行为养成习惯,习惯变为性格,性格决定命运。

192. Youth calls for pleasure, pleasure calls for love. 青春需要快乐,快乐需要爱情。

193. Tastes differ. / Every man has his taste. / There is no accounting for taste.
萝卜白菜各有所爱。/人各有所好。

194. It's up to the woman to make the man. /The woman makes the man.
一个成功男人的背后总有一个优秀的女人。

195. She is an introvert but I am an extrovert. 她性格内向,而我则外向。

196. Don't be mad. I'm sure you'll go with another fine lady someday.
别太伤心,我保证你会很快找到另一半的。

197. No man is born perfect. 没有人生来就完美。

198. Sorry, I am tone-deaf. 对不起,我五音不全。

199. I don't have the nerve to sing in front of people. 我不敢在大家面前唱歌。

200. Come on, Ben; look at the top ten of this week's top chart. Which is your favorite in the list? 本,来看看本周的排行榜前十名。你最喜欢哪首歌?

201. Her voice rose and fell with emotion. 她的嗓音时高时低,充满了激情。

202. We were quite impressed. I had no idea you had such a beautiful soprano voice.
我们被你的演出所深深地打动。我不知你竟有这么一副美妙的女高音嗓子。

203. I must say I have a strong preference for classic music.
我得说,我对古典音乐有强烈的偏爱。

204. There is something wrong with my computer. Can I use yours to type my paper?
 我的电脑坏了。能用你的电脑打篇论文吗?
205. I'm addicted to net-chat. 我对网上聊天上瘾。
206. Do you know where I can get some general chat software?
 你知道我在哪儿能买到常用的聊天软件?
207. I'm trying to send some photos to my friend, but they keep on bouncing back.
 我试图给我的朋友发照片,但它们老是被退回。
208. Maybe your files are too large, or your attachments have virus.
 也许你的文件太大,或是你的附件有病毒。
209. Of course. I can't live without the Internet. 当然。没有网络我就活不下去了。
210. What are you doing with it? 你在网上都干什么呀?
211. Are you a nethead/ cyber worm? 你是个网虫吗?
212. Computers can gather a wide range of information for many purposes.
 计算机能为多种目的搜集广泛的信息。
213. Computers can store information and pour it out whenever it is needed.
 计算机能储存信息,并在人们需要的时候将信息输出。
214. Computers have already changed the lives of millions of people.
 计算机已改变了数百万人的生活。
215. But I still must say that chatting online is a waste of time.
 但我还是认为上网聊天是在浪费时间。
216. You should learn how to make the most use of the campus wide web.
 你要学会怎样最充分地利用校园网络。
217. You should be careful when you present your personal information for which encryption is absolutely necessary. 不管怎样,提交个人信息时都要仔细,尽量使用加密传输。
218. What's the difference between hackers and crackers? 黑客和骇客有什么不同?
219. Most hackers love to explore computers and computer systems for their own sake; crackers try to get through firewalls and password systems, and are looked down by many hackers.
 大多数黑客从个人利益出发,研究计算机和计算机系统;骇客企图突破防火墙和密码系统,为黑客所不齿。
220. Is Water Sprinkling Festival official? 泼水节是法定节日吗?
221. Can you say something abut the origin of the Dragon-Boat Festival?
 你能说说龙舟节的来历吗?
222. Halloween is a holiday that Americans celebrate every year. It comes on October 31.
 10月31日是万圣节,这是美国人每年都要庆祝的节日。
223. On April Fools' Day, people play all kinds of tricks on others, and the one easily taken in is called April fool.
 在愚人节那天,人们开各种各样的玩笑,容易上当的人被称作"四月傻瓜"。
224. Christmas spirit means it's better to give than to receive. 圣诞精神就是奉献多于索取。
225. I like the Spring Festival best of all. Think of the big feast on the Eve! Also the special TV programs, firecrackers, and the games to play.

我最喜欢春节。想一想除夕的晚宴！还有特别电视节目、烟花炮竹和可玩的游戏。

226. We set off firecrackers during the festival to welcome the New Year as well as to frighten away evil spirits. 我们在春节燃放烟花炮竹是迎新年，同时也是为了驱逐鬼神。

227. Old people say the whole year will be as good or as bad as New Year's Day itself, and bad or rude words on the day will bring a bad year.
老年人说，整个一年就像新年这天一样可好可坏。这一天说了粗俗话会带来坏运气。

228. Did you see the statue of Confucius launched by the China Confucius Fund?
你看到中国孔子基金会发布的孔子标准像了吗？

229. Yes, I did. It doesn't quite match the Confucius image in my mind though.
是的。但它不完全是我心目中的孔子形象。

230. Confucius was a great philosopher, an educator, a politician, as well as the founder of Confucianism, which still has a tremendous influence over people today.
孔子是伟大的思想家、教育家、政治家，也是儒学的创始人，对中国人的生活和思想依然有着众多的影响。

231. As far as I know, about five to six million Chinese students are currently studying *The Analects* of Confucius. 就我所知，中国有五六百万的学生在学习《论语》。

232. Confucianism is the backbone of Chinese culture, which stresses fairness and harmony in human relationships, as well as the individual's social responsibility for the country.
儒家思想是中国传统文化的主干。它强调的是为人处世的正派、人际关系的和谐以及个人对国家的责任感。

233. For Confucius, political honesty is based on individual ethical integrity.
在孔子看来，政治的廉洁是以人品的正直为基础的。

234. Confucianism emphasizes "courtesy" and "respect" when dealing with people or nature so it should be very beneficial for building harmony in any society.
孔子学说提倡以"礼"来处理人际关系及人与自然的关系，对于和谐社会的构建大有益处。

235. You can say that again. A scholar once said that answers concerning our survival can be found in the wisdom of Confucius, even though he lived more than 25 centuries ago.
说得对。正如一位学者所说，21世纪的生存问题，必须回到25个世纪之前孔子的智慧中去寻求解决的答案。

236. It is said that film is a sensational one. Is it subtitled in both Chinese and English?
据说那部影片引起轰动。有中英文字幕吗？

237. I was deeply impressed by the acting and the music of it. /The acting and the music of it impressed me very much. 这部电影的演技和音乐给我留下了深刻的印象。

238. When a good film is on, there is always a full house. / When a good film is on, there's no seat left in the cinema. 每当有好的电影时，电影院总是爆满。

239. I'm sorry, but it's a bad movie. The plot is stupid, and the script is poorly written.
我不得不说，那是一部烂片。情节白痴，剧本也写得差。

240. I'm tired of cowboys and Indians as all those films are the same. What else is showing?
我看腻了牛仔和印第安人片。那些片子千篇一律。还有别的电影吗？

241. I don't care for a detective film. It makes me nervous. 我对侦探片不感兴趣,它使我紧张。
242. By the way, a western, an adventure, a war, a violent, a love story, or a science-fiction movie, which of them do you like best?
顺便问一下,西部片、探险片、战争片、暴力片、爱情片、科幻片,你最喜欢哪种?
243. I'd like to see a suspense/documentary/cartoon/thrilling film.
我喜欢看悬念片(纪录片/动画片/惊险片)。
244. Blue cinema corrupts the souls of people. 黄色电影腐蚀人们的灵魂。
245. I think *Spiderman* is the best movie. 我认为《蜘蛛侠》是最好的电影。
246. There is still some imperfection in the film. 这部电影还有许多缺憾之处。
247. The film has got this year's Oscar Award. 这部电影获得了今年的奥斯卡奖。
248. Every week, our students can enjoy movies in our multimedia classrooms.
每周,学生可以在多媒体教室欣赏电影。
249. Is there anything worth watching on another channel?
另一个频道有什么值得看的节目吗?
250. Let's switch to 12. There's a crime thriller. /Let's turn to 12. There's a crime thriller.
我们把电视转到12频道吧,那儿在放映一部侦探惊险片。
251. What's on the box tonight? 今晚有什么电视节目?
252. The movie was cut (censored) here and there. 那部电影被删减得很严重。
253. The movie was blurred (blocked) out here and there. 那部电影让人看得不明不白的。
254. I have always played supporting roles (played the second fiddle). 我总是演配角。
255. It was a tear jerker. 那是部催人泪下的电影。
256. As far as I am concerned, there are too many police shows and not enough educational programs. 就我个人来讲,我觉得关于警察的节目太多,而教育类的节目又不够。
257. I hear that China is the first country where tea was found drinkable.
听说中国是第一个发现茶是可饮用的国家。
258. Tea-drinking is a matter that many people can't dispense with in their daily life.
喝茶是许多人日常生活离不开的事情。
259. Good-quality tea must go together with good-quality water. 好茶必须有好水相伴。
260. In tea-making, we must carefully select high-quality tea-leaves, suitable water for infusing tea, and a good tea-set. 泡茶时,要讲究茶叶、泡茶用水和茶具。
261. My parents are fond of tea-drinking. Under their influence, I have also formed such a habit.
我父母爱喝茶。我受他们影响,也养成了喝茶的习惯。
262. As soon as the boiling water is poured into the boccaro pot with tea-leaves placed, the fragrance of the tea will permeate through the room.
将沸水注入装好茶叶的紫砂壶,立刻清香四溢。
263. High-quality tea is generally characterized by its excellence in color, smell, taste and shape.
好茶一般都是色、香、味和形兼备。
264. The tea-leaves of various kinds soaked in water will take on different colors, some being yellowish green, some others orange yellow, and still some others pale red or dark red.

不同种类的茶叶浸泡在水中会呈现不同的颜色,有的黄绿,有的橙黄,有的浅红,有的暗红。

265. The tea-leaves of different kinds vary in flavor. Some taste strong, some others weak, and still some others mellow or fresh, causing people to feel differently.
不同种类的茶叶具有不同的滋味。有的浓烈,有的清淡,有的香醇,有的鲜爽,会给人带来不同的感受。

266. Tea represents thriftiness and cleanliness. 茶是节俭和清廉的象征

267. A cup of tea not only serves social and economic purposes, but also political purposes as well. 茶不但有社会功能,经济功能,还有政治功能。

268. Green tea is good for longevity and combating cancer. Red tea is good for keeping the stomach warm. 绿茶有延年益寿和抗癌的作用。红茶有暖胃的作用。

269. Life is lifeless without health. 没有健康就没有生命。

270. A meaningful life is a life based on health. 有意义的生活是以健康为基础的。

271. Jogging is an easy fat-consuming exercise. 慢跑是容易消耗脂肪的运动。

272. I'm only combining work with pleasure. There is no point talking about something else without being good in health. 我只是劳逸结合。没有好的身体,其他就无从谈起。

273. You must not pledge your own health. 身体健康不能靠誓言。

274. I try to keep in shape. 我在努力保持体型。

275. If you exercise regularly, you can speed up your metabolism.
有规律的运动会促进你的新陈代谢。

276. I have a fast metabolism. 我精力旺盛。

277. You seem to be a little out of shape these days. 你好像最近身体不太好。

278. His general condition is getting worse. 他的身体状况在下降。

279. Today I'm under the weather. / I'm not myself today. 我今天感到不舒服。

280. I'm on a diet now. 我在减肥。

281. Overeating may bring about over-nutrition. 吃得过多会造成营养过剩。

282. A diet that is high in fat may cause obesity. 高脂肪的膳食会导致肥胖症。

283. My sleeping cycle is off. 我的生物钟乱了。

284. You should get regular medical checkups. 你要定期做体检。

285. You have to eat three square meals a day. 一日三餐要搭配合理。

286. I have a cold sore on my tongue. 我舌头溃疡了。

287. I was on the toilet all night. 我昨夜腹泻不止。

288. Starve a fever, feed a cold. 发烧要少吃,感冒要多吃。

289. It seems you are recovering yourself well. 看上去你身体正在恢复。

290. You seem to be fully recovered from the illness. 看上去你已完全恢复健康了。

291. I've tried to give up smoking several times, but in vain.
我已经尝试了几次戒烟,但是都未成功。

292. In my opinion, you have no choice. Either you make a real effort or there's no chance of feeling better.
我认为你没有别的选择。要么你真正努力把烟戒掉,要么你就无法治好病。

293. You must cut it down gradually and I could prescribe some kind of tranquilizer.
你必须逐渐减少吸烟的数量,我再给你开一些镇静剂。
294. Smoking is the easiest thing in the world to give up. I have done it hundreds of times! 戒烟是世界上最容易的事。我都戒了好多次了!
295. Welcome to Guang Ming Hotel. May I help you? 欢迎光临光明酒店。能为您效劳吗?
296. Hello. This is Room Reservations. Can I help you?
您好!这是客房部。可以为您效劳吗?
297. Yes. I'd like to book two twin rooms for next Friday.
是的。我想预定下周五的两个双人间。
298. That's fine, Sir. Conjoining rooms or adjoining rooms?
好的,先生。您想要相连的房间还是相邻的房间?
299. Any difference? 有什么区别吗?
300. Conjoining rooms actually have a door, so you can walk into the other people's room. Adjoining rooms are next to each other.
相连的房间之间有门。您可以在房间之间走动。相邻的房间只是彼此相邻。
301. Adjoining rooms, please. 相邻的吧。
302. With or without bath? 带不带浴室?
303. Preferably with bath. 最好带浴室。
304. Do you have any rooms available? 有空房间吗?
305. Is it possible to make reservations? 可以在你们旅馆预订房间吗?
306. I'm afraid not. We're completely booked up. (Sorry, all the rooms have been reserved.)
对不起,房间都已订出去了。(全都被预订了。)
307. Could you fill out the registration form, please? 请填写这张登记表好吗?
308. What facilities do you have? 你们这里都有什么设备?
309. What sort of amusements do you offer? 你们宾馆提供什么娱乐活动吗?
310. May I deposit my valuables here? 我可以在这儿存放贵重物品吗?
311. I'd like a room with a sea view. 我想要个能看到大海的房间。
312. The room comes with a complimentary breakfast. 早餐免费供应。
313. The dinner is on the house. 晚餐免费。
314. Could I have a wake-up call at 6 tomorrow morning?
请你明天早上6点用电话叫醒我,好吗?
315. How would you like to pay? 你打算如何付款?
316. By American Express Card. 用美国运通信用卡。
317. May I take your order, sir? 先生点菜吗?
318. Let me take a look at the menu. 让我看看菜单。
319. What's the special for today? 今天的特色菜是什么?
320. Today's special is roast pork chops. 今天的特色菜是烤猪排。
321. How would you like your steak? 请问你的牛排要几分熟?
322. Bloody./Rare./Well done. 生的。(三分熟。全熟。)
323. How delicious! Tender and crisp. 味道真好!又嫩又脆。

324. A Chinese dinner usually starts with assorted cold dishes.
中国菜通常都是以什锦冷拼盘开始的。
325. I'd like to try some of the traditional dishes of this area. 我想品尝一下本地区的传统菜肴。
326. Aren't you a picky eater? 你不偏食吧?
327. How do you eat your food: bland, salty, or hot and spicy? 你喜欢清淡、咸还是辣的食物?
328. I'm not used to eating Chinese food because it's too greasy.
中国菜太油腻了,我还不太习惯。
329. Chinese food stresses color, smell and taste. Is this correct?
中国菜讲究色、香、味俱全,对吗?
330. Correct. This is why people also refer to food as mei shi, meaning beautiful food. The primary element is color because only a good color combination can arouse people's appetite.
对,所以称为美食。食物最基本的元素是色泽,因为只有好的色泽搭配才能引起食欲。
331. Can you wrap it up for me? It's to go. 能给我打包吗?我要带走。
332. It's my treat this time./Be my guest. It's my round/treat/shout. 这次我请客。
333. Let's go Dutch. 这次我们各自付账吧。
334. The cake really looks inviting. 蛋糕太诱人了。
335. This red wine really hits the spot. 这红葡萄酒真的很合口味。
336. I can drink more than you./ I'll drink you under the table. 我比你能喝。
337. I got really drunk /intoxicated. /I feel tipsy. 我真喝醉了。/我有点醉了。
338. The song goes,"Drink to me only with your eyes, and I will pledge with mine; or leave a kiss within the cup, and I'll not ask for wine."
歌词唱道:"只需你那秋波同我干杯,我会以深情的目光相对;若你在杯中留一个亲吻,则比美酒令人心醉。"
339. Let's drink to our health and success. Cheers! /Posit! / Toast! /Down the hatch!
为了我们的成功和身体健康,干杯!
340. And here is a bottle of Chinese Mao-tai. 这瓶茅台酒送给您。
341. That is thoughtful of you. I have heard that it packs quite punch.
你想得太周到了。听说这是一种度数很高的烈性酒。
342. Allow me to express my heartiest congratulations. 请允许我表示最衷心的祝贺。
343. Please accept my warmest congratulations on your marriage.
请接受我为你们喜结良缘的祝福。
344. We painted the town red last night. 昨晚我们彻夜狂欢。
345. Who's speaking, please? / Who is this, please? 请问您是哪位?
346. Hold on, please. /Hold the line, please. /Just a second, please. 请稍等一下。
347. I'm sorry to have kept you waiting. 对不起,让您久等了。
348. Can I leave a message? 我能留个口信吗?
349. Please hang up the phone. 请挂电话吧。
350. I'm sorry, I must have misdialed. 对不起,我好像打错了。
351. There's no one here by that name. 这里没有您说的那个人。

352. It's a dead number. 这是个空号。
353. We have a bad connection. 电话线好像有毛病。
354. What number did you dial/call? 你打的是什么号码?
355. There is a call for you. / You are wanted. 有你电话。
356. I'll have an important meeting in five minutes. Please tell him to call back in 30 minutes.
抱歉,五分钟后我要参加一个重要会议,请他三十分钟后再打来。
357. He is not currently available. 他现在不能接电话。
358. May I take a message? 有什么要我转达的吗?
359. Your voice is echoing. I can't hear you well. 有点回音,听不清楚。
360. We came up from behind and won. 我们反败为胜。
361. We had five consecutive wins. / We won five games in a row. 我们五连胜。
362. We paid dearly for the victory. 我们以巨大代价取得了胜利。
363. We won the game by a narrow margin. 那场比赛赢得悬。
364. The game ended in a tie (draw). 比赛打成平手(握手言欢)。
365. He accepted his loss clearly./ He lost very gracefully. 他输得很优雅。
366. Don't complain. We lost fair and square. 别抱怨了,我们输得很坦荡。
367. We are down 6 to 7, but still have a chance of beating them.
我们6比7失败,但我们还有赢的机会。
368. We have a six to three advantage. 现在我们是6比3领先。
369. The game will go into overtime. 比赛将进入加时赛。
370. Who will be elected as the MVP (Most Valuable Player) of the year?
谁将当选"年度最佳选手"?
371. Do you have the guts to sing in front of people? 你有勇气在别人面前唱歌吗?
372. What's your karaoke specialty? 你唱卡拉OK有什么拿手的歌吗?
373. You can join me in a duet. 我们可以来个二重唱。
374. Can you imagine a life without music? 你能想象没有音乐的人生吗?
375. It would be unbearable. The world would then be full of noises, but not music.
那肯定令人忍受不了,世界会充满噪音而不是音乐。
376. How is music different from noise? 音乐和噪音是怎样区别的?
377. Music generally has a pattern and good quality which is pleasing to our ears while noises are only irritating. 音乐一般有组织而且音质悦耳动听,噪音则只会令人感到烦躁。
378. He is tone deaf. 他没乐感。
379. You make a better door than a window. Please get out of the way. /You are blocking my view. Please get out of the way. 你挡住了我的视野。请让开一下。
380. Excuse me but would you save my seat? 打扰一下,能帮我看一下位子吗?
381. He has taken this kind of music to the extreme. 他把这种音乐演绎到极致。
382. The actor's sun has been shining all these years. 这个演员这几年一直是红星高照。
383. Her debut recording proved immensely popular. 她的首张唱片大受欢迎。

384. He has indeed been riding the gravy train, but you bet every flow must have its ebb. I don't think the sun will always be shining on him.
这几年他确实很走运,但你相信潮水有涨有落,我不信他总会这样走运。
385. What sort of public transportation is nearby? 附近有什么公交系统?
386. How often do the buses run? 汽车多长时间一趟?
387. The buses leave every twenty minutes. 汽车每二十分钟一趟。
388. What does it cost to take the bus down-town? The fare is a flat rate of 1 Yuan.
坐公交车到城里多少钱? 统一价一元。
389. Every transfer station is full of passengers changing trains.
每个换乘站都挤满了要换车的乘客。
390. The road is under construction, so traffic is backed up.
道路正在修筑过程中,所以交通很拥挤。
391. The subways are really crowded during the rush hours. 交通高峰时地铁特别拥挤。
392. Follow the rules. /Don't violate rules (regulations). 请遵守规则。
393. Do you want me to trim your moustache? 你想修理一下胡子吗?
394. No. Just a hair-cut, please. Trim it at the back and the sides.
不。只剪发。后面和两边都修一修。
395. How do you like your hair set? 你喜欢头发做成什么式样?
396. I want a trim and perm. 我想剪短一点,然后烫发。
397. What color would you dye it? 您要染什么颜色?
398. Please dye my hair brown. 请把我的头发染成棕色。
399. Leave them as they are, please. 请照老样子。
400. Make my hair the latest style/the most popular style please. 请给我做最流行的发式。
401. She has shoulder-length hair. 她留着披肩发。
402. Your hair cut is stylish. 你的发型不错。(你的发型很入时。)
403. I don't like dandruff. 我讨厌头屑。
404. Do you have any dandruff shampoo? 你们有去屑洗发水吗?
405. What shampoo do you prefer? 你喜欢什么洗发剂?
406. Change your cell phone to the vibration mode during our meeting.
开会时请把手机调到振动状态。
407. The fax you sent did not come through clearly. 你发的传真有些不清楚。
408. Just put the letter face down, dial the number, and push the button. It's easy.
把写有字的一面放下,在拨完号后按下按钮,很容易的。
409. It's illegible. It's blurred. 很模糊,无法辨认。
410. He is a computer illiterate. 他是个电脑盲。
411. I got your e-mail but it was all gibberish, so I couldn't read it.
我收到你的邮件,但不清楚,难以辨认。
412. Laptop computers are more expensive than desktop computers. 笔记本电脑比台式电脑贵。
413. I'm hooked on computers. 我迷上电脑了。
414. Can you find the password? / Can you break the code? 你能解密码吗?

415. The government plans to cut taxes in order to stimulate the economy.
政府为了刺激经济准备推出减税计划。

416. The economy bottomed out last year. 去年经济进入低谷。

417. Is that a temporary recession or a depression? 那是暂时的经济不景气,还是经济大萧条?

418. Is it a bull market or a bear market? 股市是牛市还是熊市?

419. This bull market has had the longest run in history. 这次牛市在历史上延续时间最长。

420. A bear market could be just around the corner. 熊市很可能就在眼前。

421. I dabble in the stock market. 我炒股。

422. The economy is getting back on its feet. 经济正在好转。

423. The stock index is surging upwards these days. 最近股票指数一直上升。

424. He bought only blue chip stocks. 他只买蓝筹股。

425. Share prices fluctuate with market and political climates.
股票价格随着市场行情和政治气候的变化而变化。

426. Prices are soaring these days. / Prices are skyrocketing these days. 最近物价急升。

427. Let's discard this inflated, bubble economy. 让我们抛弃过热的泡沫经济。

428. Investors want a high return on their money. 投资者希望他们的钱有高收益。

429. How wonderful it is to be in love! It's love at first sight! He is my Romeo!
恋爱真是件美好的事! 我对他一见钟情,他就是我的罗密欧。

430. My love will grow, like a river, it'll flow. 我对你的爱,像河水滔滔不息。

431. It can't be dry, and can't die. 它永远不会干涸,不会枯竭。

432. You have very good taste in women. 你选女朋友眼光太高了。

433. What would your ideal date be like? 你的理想对象是什么样的?

434. He'd be handsome, have brains and a lot of money. 他要英俊、机智、有钱。

435. She was so radiant, so full of fun, so pleased with life.
她是那么光芒四射,风趣幽默,开心快活。

436. He'd be clever, rich and funny. 他要聪明、富有、幽默。

437. That means he was head over heels in love with you. 那就是说,他被你迷住了。

438. Love makes the world go around. 有爱能使鬼推磨。

439. They seem to have lost that loving feeling. /The fire seems to have gone out of their love.
他们好像没有爱情了。

440. Long absent, soon forgotten. 久别情疏。

441. Though she is plain, she's an excellent cook. /She is great shakes at cooking.
她长相一般,但菜做得很好。

442. Are you a henpecked husband? 你是"妻管严"吗?

443. He's still available. 他仍然未婚。

444. Their marriage was arranged. / That was an arranged marriage. 他们的婚姻是包办的。

445. A great marriage is not when the "perfect couple" comes together.
伟大的婚姻不是"完美夫妻"结合的婚姻。

446. Love begins with a smile, grows with a kiss and ends with a teardrop.
微笑萌生爱情,亲吻带入佳境,泪水洗尽痴情。

447. Marriage is like a beleaguered fortress: those who are outside want to get in and those inside want to get out.
婚姻犹如被围困的城堡:外面的人想冲进去,里面的人想冲出来。
448. Marriage may be compared to a cage: the birds outside despair to get in, and those within despair to get out. 有人把婚姻比做鸟笼:外边的鸟想飞进来,里面的鸟想飞出去。
449. Love is a hidden fire, a pleasant sore, a delicious poison, a delectable pain, an agreeable torment, a sweet and throbbing wound, a gentle death.
爱是看不见的暗火,惬意的疼痛,美味的毒药,叫人愉快的伤感,舒服的折磨,带来快感和抽搐的创伤,安详的死亡。
450. A sweetheart is a bottle of wine; a wife is a wine bottle.
情人是美酒,虽然沁人心脾,一时淋漓酣畅,可是喝完就消弭于无形;而妻子是酒瓶,酒喝完了,瓶子还与你朝夕相伴漫漫人生。
451. Young love is a flame; very pretty, often very hot and fierce, but still only light and flickering. The love of the older and disciplined heart is as coals, deep burning, unquenchable.
青春的爱是火焰;非常之优美,又非常之炽热和猛烈,但又是闪烁和摇曳的。苍老和经过历练的心,他们的爱则像是热炭,烧得透,难扑灭。
452. Friendship is a prodigal, but love is a miser. 友谊是慷慨的,爱情是吝啬的。
453. When a man sits with a pretty girl for an hour, it seems like a minute. But let him sit on a hot stove for a minute and it is longer than an hour. That is relativity.
当一个男人和一个漂亮姑娘坐在一起时,一个小时就像一分钟。而让他在火热的炉子上坐一分钟——这一分钟比一小时都长。这就是相对论。
454. At the beginning beauty is attractive, but when it is left at home for three days, who will look at it? 乍一看,花容月貌惊若天人,但在家里放上三天,谁还会再瞅它一眼呢?
455. The worst way to miss someone is to be sitting beside them knowing you cannot have them.
念意中人最糟糕的莫过于,你尽可与其比肩而坐,却心知与之无缘。
456. Love, with very young people, is a heartless business. We drink at that age from thirst, or to get drunk. It is only later in life that we occupy ourselves with the individuality of our wine.
就少男少女而言,恋爱是件不甚用心的事情。在那个年龄我们口渴了就想饮酒,不管什么酒都可以喝得烂醉,只是到了成年才喝适合个人口味的酒。
457. Marriage is a book of which the first chapter is written in poetry and the remaining chapters in prose. 婚姻是一本书,它的第一章是诗,而其余各章则是散文。
458. Love is wisdom in action. Love is action and no action together. Love is all that is. Love transcends mind. Love is an effervescent feeling that seems to escape definition.
爱是身体力行的智慧。爱是有为和无为的结合。爱是一切。爱超越了理智。爱是一种无法定义却又令人兴奋的感觉。
459. It's the first time for me to prepare for the exams of so many courses. I feel I am really at a loss. 这是我第一次准备这么多考试,我真的感觉有点不知所措。
460. There are usually two forms of exam questions: subjective questions and objective questions.
考试题型一般有两种,即主观题和客观题。

461. I perform better on tests when I cram. 我在考试前临时抱佛脚,通常会发挥得很好。
462. How did you do on your chemistry mid-term? 你化学期中考试考得怎么样?
463. I failed my exam. What a shame! 我没及格。真糟!
464. He gets straight A's in all subjects. 他所有科目都得"优"。
465. My grades are not high. I need to do my GRE well to get to graduate school.
    我的分数不高。我得好好考GRE才能上研究生院。
466. Do you think it wise to stay up all night studying for the test?
    你觉得一整夜不睡觉复习功课是聪明之举吗?
467. How you get by with so little rest is a mystery to me.
    我真奇怪你怎么能睡那么少,还那么有精神。
468. Could you tell me how to review the entire text? 你能否告诉我怎么复习整个课文?
469. I think my notes should be helpful. 我觉得我的笔记会有助于我的复习。
470. Every wise student knows how to avoid these last-minute cram sessions before an exam.
    聪明学生都知道如何避免临时抱佛脚。
471. The heat is killing me. 天真热(我热得要死。)
472. It's misty./It's foggy./It's overcast today./ It's gloomy.
    天(灰)雾蒙蒙的。(今天天色阴暗。)
473. It's snowing heavily./The snow's falling thick and fat. 大雪纷飞。
474. Horrible weather, isn't it? Cold and rainy. 天气糟透了,不是吗? 又冷又下雨。
475. The weather is so changeable that I can hardly get used to it.
    这里的气候变化无常,我很难适应。
476. The weather up there is awful and it's cold and damp. 那里的天气太差了,又冷又潮。
477. It's driving me crazy! But it's supposed to be sunny by the end of this week.
    这种天气快把我逼疯了。不过这个周末天气会好的。
478. The summer here is terribly hot. Do you remember the day our air conditioner broke down? The temperature stayed above one hundred for four straight days.
    这里夏天热得够呛。你还记得我们的空调机坏了的那天吗? 气温连续四天保持在华氏100度以上。
479. Do you have something special in mind for the coming holiday?
    马上就要放假了,你有什么与众不同的计划吗?
480. I want to see the places of interest in Xi'an. Can you arrange a tour for me?
    我想看看西安的名胜古迹。你能帮我安排一趟旅游吗?
481. There is a five-day package tour. You will have 5 full days in the city. It is a general tour of the city.
    有一个5天的包价旅游。您将在那座城市里玩上5整天。这是对整个城市进行游览的旅行。
482. It's sunny and warm, and the flowers are in blossom. It's just the weather for an outing.
    阳光明媚,春暖花开,正是郊游的好天气。
483. Let's fix the sightseeing schedule for this week. 我们把本周的观光计划定一下吧。

484. Could you recommend some historic sites worth visiting?
请给介绍一下值得观光的景点好吗?

485. Here's a copy of the itinerary for our tour. What do you think of it?
这个是我们的旅游路线,你觉得如何?

486. The tour of Guilin was a feast for my eyes. 桂林一游使我大饱眼福。

487. We hear that it's worth going. It's absolutely fascinating.
听说真值得一去,那里绝对令人着迷。

488. it's a popular place for people to relax and picnic in their spare time.
这是人们常来放松休息和野炊的地方。

489. That is really a famous tourist attraction. 那真是一个有名的旅游胜地。

490. The combination of wind, sand and sea is really fascinating.
海风、白沙、海水的结合的确迷人。

491. It is relaxing to be around nature. 投入大自然的怀抱令人心旷神怡。

492. The sunrise as seen from the mountaintop was a tremendous spectacle.
从山顶看日出景象蔚为壮观。

493. Its gleaming sands and backdrop of pinewoods and distant hills lend it a pleasant and restful atmosphere. 这儿沙滩闪烁,松林掩映,远山连绵,自有一种心旷神怡的气氛。

494. Unfortunately little is left of the former splendor. 可惜,昔日壮观,所剩无几。

495. Walking in the mountains helps keep you fit. 在山间散步有助于保持身体健康。

496. From up here we can have a bird's eye view of the city. 从这儿我们可以鸟瞰这座城市。

497. The great attraction for visitors is the National Museum. 最吸引人的是国家博物馆。

498. There are lots of historical relics and art treasures in it. 里边有好多历史文物和艺术珍宝。

499. Most of the unearthed relics remain intact. 大多数出土文物仍然保持完整无缺。

500. The Great Wall was the embodiment of the wisdom of the ancient Chinese people.
长城是古代中国劳动人民智慧的结晶。

501. The Palace Museum attracts thousands of visitors each day with its magnificent architecture and precious collections of cultural and art objects.
故宫博物馆的辉煌建筑以及宝贵的文化、艺术品每天都吸引着数千旅游者前来参观。

502. The landscape in Guilin is characterized by its "green hills, clear water, pretty rocks, and grottoes." 桂林风景的特点是"山青、水秀、石美、洞奇"。

503. I enjoyed my trip very much and it was memorable experience to me.
我玩得非常痛快,是一个难以忘怀的经历。

504. I want a cheapest ticket with an open return. 我要张最便宜返程时间不定的票。

505. There is a 40% discount. That happens once in a blue moon.
现在打六折。千载难逢的好机会。

506. Would you tell me where the baggage claim is, please? 请问在哪儿托运行李?

507. There is an overweight of five kilos, and you'll be charged for it.
超重五千克,你要交超重费。

508. You should get to the airport two hours ahead of your flight time.
你应当在飞机起飞前两小时到达机场。

509. I feel so much pressure in my ears when I'm flying. 我坐飞机会耳鸣。

510. Please put your seat up. We'll be serving dinner shortly. 请把椅子调正。马上供应晚餐。

511. Do you want to send it by air mail or surface mail? 你想寄航空信还是平信？

512. How much does it cost to mail it first-class? 寄平信要多少钱？

513. I want to have this letter registered, please. 这封信我想寄挂号。

514. Would you please weigh this parcel to see what the postage is?
请称一下包裹看看邮资是多少？

515. I'd like to send this document by Federal Express. 请把这些文件寄特快专递。

516. How much is the postage for this postcard to U.S.? 往美国寄一张明信片要多少钱？

517. I guess someone must have already checked it out. 我想这本书肯定是让人借走了。

518. I'd like to take those two out and return these four. 我想借那两本，还这四本。

519. Will you inform Tom to return the library books tomorrow? They are due now.
请通知汤姆明天把图书馆的书还了好吗？书到期了。

520. I just got an overdue notice from the library. 我刚接到图书馆的一张过期罚款单。

521. Good resources for research are primarily found in the library.
一般来说图书馆是做研究获取资料的好地方。

522. I'd like to get an early start on my research paper. 我希望早点开始写论文。

523. I'd like to explore that problem, but I'm not sure how to go about it.
我想探讨一下那个问题，但不知道该怎么入手。

524. Try to digest the information thoroughly, and then write it down in your own words.
尽量充分地分析信息，然后用自己的话写出来。

525. I'm sorry, Professor Barkley, but I haven't finished my term paper. Can I get an extension?
对不起，巴克雷教授，我没写完学期报告。能给我延期吗？

526. What are the procedures and conventions which must be followed in writing a paper?
写论文必须遵循什么步骤和原则？

527. When writing a paper, you need to do a lot of research before you can begin writing. Ten or fifteen sources are usually the minimum number for a paper.
写论文前需要做大量的研究工作。一篇论文通常至少要有10至15个来源。

528. I'm glad to tell you that the University Academic Committee has reviewed all of your documents and will grant you the degree of the Master of Arts. My sincere congratulations.
我很高兴地告诉你，大学学术委员会复查了你的材料，并将授予你文学硕士学位。我真诚地恭贺你。

529. Thank you Dr. Johnson. I'm very grateful for all you have done to help me with my academic program over the past three years. I wouldn't have been able to complete my studies without your advice and guidance.
谢谢，杰克逊博士。我非常感谢您在过去三年中在指导我专业方面所做出的一切努力。没有您的建议和指导，我是不可能完成学业的。

530. Your success has depended on your wisdom and courage as well as your desire for knowledge. I'm really very proud of you.
你的成功来自于你的智慧和勇气以及你对知识的渴望。我真为你感到自豪。

531. The US dollar has been very weak lately. 近来美元很疲软。

532. What's the exchange rate at the present time? 最近的兑换率是多少？

533. One pound is worth fifteen *yuan*. 1镑可以换15元。

534. One US dollar is valued at eight *yuan* and ten cents in cash.
　　1美元可以兑换8.1元的人民币现金。

535. Do you charge any commission? 你们收手续费吗？

536. May I open an account with your bank? 我可以在你们银行开账户吗？

537. Would you like to open a checking account or a savings account?
　　您开支票账户还是开现金账户？

538. Do I have to make a minimum deposit in order to open an account?
　　开户要有存款最低限度吗？

539. How is the interest paid? 利息怎么算？

540. Interest is paid on the money held in a savings account. 利息就放在现金存款的账上。

541. Please fill in this form and print your name and address in capital letters.
　　请填写这张表,您的名字和地址用大写字母填写。

542. How much money do you plan to deposit in your account? 您准备存多少钱？

543. All bank charges and credits are recorded on your monthly statement.
　　您每月的所有开支与利息都记录在您的清单上。

544. I want to withdraw $500 from my deposit account. 我想支取500美元。

545. I'm afraid you can't make an overdraft. 恐怕您不能透支。

546. "Overdraft" means to overdraw a check for a sum in excess of one's credit balance in bank.
　　透支就是开的支票款超过了在银行的存款余额。

547. Now I want to close my account with you. 我想把我的账户结清。

548. Out of the $35 I received, your change is 40 cents. 我收你35美元,找你40美分。

549. You short-changed me. 你少找我钱了。

550. I'd like to open a bank account with you. 我想开个账户。

551. I want to withdraw 600 *yuan* from my account. 我想从账户里取600元。

552. I'd like to deposit 1000 *yuan* into my account. 我想往账户里存1000元。

553. I'd like to cash this check, please. 我想将这张旅行支票兑现。

554. Please key in your code. 请输入密码。

555. It is a great pleasure for me to have this opportunity for the interview.
　　能有这个机会参加面试,我感到非常高兴。

556. We looked over your resume and thought you might be a good candidate.
　　看了你的简历,我们认为你是个不错的人选。

557. Did you get any honors or rewards at your university?
　　你读大学时有没有获过什么荣誉或奖励？

558. I won the university scholarship for three years in succession. 我连续三年获得了奖学金。

559. Do you have some certificates on computer? 你有计算机等级证书吗？

560. Yes, I have NCRE certificate, rank 2. 是的,我有全国计算机二级等级证书。

561. I guess you can do the work when it fits into your own schedule.
我想如果这份工作和你的时间表不冲突,你可以做。

562. I would expect the appropriate rate of pay for a person with my experience and educational background. 我希望能得到与我的经验和学历相匹配的待遇。

563. I can type 60 words per minute and I take shorthand at 80 words per minute.
我打字的速度是每分钟60字,速记是每分钟80字。

564. Building up your computer skills is a good preparation for lots of jobs.
掌握电脑技能对很多工作都会有用的。

565. I believe that I'll have a great deal to learn from and to contribute to your company.
我相信我能从你们公司学到很多东西,也能为你们做很多贡献。

566. I can't say that I am good at it but I surely know something about architecture.
我不敢说我做得很好,不过我确实对建筑方面有所了解。

567. Can you sell yourself in two minutes? Go for it. 你能在两分钟内自我推荐吗? 大胆试试。

568. I'm very happy that I am qualified for this interview. 能有机会参加面试我感到很荣幸。

569. Don't start with your date of birth. Summarize your career and education, but don't recite a list. 不用提及你的出生日期。概括说出你的工作经验和学历,但请勿背诵。

570. I am an extrovert, easy-going girl. 我是一个外向并且容易相处的女孩。

571. The main qualities are preparedness to work hard and ability to learn. In addition to reading, I also like to play PC games.
主要素质是吃苦耐劳和很强的学习能力。除了阅读,我也喜欢玩电脑游戏。

572. English has been a global language for communication. If you learn this language well, it will help you in getting an ideal job.
英语已成为人们交流的一门全球性语言。如果你把英语学好了,它必将有助你谋求一份理想的职业。

573. I would like to talk with you regarding your qualifications for this position, OK?
我想就你应聘这一职务的资质同你谈一谈,好吗?

574. I can communicate with foreigners easily. They say my English is quite good.
我能轻松地和外国人沟通。他们都说我的英语相当好。

575. I've received Excellent Teaching Awards in the past two years in succession.
我连续两年获得教学优秀奖。

576. What do you think of yourself? (What kind of person are you?)
你觉得自己是个什么样的人?

577. For my personality, I think I'm very honest and I have a strong sense of responsibility. In general, I'm very easygoing, but I get very serious and cautious when I work.
性格方面,我觉得自己是一个坦诚和富有责任感的人。大体来说,我很随和,但我在工作的时候很认真也很小心谨慎。

578. To tell you the truth, I feel I can think independently and work cooperatively.
老实说,我认为我能独立思考并能与人合作。

579. I'm very responsible. I can make fast decisions, and I do not need much supervision. I enjoy completing challenging tasks.
我是一个责任心很强的人。我做事果断,而且我工作时不需要上司的监督。我乐于完成有挑战性的任务。

580. I think my greatest shortcoming is that I'm a poor talker and I'm very reserved when speaking in public. I need to work hard at that.
我想我最大的缺点就是我不大会说话。在大庭广众下,我很沉默。我必须在这方面努力改进。

581. What kind of personality do you think you have? 你认为你有怎样的个性?

582. To do me justice, I am a curious person, and I like to learn new things.
说句公道话,我是一个充满好奇心的人,而且喜欢接触新事物。

583. What is your philosophy of life? 你的人生哲学是什么?

584. Do you have any special skills? 你有什么特殊技能吗?

585. Yes, I have a good command of secretarial skills. 有。我通晓秘书技能。

586. Have you received any honors or rewards? 你有没有获得过什么荣誉或奖励?

587. Yes. I got the title of "Advanced Worker" in 2007 and 2008.
得过。我于2007年和2008年获得了"先进工作者"的称号。

588. If you are hired, your salary will be 3,000 RMB per month. How does that sound to you?
如果你被雇佣,你的月薪是3000元。你觉得如何?

589. Well, I can't really say. Pay is not everything. What I value most is job satisfaction.
我的确没法提。薪水不是一切。我看中的是工作的乐趣。

590. As for salary, I leave it to you to decide after experience of my capacity.
至于薪水,还是等检验了我的能力后由你们决定。

591. You'll have a starting salary of 3,000 *yuan* a month. 你初始工资是一个月3000元。

592. To be frank, I don't think the company's salary structure is perfect.
坦白说,我认为公司的薪资结构并不完善。

593. I got a job starting at $2500. 我一工作就拿2500美元。

594. It's a nice job except when it rains, snows or gets too hot or too cold.
这工作不错。就是赶上下雨、下雪,或者太冷、太热时不太好。

595. I guess all jobs have drawbacks. 我想什么工作都有这样或那样的缺点。

596. May I call at your office sometime this week? 本周我能去你办公室拜访你吗?

597. I'm afraid not. I'm fully booked up tomorrow. 恐怕不行,我明天安排已满。

598. Could you tell me if there's anything special (particular) to be discussed?
你能告诉我有什么特别的事要谈吗?

599. Is it convenient to change our appointment from Friday to Sunday, at the same time?
不知能否将我们的约会由周五改到周日,时间不变?

600. I don't want to go just to go. I really want to accomplish something.
我并不是为了出国而出国,我是真想有所作为。

601. When is the deadline for admission application? 申请入学的最后期限是什么时候?

602. How can I apply for financial aid? 我怎么申请经济资助呢?

603. If you expect to study in the United States next fall, you should make an application now.
要是你想明年秋天去美国学习,你现在就得申请了。

604. I'm having trouble filling out this application form. 我不知道怎么填这张表。

605. What's the tuition for international students? 留学生的学费是多少?

606. Do you get the visa of America? 你拿到美国的签证了吗?

607. They informed me of the denial of my visa application.
他们通知我,我的签证已被拒绝了。

608. I got an offer from LSE last week.
上周我得到了伦敦大学政治经济学系的入学通知书。

609. How did you get the offer? 你是怎样得到通知书的?

610. First, I sent my graduation diploma, degree certificate and academic report. Then I took the TOFFL and GMAT exam and got very good scores.
首先,我寄了我的毕业证书、学位证书和成绩单;然后,我参加了托福和GMAT考试,并且得到了很好的分数。

611. That university seems very selective. 那所大学竞争很激烈。

612. I haven't made up my mind yet. Maybe I will choose some school in the east.
我还没决定去哪儿。可能我会去东部的学校。

613. A job is a job, and we've got to earn money to pay our tuition.
工作就是工作,我们必须挣钱交学费。

614. I'd like to apply for a part-time job. 我想申请一个临时工作。

615. Good luck to your interview. 祝你面试时有好运。

616. I need to take an English conversation course to improve my spoken English.
我需要选英语会话课来提高我的英语口语。

617. I am looking for something interesting to finish off my electives.
我想找门有意思的课来完成我的选修课。

618. Are your required courses more difficult than your electives?
你的必修课比选修课难吗?

619. I got held up by the traffic jam. 我路上堵车了。

620. Which train should I take to Shanghai? 到上海我该坐哪趟车?

621. We can sleep to Nanjing on this evening departure morning arrival train.
我们可以在这班夕发朝至的列车上睡到南京。

622. I'd like to reserve two one-way tickets to New York for tomorrow.
我想预订两张明天去纽约的单程(飞机)票。

623. I'm terribly sorry. All the day flights have been booked out.
非常抱歉,所有白天的航班都订出去了。

624. I'm afraid a night flight is not suitable for me. 恐怕夜间航班对我不合适。

625. What's the difference in price between a day flight and a night flight?
白天航班和夜间航班在价格上有什么不同?

626. The fee difference could be about RMB1000 *yuan* from Beijing to Chicago.
从北京到芝加哥的机票差价可达1000元人民币。

627. Would you recommend to me the best route and the best train to Changzhou?
您能向我推荐去常州的最佳路线和最好的车次吗?

628. The No.37 Express Train is equipped with a new air-condition system and it's much faster.
37次特快列车装有新式的空调设备,而且运行得也特别快。

629. The through train No.368 and No.374 will take you nearly a day to get to Changzhou and they're old air-conditioned trains.
368次和374次直快列车是旧空调车,而且你得花上几乎一天的时间才能到达常州。

630. Can I cancel my reservation on August 9 and make a new reservation on August 10?
我可以取消8月9日的订票,重新订一张8月10日的票吗?

631. Do I have to go through complicated formalities if I ask to refund my ticket?
我如果要求退票,手续复杂吗?

632. No, but a certain amount of money will be deducted from your ticket.
不复杂,但是要从机票中扣掉一部分钱。

633. Do you happen to know any regulations concerning ticket refunding in the railway services?
你知道铁路部门关于退票方面的有关规定吗?

634. Generally speaking, you'll have a profound refund if you give your notice before the train starts at the terminal.
一般来说,在火车的起点站,如果你在火车发车之前提出退票,你可以得到全部的退款。

635. The train is well air-conditioned. 这列火车装备了良好的空调系统。

636. The sleeping car is so clean and tidy. 卧铺车厢里既干净又整齐。

637. Oh, the jerk was so great that I almost lost my balance.
哎呀,车颠得这么厉害,我差点失去了平衡。

638. The Railway Services wishes to announce that all trains have been delayed because of heavy snow. 铁路管理局宣布,因为大雪,所有的火车都晚点了。

639. Excuse me, could you tell me the way to 28 Street? 劳驾,您能告诉我去28大街怎么走吗?

640. Turn right at the next corner. 到前面拐弯处向右拐。

641. Would you tell me which bus to take to get to Capital Hill?
请问,我乘哪路公共汽车才能到国会山?

642. Where do I change buses if I go to Charles Street by bus?
如果我乘公共汽车去查尔斯大街,在哪儿换车呢?

643. Turn left at the intersection of the 12th Avenue and the 8th Street.
在第12条林荫道和第8条大街的交界处向左拐。

644. You may get lost on the short-cut. 你走捷径有可能迷路。

645. Following the zigzag up to the top of the hill, you'll find the temple.
顺着拐弯的小路走到山顶,你就看到那座庙宇了。

646. It's within walking distance. 不远,可以步行去。

647. It takes twenty minutes to walk there. 有20分钟的路程。

648. Go along this road as far as the third crossroads. /Walk down this road as far as the third crossroads. 沿着这条路走,一直走到第三个交叉路口。

649. Can I have a refund on this cap? 这顶帽子能退款吗?

650. Can I have my money back on this radio? 这台收音机能退钱吗?

651. I'd like to have a look at the famous brand name items (some of the famous brands). 我要看名品牌的商品。

652. I hope you have exactly the same brand, same size and same design. 我希望你们有同样牌子、同样尺码、同样款式的。

653. How long is the warranty on it? 保修多长时间?

654 There is a warranty on this one. 这件产品有售后保修服务。

655. The price of this laptop computer took a big nosedive. 这款笔记本电脑价格暴跌。

656. The price was recently marked down. 最近价格下调了。

657. This conditioner is an excellent buy. 这个空调买得很划算。

658. You were overcharged./That's a rip-off./You got ripped off./You paid for it through the nose. 你被宰了。

659. Can I get a discount on this? 这个能打折吗?

660. They are having a special offer: $20 each or three for $50. 这些特价出售,一个二十美元,三个五十美元。

661. How much do I have to pay up front for a new car? You have to make a ten-percent down payment. 新车要交多少预付金? 要先交10%的预付金。

662. You can get it without breaking the bank. 你不必花大钱就能买这东西。

663. Is this brand name real? /Is it the real McCoy? 这些是真品吗?

664. Nowadays all the products are marked with bar codes. 最近所有的商品都用条形码标注。

665. I got it at a white elephant sale. 我在处理品商店买的。

666. I'm a regular customer here. / I patronize this shop regularly. 我是这儿的常客。

667. The most popular color this year is black, and the style fits you well. 今年最流行的就是黑色,而且这款式也适合你。

668. May I say how elegant you look with this necktie? 我想说您戴这条领带真潇洒。

669. I'd like to buy a tie to match this suit. 我想买条领带搭配这套衣服。

670. Don't overwhelm your look with a scarf. 别让围巾盖过你的整体造型。

671. Don't think a scarf can save a bad outfit. 别以为围条围巾就能挽救失败的衣着。

672. The most important part of personal style is your person. 个人风格最重要的一部分就是要穿出真我。

673. Please show me what's in vogue/style/fashion. 请给我看一下现在最时兴的。

674. Your tie goes well with that shirt. 你的领带很配这件衬衫。

675. You are wearing your clothes inside out. 你衣服穿反了。

676. This dress is too low-cut/revealing/immodest for me to wear. /This dress is loud /gaudy/ flashy for me to wear. 这件衣服太低胸/俗艳了(暴露/不庄重),我不能穿。

677. Are all the shirts a uniform price? 衬衫都是统一价吗?

678. You must have a receipt to get a refund. 如果想退货请保留收据。

679. Learn on describing a person with signs. 学着用星座来描述一个人。

680. The time of your birthday decides your star sign. 每个人的星座是由他的生日决定的。

681. Scorpio is the most mysterious. 天蝎座是最神秘的星座。

682. Aquarius is the friendliest of the star signs. 水瓶座是所有星座中最友善的星座。
683. Pisces is the most romantic one. 双鱼座是最浪漫的星座。
684. Some people believe that people born under the same star sign share similar characteristics.
 有些人相信星座相同的人有共同的性格特点。
685. The murderer was still at large. 杀人犯依然逍遥法外。
686. Justice has long arms. 法网恢恢。
687. He lost at court. / He took the beating in court. 他在法庭上败诉了。
688. Your honor, we find the defendant guilty (not guilty).
 法官大人,我们对被告做出有罪(无罪)的判决。
689. We could not reach a consensus on a verdict. 由于意见不一致,我们还没有做出最后判决。
690. I plead the Fifth (Amendment). 我有保持沉默的权利。
691. Objection sustained/denied. 反对无效。
692. Order in the court. 请遵守法庭秩序。
693. The jury will adjourn to its quarters and deliberate the verdict.
 陪审团会休庭,然后秘密商讨判决。
694. The plaintiff accused the defendant of fraud. 原告指控被告犯了欺诈罪。
695. The witness's testimony sounds convincing. 目击者的证词听起来令人信服。
696. Nature is not over-merciful in its treatment of delinquents.
 大自然对于罪人是不会过于心慈手软的。
697. A good name is easier lost than won. 名誉失之易,得之难。
698. You mustn't do that. It will blot your copybook.
 你千万不要这么干,这会玷污你自己的名声。
699. He that has a tongue in his head may find his way anywhere. 遇事多问,随处可行。
700. A burden of one's choice is not felt. 爱挑的担子不嫌重。
701. Progress is the activity of today and the assurance of tomorrow.
 进步是今天的活动,明天的保证。
702. The man who has made up his mind to win will never say "impossible."
 凡是决心取得胜利的人是从不说"不可能"的。
703. If winter comes, can spring be far behind? 冬天来了,春天还会远吗?
704. Man cannot discover new oceans unless he has courage to lose sight of the shore.
 人只有鼓足勇气,告别海岸,才能发现新的大洋。
705. Time drops in decay, like a candle burnt out. 时间一点点地流逝,如同蜡烛慢慢燃尽。
706. No road of flowers leads to glory. 没有一条通向荣耀的道路是铺满鲜花的。
707. I might say that success is won by three strings: first, effort; second, more effort; third, still more effort. 可以说成功要靠三件事才能赢得:努力、努力、再努力。
708. Meet success like a gentleman and disaster like a man. 优雅地迎接成功,勇敢地面对挫折。
709. Care and diligence bring luck. 谨慎和勤奋才能抓住机遇。
710. Nothing is impossible to a willing heart. 心头有志愿,无事不可能。
711. Life is like a play: it's not the length, but the excellence of the acting that matters.
 生活就像一场演出,重要的不是长度而是演出精彩与否。

712. There is nothing permanent except change. 唯有变化才是永恒的。
713. Ambition never dies until there is no way out. 不到黄河心不死。
714. Every extremity is a fault. 万事过分都是差误。
715. Plain living and high thinking. 生活俭朴,思想高远。
716. Fine character is superior to wisdom. 良好的个性胜于卓越的才智。
717. The bough that bears most, hangs lowest. 结果最多的枝头,垂得最低。
718. Gather your rosebuds while you may. 花开堪折直须折,莫待无花空折枝。
719. You can't step twice into the same river. 人不能两次踏入同一条河流。
720. One flower makes no garland. 一朵花做不成一个花环。
721. Hard work keeps away poverty; toleration keeps away violence.
以勤为富则不贫乏;以忍为力则不暴戾。
722. He who risks nothing gains nothing. 不入虎穴焉得虎子。
723. Faults are thick where love is thin. 一朝情意淡,样样不顺眼。
724. A fault once denned is twice committed. 一次不认错,必定再犯错。
725. Weak men wait for opportunities; strong men make them. 弱者等待机会,强者创造机会。
726. Experience is a school from which one can never graduate. 经验无止境。
727. Good temper is the best coat for any man in social activities.
好脾气是一个人在社交中能穿着的最佳外套。
728. He who questions nothing learns nothing. 无所问者无所获。
729. One of the first principles of perseverance is to know when to stop perseverance.
忍耐的首要原则是知道什么时候停止忍耐。
730. No pain, no palm; no thorns, no throne; no gall, no glory; no cross, no crown.
没有播种,何来收获;没有辛劳,何来成功;没有磨难,何来荣耀;没有挫折,何来辉煌。
731. Something attempted, something done. 有所尝试,就有所作为。
732. What we love to do, we find time to do. 我们喜欢做的事,总能找到时间去做。
733. Experience is the child of thought, and thought is the child of action. We cannot learn men from books. 经验是思想之子,思想是行动之子,了解他人不可以书本为据。
734. An idea that is developed and put into action is more important than an idea that exists.
有了想法并将之付诸行动对比徒有空想更重要。
735. The roots of education are bitter, but the fruit is sweet.
教育的根是苦涩的,但其果实是香甜的。
736. Education is a progressive discovery of our own ignorance.
教育是一个逐步发现自己无知的过程。
737. That under everyone's hard shell is someone who wants to be appreciated and loved.
在某些人的坚硬外壳下,也有渴望被欣赏和被爱的一面。
738. Time was a swiftly flowing river that had no shore, no boundaries. Its seasons were not winter, spring, fall or summer, but birthdays and joys and troubles and pain.
岁月似无边无涯的激流。一年四季不是春、夏、秋、冬的更迭,而是由生日的欢悦、生活的乐趣、烦恼和痛苦所交织而成的。

739. However, though it has brought mankind merits, some undesirable side-effects have gradually come to the surface. 尽管它给人类带来好处,但一些副作用也渐渐表现出来。

740. Achievements provide the only real pleasure in life. 有所成就是人生唯一的真正乐趣。

741. Life consists not in holding good cards, but in playing well those you hold.
生活不在于握有一手好牌,而在于把手里的牌打好。

742. Education does not mean teaching people to know what they do not know; it means teaching them to behave as they do not behave.
教育不在于使人知其所未知,而在于按其所未行而行。

743. What sculpture is to a block of marble, education is to the soul.
教育之于心灵,犹如雕刻之于大理石。

744. Good painting is like good cooking: it can be tasted, but not explained.
好画犹如佳肴,只可意会,不可言传。

745. Painting is silent poetry, and poetry is a speaking picture.
画是无言之诗,诗是有声之画。

746. The landscape belongs to the man who looks at it. 风景属于看风景的人。

747. Minds that have nothing to confer find little to perceive.
固执己见的人终将发现自己领悟甚少。

748. He who neglects learning in his youth, loses the past and is dead for the future.
少壮不努力,老大徒伤悲。

749. Nothing in the world is more dangerous than sincere ignorance and conscientious stupidity.
世上再也没有比纯粹的无知和认真的愚蠢更危险的了。

750. A hedge between keeps friendship green. 君子之交淡如水。

751. A rolling stone gathers no moss. 滚石不生苔,转业不聚财。

752. Caution is the parent of safety. 小心驶得万年船。

753. Empty vessels make the greatest sound. 石磨无声空磨响,满瓶不动半瓶摇。

754. Fools learn nothing form wise men, but wise men learn much from fools.
愚者不学无术,智者不耻下问。

755. If you make yourself an ass, don't complain if people ride you. 人善被人欺,马善被人骑。

756. Many things grow in the garden that were never sown there.
有心栽花花不发,无心插柳柳成荫。

757. He who does not advance loses ground. 逆水行舟,不进则退。

758. One swallow does not make a summer. 一花不是春,独木不成林。

759. Don't bite more than you can chew. 贪多嚼不烂。

760. While the grass grows, the steed starves. 远水解不了近渴。

761. Faith will move mountains. 只要功夫深,铁杆磨成针。

762. That is gold that is worth gold. 实至名归。

763. High aims form high characters, and great objects bring out great minds.
崇高的目标造就崇高的品格,伟大的志向造就伟大的心灵。

764. A good thing is known only within one's family, but a bad thing is known far and wide.
好事不出门,坏事行千里。

765. He who does not learn when he is young will regret when he is old.
少壮不努力,老大徒伤悲。

766. The fish always stinks from the head. 上梁不正下梁歪。

767. Failure teaches success. 失败是成功之母。

768. There is a black sheep in every flock. 十个指头不一般齐。

769. Don't look a gift horse in the mouth. (=Don't judge a gift by its value.)
千里送鹅毛,礼轻情意重。

770. The spirit is willing but the flesh is weak. 心有余而力不足。

771. Continuous effort is the key to unlock our potential. 持续的努力是开启潜力的钥匙。

772. Don't count your chickens before they are hatched. 鸡蛋未孵,勿先数雏。

773. When Greek meets Greek then comes the tug of war. 两雄相遇,其斗必烈。

774. Beauty is in the eye of the beholder. (= Beauty lies in the lover's eyes.)
情人眼里出西施。

775. Beggars can't be choosers. (=Whoever facing an unfavorable circumstance must make concessions to survive.) 人在矮檐下,不得不低头。(讨饭难减嘴。)

776. Actions speak louder than words.(=Taking actions is more convincing than speaking.)
说一尺,不如行一寸。

777. Give a dog a bad name and hang him. 众口铄金,积毁销骨。

778. It takes two to tango. (= Certain activities require mutual cooperation to achieve a common goal.) 一足不成步,独拍不成声。

779. You don't get something for nothing. (=It's impossible to gain anything without an effort.)
一分耕耘,一分收获。(人要勤劳,地要勤刨。)

780. Once bitten, twice shy. (= If one has been hit hard by something, he will be afraid of a similar thing or situation for a long time.)
一朝蛇咬脚,十年怕踩草。(一次挨蛇咬,二次不拔草。)

781. All that glitters is not gold. (=Nothing should be judged by its appearance.)
光头圆顶不一定都是和尚。(名山不在高。)

782. One boy is a boy, two boys half a boy, three boys no boy.
一个和尚挑水吃,两个和尚抬水吃,三个和尚没水吃。

783. It takes three generations to make a gentleman. 十年树木,百年树人。

784. Men should have high aspirations; students should study perseveringly.
人贵有志,学贵有恒。

785. Every man is mad on some point. 人非圣贤,孰能无过。

786. Do not do to others what you would not like yourself. 己所不欲,勿施于人。

787. Do to others as you would be done by. 以己所欲,施之于人。

788. All bread is not baked in one oven. 人心不同,各如其面。

789. He who does not advance falls backward. 不进则退。

790. A crooked stick will have a crooked shadow. 上梁不正下梁歪。

791. Friends agree best at distance. 君子之交淡如水。

792. What are the odds so long as you are happy. 知足者常乐。

793. Everyone for himself, the devil takes the hindmost. 人不为己,天诛地灭。
794. Speak of the wolf, and you will see his tail. 说曹操,曹操到。
795. Better be the head of a dog than the tail of a lion. 宁为鸡头,不为牛后。
796. A thousand-li journey is started by taking the first step. /A thousand-li journey starts with the first step. 千里之行,始于足下。
797. Several men, several minds. 千人千品,万人万相。
798. United and having the same faith, we have wits as keen as a sword's blade.
大家一条心,锋利可断金。
799. Coming events cast their shadows before. 山雨欲来风满楼。
800. If you want to do your job well, you must have good tools first. 工欲善其事,必先利其器。
801. Great minds think alike. 英雄所见略同。
802. Without braving storm and wind, a sapling cannot grow into a tall tree.
不经风雨长不成大树。
803. He, who knows nothing but pretends to know everything, is indeed a good for nothing.
不懂装懂,永世饭桶。
804. The cleverest housewife cannot cook a meal without rice. 巧妇难为无米之炊。
805. If you have tasted the bitterness of gall, you know better the sweetness of honey.
吃过黄连苦,更知蜜糖甜。
806. Do not all you can, spend not all you have, believe not all you hear, and tell not all you know. 不要为所能为,不要花尽所有,不要全信所闻,不要言尽所知。
807. By mass efforts, things can be easily done; if working alone, you can achieve none.
众擎易举,独力难成。
808. It takes more than one cold day for the river to freeze three feet deep. /Rome was not built in a day. 冰冻三尺,非一日之寒。
809. Injuring all of a man's ten fingers is not as effective as chopping off one.
伤其十指,不如断其一指。
810. Take the whole into consideration, but do the job bit by bit. 大处着眼,小处着手。
811. In time of abundance, you should always think of time of want.
常将有时想无时,莫到无时想有时。
812. Cry with one eye, and laugh with the other. 啼笑皆非。
813. Although intensive study is hard, its fruit is sweet. 勤学虽苦,其果却甜。
814. He who has a mind to beat his dog will easily find his stick. 欲加之罪,何患无辞。
815. Many a little makes a mickle. 聚沙成塔,集腋成裘。
816. Forewarned, forearmed. 凡事预则立,不预则废。
817. Dogs sway their tails not so much in love to you as to your bread. 醉翁之意不在酒。
818. He devoted himself entirely to the service of the people until his death.
鞠躬尽瘁,死而后已。
819. If you don't aim high, you will never hit high. 不立大志,难攀高峰。
820. Smart as a rule, but this time a fool. 聪明一世,糊涂一时。
821. The leopard cannot change its spots. 江山易改,本性难移。

822. When the snipe and the clam grapple, the fisherman profits. 鹬蚌相争,渔人得利。

823. As distance tests a horse's strength, so time reveals a person's heart.
路遥知马力,日久见人心。

824. Many kiss the baby for the nurse's sake. / One talks about one thing, but tries to do another.
醉翁之意不在酒。

825. Loving comes by looking. 窈窕淑女,君子好逑。

826. Sickness comes on horseback but goes on foot. 病来如山倒,病去如抽丝。

827. Don't say that you have started too early, for many people are already on the way.
莫道君行早,更有早来人。

828. Running water does not get stale; a door-hinge is never worm-eaten. 流水不腐,户枢不蠹。

829. Beauty may have fair leaves, yet bitter fruit. 金玉其外,败絮其中。

830. Man cannot be always fortunate, just as flowers do not last forever.
人无千日好,花无百日红。

831. Listen to both sides and you will be enlightened; heed only one side and you will be benighted. 兼听则明,偏听则暗。

832. The grass is greener on the other side. 这山望着那山高。

833. The unexpected always happens. 天有不测风云,人有旦夕祸福。

834. Times try all. 路遥知马力,日久见人心。

835. Nothing is so strong as gentleness; nothing is so gentle as strength. 刚者至柔,柔者至刚。

836. A thousand cups of wine are too few when drinking with close friends. 酒逢知己千杯少。

837. A small leak will sink a great ship. 千里之堤溃于蚁穴。

838. All good things must come to an end. 天下没有不散的宴席。

839. Birds of a feather flock together. 一丘之貉。

840. World is but a little place, after all. 天涯原咫尺,何处不逢君。

841. Without the piercing chillness of the snowfall, where comes the fragrant whiff of the plum blossoms? 没有一雪彻骨寒,哪来梅花扑鼻香。

842. No pains, no gains. 宝剑锋从磨砺出,梅花香自苦寒来。

843. Don't waste your precious time, for youth, once spent, will never come again.
光阴勿虚度,青春不再来。

844. God helps those that help themselves. (=People should rely on themselves to overcome difficulties or correct mistakes.) 自助者天助。(天上下雨地上滑,各自跌倒各自爬。)

845. Living near the river, one knows the nature of fish; living near the mountain, one can distinguish the sounds made by birds. 近水知鱼性,近山知鸟音。

846. History tells us that modesty leads to success and conceit, to failure.
历览古今多少事,成由谦逊败由奢。

847. A healthy mind is in a healthy body. 健全的思想寓于健全的体魄之中。

848. Good fences make good neighbors. (= It is better to keep a certain distance between relatives and friends if they want to maintain a good relationship.)
好兄弟高打墙,亲戚朋友远离乡。

849. As heaven maintains vigor through movement, a gentleman should constantly strive for self-perfection. 天行健,君子以自强不息。——尤维纳利斯(诗人)

850. Our deeds determine us, much as we determine our deeds.
什么样的人便决定了干什么样的事;同样,干什么样的事决定了是什么样的人。——艾略特(诗人、剧作家、批评家)

851. "I'll try" does great things every day, "I can't" gets nothing done.
"我试试",则每日皆成大事;而"我不行",则一事无成。——罗塞蒂(画家、诗人)

852. Follow your own course, and let people talk.
走自己的路,让别人去说吧。——但丁(诗人)

853. Industry keeps the body healthy, the mind clear, the heart whole, the purse full.
勤奋使身体健康,头脑清醒,心灵充实,经济充足。——西蒙(小说家)

854. All that you do, do with your might; things done by halves are never done right.
做一切事情应尽力而为,半途而废永远不行。——斯托达德(诗人)

855. When work is a pleasure, life is a joy! When work is a duty, life is slavery.
当工作是一种愉快时,它是享受!当工作是一种责任时,它是苦役。——高尔基(作家)

856. There is a skeleton in every house. 家家有本难念的经。——萨克雷(作家)

857. All happy families are like one another; each unhappy family is unhappy in its own way.
所有幸福的家庭都十分相似;而不幸的家庭各有各的不幸。——托尔斯泰(作家)

858. A contented mind is the greatest blessing a man can enjoy in this world.
知足是人生在世最大的幸事。——艾迪生(文学评论家)

859. Happiness lies in the consciousness we have of it.
幸福在于自知拥有幸福。——桑(作家)

860. Self-distrust is the cause of most of our failures.
在多数情况下,失败的原因是不自信。——博依(作家、律师)

861. Life is not all beer and skittles.
人生并非只是吃喝玩乐。——休斯(思想家、法学家、小说家)

862. The meaning of life lies in people's self-perfection.
人生的意义就在于人的自我完善。——高尔基(作家)

863. Life is always unreasonable and full of agony, but it is still interesting ultimately.
人生总是不尽合理,而且往往充满痛苦,可是归根到底它仍然充满趣味。
——门肯(批评家)

864. To succeed in a great cause, one must begin from the trivialities
要成就一件大事,必须从小事做起。——列宁

865. The value of a man, however, should be seen in what he gives and not in what he is able to receive.
衡量一个人的价值应看他奉献了什么,而不是他能得到什么。——爱因斯坦(科学家)

866. There are three ingredients in the good life: learning, earning and yearning.
美好生活的三要素是:学习、收获、向往。——莫利(作家)

867. Life is ten percent what you make it and ninety percent how you take it.
生活有百分之十在于你如何塑造它,有百分之九十在于你如何对待它。——柏林(作曲家)

868. It is harmful to be self-conceited, while good to be humble.
满招损,谦受益。——《尚书》

869. Optimist: a man who gets treed by a lion but enjoys the scenery.
乐观主义是被狮子逼上了树仍然在欣赏风景的人。——温切尔(记者)

870. An optimist stays up until midnight to see the New Year in. A pessimist stays up to make sure the old year leaves.
乐观者等到午夜以迎新年,悲观者守到午夜以别旧岁。——大仲马(作家)

871. The great end of life is not knowledge but action.
人生的伟大目标不在于知,而在于行。——赫胥黎(生物学家、教育家)

872. The real purpose of books is to trap the mind into doing own think.
书的真正目的在于诱导头脑去思考。——莫利(小说家)

873. Book is the nutrient of the whole world. A life without books is like a life without sunlight; wisdom without books is a wingless bird.
书籍是全人类的营养品。生活里没有书籍,就好像没有阳光;智慧里没有书籍,就好像鸟儿没有翅膀。——莎士比亚(剧作家)

874. The good life is one inspired by love and guided by knowledge.
爱,激励美好生活;知识,指引美好生活。——罗素(数学家、哲学家)

875. Knowledge is the food on the journey of life.
知识是人生旅途中的粮食。——雨果(作家)

876. The first step to knowledge is to know that we are ignorant.
迈向有知的第一步,是要知道自己无知。——塞西尔(政治家)

877. The more we study, the more we discover our ignorance.
我们越是学习,越是发现自己无知——雪莱(诗人)

878. Reading is to the mind what exercise is to the body.
读书之于心灵,犹如锻炼之于身体。——爱迪生(发明家)

879. Reading makes a full man, conference a ready man, and writing an exact man.
读书使人充实,讨论使人机智,笔记使人准确。——培根(作家、哲学家)

880. Cultivation to the mind is as necessary as food for the body.
学习对于头脑,如同食物对于身体一样不可缺少。——西塞罗(政治家、演说家)

881. Never be tired of learning, never be wearied of teaching.
学而不厌,诲人不倦。——孔子(思想家、教育家、儒家学派创始人)

882. The three foundations of learning: seeing much, suffering much, and studying much.
求学的三个基本条件:多观察、多磨砺、多研究。——卡瑟(作家)

883. If three of us are walking together, at least one of the other two is good enough to be my teacher. 三人行必有我师焉。——孔子

884. Too much clearness is folly. 聪明过分,反成愚蠢。——梭伦(政治家、诗人)

885. It is not wise to be wiser than necessary. 聪明过了头,就不是聪明。——基诺(剧作家)

886. Education has for its object the formation of character.
教育的目的在于品质的形成。——斯宾塞(哲学家)

887. Education is not the filling of a pail, but the light of a fire.
教育不是注满一桶水,而是点燃一把火。——叶芝(诗人、剧作家)

888. Example is always more efficacious than precept.
身教胜于言教。——约翰逊(作家、批评家)

889. All the master scholars in the history must experience three periods: "Cold wind withered the green trees last night; Upstairs alone, I saw the road stretching to the endless," this is the first period; "No regret to be underweight, I am willing to wither for my sweetheart," the second; "After searching everywhere for him in vain I looked back suddenly and found that he was in the dim corner," the last period.
古今之成大事业、大学问者,必须经过三种境界:"昨夜西风凋碧树,独上西楼,望尽天涯路",此第一境也;"衣带渐宽终不悔,为伊消得人憔悴",此第二境也;"众里寻他千百度,蓦然回首,那人却在灯火阑珊处",此第三境也。——王国维(文学家、美学家、历史学家)

890. In front of my bed flooded with moonbea, / I mistook for frost appears on the floor. / lifting my head trying to watch the moon, / I drooped again for missing our hometown.
床前明月光,疑是地上霜。举头望明月,低头思故乡。(《静思夜》 唐·李白)

891. AN EXCELLENT SCENE—Du Fu   Tang Dynasty
Two yellow orioles are singing atop the green willows, / A flight of white egrets are flying up toward the sky; / You see the eternal snow from western peak via window; / A long-trip boat from Eastern Wu moored near the door.
两个黄鹂鸣翠柳,一行白鹭上青天。窗含西岭千秋雪,门泊东吴万里船。(《绝句》 唐·杜甫)

892. CLOTH OF GOLD—Anonymous   Tang Dynasty
I advise you not to cherish the cloth of gold, / But to honor the days of youth. / When flowers bloom they need be plucked; / Wait not to grasp in vain at empty twigs.
劝君莫惜金缕衣,劝君须惜少年时。有花堪折直须折,莫待无花空折枝。(《金缕衣》 唐·无名氏)

893. SPRING DAWN—Meng Haoran   Tang Dynasty
I overslept unaware of daybreak in spring. / Have heard birds crying almost everywhere. / A nightlong of noise from winds and rains. / A wonder the fallen flowers are countable.
春眠不觉晓,处处闻啼鸟。夜来风雨声,花落知多少。(《春晓》 唐·孟浩然)

894. CHING MING FESTIVAL—Du Mu   Tang Dynasty
Continuous drizzle on Ching Ming Death Festival days. / Pedestrians on the roads seem to be losing balance. / When I try to inquire the whereabouts of an alehouse, / The cowherd points at distant Apricot Flower Village.
清明时节雨纷纷,路上行人欲断魂。借问酒家何处有,牧童遥指杏花村。(《清明》 唐·杜牧)

895. SCRIPT ON RETURNING HOME—He Zhizhang   Tang Dynasty
I left in boyhood days now returned maturely old. / Native accent unchanged tho' grey temple hastened. / Seeing the children couldn't recognize each other, / Laughingly they'd asked whence comes this visitor?

少小离家老大回,乡音无改鬓毛衰。儿童相见不相识,笑问客从何处来?(《回乡偶书》 唐·贺知章)

896. THE DEER STOCKADE—Wang Wei Tang Dynasty

Not a single soul amidst an empty hill, / Though I still hear sounds from people. / Sun light is reflecting in deep forest, / It lightens too on the greenish mosses.

空山不见人,但闻人语响。返景入深林,复照青苔上。(《鹿柴》 唐·王维)

897. DOWN TO JIANG LING—Li Bai Tang Dynasty

Bade farewell to Baidi City amidst colored clouds in the more, / I returned to the thousand-li Jiang Ling negotiated in one day. / Gibbons were howling incessantly on both Yang Zi River's banks; / The light boat meanwhile managed to pass thousands of mountains.

朝辞白帝彩云间,千里江陵一日还。两岸猿声啼不住,轻舟已过万重山。(《下江陵》 唐·李白)

898. ON ASCENDING GUAN QUE TOWER—Wang Zhihuan Tang Dynasty

The sun is diminishing behind the mountains, / While Yellow River keeps flowing to the sea. / Exhausting my eyes to a thousand li further, / I am ascending one more storey of the tower.

白日依山尽,黄河入海流。欲穷千里目,更上一层楼。(《登鹳雀楼》 唐·王之涣)

899. RIVEER SNOW—Liu Zongyuan Tang Dynasty

Birds disappeared amidst thousands of mountains, / Not a single man is seen on the countless paths. / An old man with straw hat sits on the lone boat, / He is fishing alone along the cold snowed river.

千山鸟飞绝,万径人踪灭。孤舟蓑笠翁,独钓寒江雪。(《江雪》 唐·柳宗元)

900. The moon had sunk when crows were crying amidst frosty sky, / Riverside maple and fisherman's lamp faced my uneasy sleep. / There was the Hanshan Temple located at suburban Gusu City, / Midnight tolling of bell was heard on the passenger's boat.

月落乌啼霜满天,江枫渔火对愁眠。姑苏城外寒山寺,夜半钟声到客船。(《枫桥夜泊》 唐·张继)

常用句型100例

1. **anything but** "决不,根本不"。该句型具有较强的强调意味,后面直接跟所否定的内容,相当于"far from",表示"根本不……"。例如:

   The fruit here is anything but cheap.
   这儿的水果根本不便宜。
   Though we love peace, we are anything but cowards.
   我们热爱和平,但决不是懦夫。

   相关句型:

   1) not... at all 常用于句尾,表示"一点也不……,根本不……"。例如:
      I don't hate the idea at all.
      我一点也不讨厌这个主意。

   2) nothing but 指"只有,只是,仅仅"。例如:
      It's nothing but a joke.
      这不过是开开玩笑而已。

   3) not ...for anything 常用于口语中,强调"决不做某事"。例如:
      I wouldn't betray them for anything.
      我绝对不会背叛他们。

2. **as...as...** "像……一样……"。该句型用于两者的比较, as 与 as 之间跟形容词或副词原级,通常主句的主语和 as-分句的主语不同,而比较的项目相同;有时也可能主语相同,而比较项目不相同。这种比较结构的否定形式是 not(...)as/so...as...。例如:

   This room is as big as that one.
   这个房间和那个房间一样大。
   The young man was as brilliant as (he was) handsome.
   这青年既帅气又聪明。
   She'll soon be as tall as her mother.
   她很快就要跟她母亲一样高了。
   I can't run as/so fast as you.
   我跑得没你那么快。

   相关句型:

   1) less...than... 相当于 not(...)as/so...as..., 后者在实际使用中更常见。例如:
      Tom behaves less politely than Jack.
      汤姆举止不如杰克有礼貌。

2) **as much/many...as...** 也表示两者的比较,但限定词much/many后面跟名词,其否定形式是not...as/so much/many...as...。例如:

The girl hasn't known so/as many people as her younger sister (has).

这女孩认识的人不及她妹妹认识的多。

3. **as far as** "远到,到……为止;就……而言"。表示程度或范围,常用于as far as I know/remember/see等,指"据我所知,尽我记得的,依我看";或as/so far as I am concerned,指"就我而言"。例如:

We didn't go as far as the others.

我们没有像其他人走得那么远。

As far as I am concerned, that water is too cold.

对我来说,水太凉了。

As /So far as my knowledge goes, there is no such word in English.

据我所知,英语里没有这样一个词。

相关句型:

1) **by far** 强调程度深,与形容词、副词的最高级或比较级连用,表示"显然,到达极为明显的程度,……得多"。例如:

She is by far the best designer in the company.

她显然是公司中最优秀的设计师。

2) **far and away** 指"很大程度上"。例如:

This pizza is far and away the best I have ever tasted.

无疑,这个比萨是我尝过最棒的。

3) **so/thus far** 迄今为止;仅到一定的程度。例如:

So far the search has yielded nothing.

到目前为止没有找到任何东西。

Let me just recap on what we've decided so far.

让我来概括一下到目前为止我们所做的决定吧。

4. **as if/though** "仿佛,宛如"。以as if开头的从句,如果表示的是与事实相反的状态,需要用虚拟语气,其中从句的谓语动词在表示与现在事实相反的状态时,用一般过去时;表示与过去事实相反的状态时用过去完成时;表示将来不太可能实现的情况,多用would, could等;但在某些语境中,如果不表示假设意义,只是说话人在判断某事的真实性,as if从句可以用陈述语气。该短语后也可以跟不定式to do sth。例如:

She treats him as if he were the fount of all knowledge.

她把他当成无所不晓。

I can remember our wedding as if it were yesterday.

我们的婚礼我记忆犹新,就像昨天一样。

He took to French as though it had been his native language.

他觉得法语就像母语一样容易学。

He looked as though butter wouldn't melt in his mouth.
他装出一副老实的样子。
He walks as if he is drunk.
他走起路来仿佛喝醉了似的。
Her guest suddenly stood up as if to leave.
她的客人突然站起来,好像要走似的。

相关句型:

1) ...be/look like... 指"像……",这里like是介词,可用于比喻。例如:
The lake looks like a mirror.
湖面如镜。
This is just like old times.
宛如时光倒转。

2) ...take after sb... 指"长得像,尤其是(外貌或行为)像(父亲或母亲等)"。例如:
You really take after your mother.
你长得真像你母亲。

5. **as it is** "事实上,实际情况是"。该短语相当于as it turns out; as things stand。例如:
The situation is getting worse, as it is.
事实上情况正在恶化。
We can go in my car, such as it is.
我们可以坐我的车去,虽然我的车子不太好。
We're busy enough as it is; don't give us more trouble.
我们够忙的了,别再来凑热闹了。

相关句型:

1) as it were "可以说是,在一定程度上是,似乎就是",用来说明说话人的措词谨慎。
He is, as it were, a walking dictionary.
他可以说是一部活字典。
The man is, as it were, a modern Holmes.
这名男子可以说是现代的福尔摩斯。
She is my best friend, my sister, as it were.
她是我最好的朋友,可以说如同我的姐妹。

6. **as/so long as** "只要……,如果……"。后面跟从句,表示"只要,如果……",有时指"既然……;由于……"。例如:
You will never cease to learn as long as you live.
活到老,学到老。
He need not step down so long as they support him.
既然他们支持他,他就不必辞职。
Any topic will do, so long as it is interesting.
只要有趣,任何话题都可以。

My parents don't care what job I do as long as I'm happy.
只要我开心,我父母不在意我做什么工作。

相关句型:

1) as long as your arm 指"很长",常用于口语中。例如:
There is a shopping list as long as your arm.
有一份长得要命的购物清单。

2) so long 指"再见",常用于口语中。例如:
So long! My dear family!
再见了!我亲爱的家人!

7. **as soon as** "一……就……"。前后分别跟两个动作,强调as soon as后的动作一发生,这之前的动作随之发生,两者时间间隔较短。例如:
I recognized him as soon as he came in the room.
他一进屋我就认出了他。
Yet as soon as one has left the starting line, money matters.
但一旦他离开了这条起跑线,钱就变得重要了。
I came as soon as I heard the news.
我一听到消息马上就来了。

相关句型:

1) as soon as possible 指"尽快",常用于句尾。例如:
We agreed to contact again as soon as possible.
我们同意尽快再次联系。

2) would (just) as soon "宁可,宁愿……也不"。多用于第一人称的语气中。需要注意的是,该句型后接从句时,从句应是虚拟语气。例如:
We would as soon go to a movie as wander about the street.
我们与其在街上闲逛,还不如去看电影。
I'd just as soon you didn't drive the car while I'm gone.
我倒是希望我不在时你不要开车。

8. **as** "尽管……,即使……"。as 的用法很多,当它作为连词引导让步从句时,从句常位于句首,且谓语部分倒装。此用法多见于书面英语。例如:
Try as she might, she couldn't start the engine.
她想尽了办法也没能发动引擎。
Busy as he is, he studies English very hard.
尽管他很忙,可他还是努力学英文。

相关句型:

1) though/although 也指"尽管,虽然",引导让步从句,但从句位置灵活,不需倒装。although 较为正式,though 多用于口语。若强调时还可以用 even though。例如:
Though they were happy, there was something missing.(相当于 Happy as they were, there was something missing.)

尽管他们很快乐,但总缺少点什么。
Although/Even though/Though everyone worked hard, we lost the case.
尽管每个人工作都很努力,我们还是输了这案子。

2) much as 表示"尽管",可引导让步从句。例如：
Much as I would like to stay, I really must go home.
尽管我想留下来,但我确实必须回家。
Much as she likes him, she would never consider marrying him.
尽管她喜欢他,但她并不打算嫁给他。

9. **be about to**　"即将,将要"。用于表示随后马上会发生的事,通常不与表示将来的副词连用。例如：
The movie is about to start.
电影即将开始。
And I know what you're about to do.
我知道你要去做什么。

相关句型：

1) be on the point of doing "即将要……"。也用于表示随后马上会发生的事,距发生时间更近。例如：
We were on the point of missing the train.
我们眼看就要误了火车。

2) be to do sth 表示"预定要做……"。多用于表示公开的预定计划等。例如：
The wedding is to be held in a month's time.
婚礼将于一个月后举行。

3) be going to sth "将要做；将要发生"。侧重表达一种打算、意图、计划做的事,或是基于现有状况做出的推断。例如：
We'll be going to discuss the matter with them.
我们打算和他们一起讨论这件事。
It's going to snow.
快下雪了。

4) will do sth 通常指当场做的决定和打算,通常不用于表示计划或安排好的事件。例如：
I will text you later.
我会迟点给你发信息的。

10. **be capable of (doing) sth**　"有能力、有才能做某事"。较为正式,常见于书面语中。例如：
Bigger aircraft would be capable of flying farther.
较大的飞机可以飞得更远。
The company isn't capable of handling such a large order.
该公司没有能力应付那么大的订单。

相关句型：

1) be able to 表示"有能力、有机会做某事"，大多数情况下可以和 can 互换。但表示过去的某种具体能力时，肯定句中只能用 was/were able to 或 managed to，而不能用 could；但否定句没有这种限制，could 既可以表示过去的一般能力，也可表示过去做某件具体事情的能力。例如：
I was able to/managed to find some useful books in the library.
我总算在图书馆找到一些有用的书。
We weren't able to/didn't manage to/couldn't catch the flight in time.
我们未能及时赶上航班。

11. **be entitled to** "有权利、有资格做某事"。指"使……享有权利，给予某人获得某物或做某事的权利"。该短语常用于被动态 be entitled to sth，也可以跟不定式 entitle sb to do sth，指"有权做某事"。例如：
Party B shall be entitled to annual leave with salary.
乙方有权享受带薪年假。
Everyone is entitled to their own opinion.
人人都有权发表自己的意见。
The other party is entitled to cancel the contract.
另一方有权撤消该合同。
He believes his daughter is perfectly entitled to marry whoever she chooses.
他相信他的女儿完全有权选择要嫁给谁。

相关句型：

1) be qualified to do sth/for sth 指"具备做（尤其是某项工作）的知识或技能，能够胜任……"。例如：
She's extremely well qualified for the job.
她完全胜任此项工作。
He's not qualified to teach in high school.
他教中学还不够格。

2) be eligible to do sth/for sth 指"合格的，有资格的，有条件做某事，如达到一定年龄等"。例如：
You could be eligible for a university scholarship.
你也许有资格获得大学奖学金。
Anyone over the age of 18 is eligible to vote.
超过18岁的人就有选举资格。

12. **be likely to/that** "可能做某事，有希望的"。这里的 likely 是形容词。例如：
Roses on Valentine's Day are likely to be expensive.
情人节那天的玫瑰可能很贵。
It's more than likely that the thieves don't know how much it is worth.
盗贼很可能不知道此物的价值。

They might refuse to let us do it, but it's hardly likely.

他们也许会不让我们做这工作,但这可能性太小。

相关句型:

1) (as) likely as not 在口语中常用,表示"很可能"。这里的likely是副词。例如:

They will turn up at the meeting as likely as not.

他们很可能会在会议上露面。

2) more likely/most likely/more than likely 此处likely也是副词,用于表示可能性较大。例如:

It's more than likely Brazil will win the World Cup.

巴西很有可能赢得世界杯。

13. **be/have nothing/something etc. to do with** "与……无/有关系"。表示句子主语与with的宾语有某种联系,其中用nothing指"毫无关联",something指"有些联系",还可以用much, little等分别表示"有较多联系"、"有较少联系"等。值得注意的是,该句型不用于进行时。例如:

It has nothing to do with you.

这与你不相干。

That has nothing to do with what we're discussing.

那与我们所讨论的内容毫不相干。

I don't know much about this project, but I know it's something to do with energy.

我不太了解这个项目,但我知道它和能源有关。

The book has something to do with domestic violence, as far as I know.

据我所知,这本书与家庭暴力有关。

相关句型:

1) be nothing to 指"对某人来说无所谓"。例如:

I used to love this house but it's nothing to me now.

我爱过这栋房子,但现在对它再也没什么感情。

2) have nothing on sb 有两个含义,一指"远比不上某人",或指"没有某人的罪证"。例如:

He is quite a good father, but he has got nothing on Mr. White.

他已经是个很好的父亲,但比怀特先生还差得远。

The police wanted to arrest him but they had nothing on him.

警察想要逮捕他,但没有他的罪证。

3) there is nothing in/to 指"某事不可信,是捏造的";而there is something in 则指"某人的话或主意等有道理"。例如:

The rumor said she was going to resign, but there's nothing in it.

有传言说她要辞职,不过这不可信。

They had to concede that there was something in his teaching methods.

他们不得不承认他的教学方法有道理。

4) there is nothing like 指"什么都比不上……，……非常好"。例如：
There's nothing like a cup of hot tea on a cold day!
冷天喝杯热茶,简直太舒服了!

14. **be of** "具有……(性质)"。用于描述特定的人或事物,of后接名词,常可用对应的形容词改写句子。例如：
She is a girl of courage.
She is a courageous girl.
她是个有勇气的姑娘。
This is a book of value.
This is a valuable book.
这是本有价值的书。
The sleeping pills are of no effect to him.
安眠药对他没有用。

相关句型:

1) be blessed with 指"在……方面有福气；幸运地享有"。例如：
She's blessed with excellent health.
她身体很好,是一种福气。

2) be endowed with 指"具有或被赋予资质、才能"。例如：
The stones are believed to be endowed with magical powers.
人们认为这些石头具有魔力。

3) be possessed of 指"具有某种品质或特征",较为正式。例如：
He was possessed of great self-confidence.
他有很强的自信心。

15. **be supposed/expected to** 这两个句型均指"被期望做……,应该做……"。其中be supposed to指"因为规定或指令而被期望做……",或是"本该发生而没有发生的某个动作"。...be expected to...则强调"被预计做……",常因职责或身份而为之。例如：
We're not supposed to smoke here.
我们不应该在这里抽烟。
The new laws are supposed to prevent crime.
这些新法令本应起到防止犯罪的作用。
Eating spinach is supposed to make you strong.
据说吃菠菜能使人强壮。
They are expected to win the election with ease.
预计他们在竞选中能够轻易获胜。

相关句型:

1) suppose 在口语中的使用频率很高,比如" I suppose..."表示"我想,我认为",或直接跟从句表示推测、建议等。例如：

I suppose you're splitting hairs.

我认为你在吹毛求疵。

Suppose your father saw you, what would he say?

你父亲要看见你,他会怎么说?

Suppose we get him wrong, what will we do then?

假如我们误会他了,那我们该怎么办呢?

2) fully expect 指"完全相信,确信某事会发生"。其他还有"half expect"指"认为某事有可能";"is (only) to be expected"指"在预料之中,相当正常";"I expect..."多用于口语中,表示"我觉得,依我看"。例如:

At the time I fully expected to find a job.

那个时候我还一心盼望找到份工作。

I looked back, half expecting to see someone.

我回过头去,猜想可能有人跟踪我。

This was to be expected.

这是预料中的。

3) What's that supposed to mean? 意为"这算什么意思呢?"这句话常用于表示对某人刚说的话感到恼火。例如:

"You want to quit? What's that supposed to mean?"

"你想退出?你什么意思啊你?"

4) What (else) do you expect? 表示"有什么大惊小怪的;你还能指望怎么?"这句话常用于评论某件令人不快但合理的事情。例如:

"Mary is sick again." "What else do you expect?"

"玛丽又生病了。""有什么好奇怪的?"

16. **both...and...** "不仅……而且……"。由 both...and...连接的并列结构表示"……和……都……"。如果该并列结构做主语,表示的意义为复数,谓语动词用复数;如果做主语的并列结构不是指两个或两个以上的人或物,而是表示单数意义,则动词用单数。例如:

Both his mother and his father have been there.

他父母二人都去过那里。

Both bread and butter is usually eaten with smoked bacon.

面包黄油在一起常与熏火腿肉搭配着吃。

相关句型:

1) 当主语后面跟 as well as, in addition to, with, along with, together with 等引导的词组时,其后的谓语动词形式也取决于主语本身的形式。在非正式语体中,也可根据"意义一致"或"就近原则"来决定随后动词的形式。例如:

The father, as well as his sons, is going to enroll.

父亲和儿子们都打算去应征报名。

An expert, together with some assistants, was sent to help in this work.

一位专家和几位助手被派去协助这项工作。

The truck along with all its contents was destroyed.
卡车及所有货物全毁了。

The basketball players as well as their coach were there.
篮球选手们和教练都在那儿。

17. **can never/ can't ...overdo/too/too much/ enough etc.** "无论怎样……都不过分"。该结构通常由否定性的谓语部分加程度副词 too/too much/enough 或是表示程度深的 overdo, exaggerate 之类的动词等构成，表示"越……越好，无论怎样……也不为过"。例如：

You can't be too polite.
你越礼貌越好。

You can never be too polite.
你越礼貌越好。

You can't be polite enough.
你越礼貌越好。

We can scarcely pay too high a price for freedom.
为了自由我们付出再大的代价也不为过。

His novel cannot be overestimated.
他的小说无论怎样评价也不会过高。

The importance of creativity cannot be overemphasized.
创造力的重要性无论怎样强调也不为过。

相关句型：

1) be too/a bit much (for sb) 指"非……力所能及，非……所能忍受，过分"。例如：

This job is too much for a new employee.
这项工作不是一个新雇员能完成的。

I thought damaging your car and expecting you to pay for it was a bit much!
弄坏了你的车还指望你自己掏腰包，我认为这有点过分！

18. **can't/couldn't help doing sth** "不可能避免做……，情不自禁做……"。强调某人因忍不住或无法抑制而做某事，help 后面跟动词 ing 形式。例如：

I can't help thinking he knows more than he has told us.
我总觉得他没把他知道的事全告诉我们。

I couldn't help hearing what you have just said.
我无意中听到了你刚刚说的那些话。

相关句型：

1) can't/couldn't help but do sth 与之类似，指"控制不住做某事"，but 后面跟动词原型。例如：

You can't help but start moving when you hear this song.
当听到这首歌的时候，你不由自主地开始移动。

2) can't help it 指"不是某人的过错"或"忍不住,无法控制自己"。例如:
　　I always make the same mistake; I just can't help it.
　　我总犯同样的错,我就是控制不了自己。
3) cannot but 指"不得不,只能",后面跟动词原型。例如:
　　She could not but walk there.
　　她不得不走到那里去。

19. **chances are (that)** "很可能……"。常用于口语中,句首可以加 The,也可以省略,表示"有机会,很可能做某事"。例如:
　　Chances are she has already heard the news.
　　很可能她已经听到这消息了。
相关句型:
1) stand/have a chance of doing sth "有可能成功……,有机会获得……"。例如:
　　If you don't try, you don't stand a chance of gaining anything.
　　如果你不尝试,将会一无所获。
2) take a chance (on sth) 指"冒险……",也常以 take one's chances 的形式出现,表示"冒险……,碰运气……"。例如:
　　He took his chances and jumped into the water.
　　他冒险跳进水里。

20. **elbow/shoulder/push etc. one's way** "用肘、肩等挤出(一条路)出去"。elbow 是"肘部",shoulder 是"肩膀",这些表示身体部位的词可作动词,表示"用肘推、用肩膀挤"等,push 表示"推、挤",此类动词后面跟 one's way (through, cross, in...),常表示在拥挤或嘈杂的情况下较困难地行走,挤出一条路。例如:
　　He elbowed his way through the crowd.
　　他从人群中挤了过去。
　　She shouldered her way through the onlookers.
　　她用肩膀挤着穿过围观的人群。
　　She pushed her way to the front of the crowd.
　　她挤到人群的前面。
相关句型:
1) feel one's way 指"(因看不清或不了解情况)摸索前进,谨慎行事"。例如:
　　He felt his way across the room, and found the light switch.
　　他摸索着走到房间的另一头,找到了电灯开关。
2) push forward 指"(不顾困难)继续前进",而 push sb/oneself forward 则指"出风头,使别人注意到……"。例如:
　　As the army pushed forward, the death toll mounted.
　　随着部队的推进,死亡人数在增加。
　　She had to push herself forward to get a promotion.
　　她必须努力表现自己以求得升迁机会。

21. **end up doing sth** "最终……,结果是……"。该句型除了后接动词ing形式外,还可跟介词短语或形容词,表示"以……结束、收场",尤指意料之外的结局。例如:
   We didn't like it at first, but we ended up cheering.
   一开始我们并不喜欢它,可最后我们却为之欢呼。
   If you go on like this you'll end up in prison.
   如果你继续这样,早晚得进监狱。
   If he carries on driving like that, he'll end up dead.
   如果他继续这样开车,总有一天会把命都丢掉。

相关句型:

1) **only to** 作结果状语多用来表示出人意料、结局令人沮丧的结果,动词多为find, learn, to be told, to be caught 等。例如:
   He hurried to the office, only to be told that he was fired.
   他急急忙忙赶往办公室,结果被告知他被解雇了。

2) **end in sth** 指"以某种特定方式结束",不用于被动态。口语中还有 it'll all end in tears 一说,指"某事以痛苦而告终,以悲剧收场"。例如:
   Their date ended in uproars.
   他们的约会最后以大吵大闹收场。

3) **the end justifies the means** 这句话指"只要目的正当,可以不择手段",常用于口语中。

4) **it's not the end of the world** 这句话的字面意思指"还未到世界末日,天不会塌下来",表示事情并不那么可怕,常用于口语中。例如:
   Failing an exam is not the end of the world.
   一次考试不及格并非世界末日。

22. **enjoy (doing) sth** "喜欢……,享受……的乐趣"。enjoy 后面跟名词短语、代词或是动词ing形式,表示"乐于做某事",还有常见结构 enjoy oneself,表示"过得愉快,玩得痛快"。例如:
   He enjoys traveling by train.
   他喜欢乘火车旅行。
   They all enjoyed themselves at the party.
   他们在聚会上都玩得非常开心。

相关句型:

1) **have a good/great/fantastic time** 均指"玩得很高兴"。例如:
   Thanks for the ride— tonight I had a good time.
   谢谢你送我回家——今晚我过得很开心。

2) **have fun** 指"玩得很愉快",这里的 fun 是名词,指"有趣而令人激动的经历或活动",常用 great/good fun。例如:
   Why don't you come with us? It'll be great fun.
   你为什么不跟我们来呢? 会玩得很痛快的。
   The children were having so much fun in the park.
   孩子们在公园玩得那么开心。

Swimming in the sea is great fun.
在海里游泳很好玩。

23. even if/though "即使……"。引导让步状语从句,表示"即使,尽管……",而主句开头不能再用but/however,相当于though/although,但语气更强。例如:
Even if we could afford it, we wouldn't go abroad for holidays.
即使我们有能力,我们也不去国外度假。
We had to go out, even though it was raining.
即使下雨,我们还得外出。
I like her, even though she can be annoying at times.
尽管她有时可能很烦人,我还是喜欢她。

相关句型:
1) even now/then 指"尽管如此(那样);即便是这样(或那样);甚至到现在(或那时)"。例如:
I explained everything, but even then he didn't understand.
我样样都解释到了,即便这样他还是不明白。
2) even so 指"尽管如此,即使这样"。例如:
There are a lot of spelling mistakes; even so, it's a quite good essay.
尽管有许多拼写错误,它仍不失为一篇佳作。

24. every time/ each time/ next time/ the first time etc. "每当……,每次……,下次……,第一次……"。这里的time指"次,回",其加限定词every, each等构成连词短语,引导时间状语从句。例如:
Every time she eats icecream she feels happy.
她每次吃冰激凌都感到很开心。
Next time you're here, let's have lunch together.
下次你到这里来,咱们一起吃午饭。
I fell in love with him the first time I saw him.
我第一次见他就爱上了他。

相关句型:
1) when 指"当……的时候",较常用。例如:
Things were different when I was young.
我年轻的时候情况并不一样。
2) while 指"在做……的时候"。当它后接的分句中动词表示动作时,动词大多使用进行时。该词还用于"虽然……,(然而)另一方面……"的场合,表示转折。例如:
The child fell while (he was) running.
那孩子跑的时候摔倒了。
I found a wallet while I was walking in the park.
我在公园散步时发现了一个钱包。
Their country has plenty of oil, while ours has none.
他们国家盛产石油,我们国家却一点也没有。

While I like the color of the dress, I don't like its cut.
我虽喜欢这裙子的颜色,但不喜欢它的剪裁。

25. **feel like (doing) sth** "想要某物或想做某事"。feel like可以指"想要……",后面跟名词或ing短语。也可以指"摸起来像……"以及"感觉自己是(某一种人)"。例如:
I felt like another cup of coffee.
我想再喝一杯咖啡。
We all felt like going swimming.
我们都想去游泳。
It's nice fabric—it feels like velvet.
这布很好——摸上去像天鹅绒。
They made me feel like one of their family.
他们使我觉得自己是他们家里的一员。

相关句型:
1) long to do sth/long for sth 指"渴望,盼望(尤其当某事不可能很快发生时)"。例如:
I long to join you.
我真想和你们一起。
Most of all, they long for an emotional connection.
最重要的是,她们渴望感情上的共鸣。

26. **for every...** "每……就有……"。用于表示一种比例。例如:
For every 5 dollars you make, you can take 2 dollars as your commission.
你每收进五美元,就可以留两美元作为佣金。
For every one who wanted chips, ten wanted hamburgers.
有一个人要吃薯条,就有十个人想要吃汉堡包。

相关句型:
1) for all后面可以跟句子成分,指"尽管";也可以跟分句,表示"对某人不重要、无所谓"。例如:
For all its simple words, the book is not easy reading.
这本书虽然用词简单,但读起来并不容易。
For all I know she's still living in UK.
说不定她还住在英国呢。
He can wait for ever, for all I care.
他可能永远等下去,我才不管呢。

27. **get (sb) anywhere/somewhere/nowhere** "有所/无所成就,有所/无所进展"。anywhere, somewhere, nowhere等在这里均表示程度,用在get后,可表示某事或某人是否取得一定进步,情况是否有了进展等。例如:
After studying hard for a term, at last I feel I'm getting somewhere.
在努力学习一学期后,我终于感到有些进步。

This line of investigation is getting us nowhere.
这种调查方式不会使我们得到任何结果。
Terry's a nice lad but he's not getting anywhere.
特里是个不错的小伙子,但没什么成就。

相关句型:

1) get it 指"明白"、"理解",相当于 I see,常用于口语中,尤其在对方多次解释之后。例如:
Oh, the paper's supposed to go in this way up. I get it.
啊,纸得这面朝上放进去,我明白了。

2) you've got me there 这个句子指"你可把我难倒了",常用于口语中。此处 get 指"使……困惑,使……烦恼"。例如:
What gets me is having to do the same thing all day long.
使我感到恼火的是每天都得干同样的事。

3) get there 指"达成目的,获得成功"。例如:
It's not easy but we're getting there.
虽然这并不容易,但我们正朝着目标迈进。

28. get/be used to (doing) sth "习惯于做某事"。这里的 to 是介词,后面接名词或动名词结构,表示"习惯于、适应于做某事"。例如:
I'm used to the noise.
我对这噪音已经习惯了。
She wasn't used to people disagreeing with her.
她不习惯别人跟她意见相左。
I'm sure I will get used to the cold weather.
我肯定会习惯这寒冷天气的。

相关句型:

1) used to do sth 指"过去惯常做某事,现在则不做了"。例如:
I used to drink, but I gave up a couple of years ago.
我以前喝酒,但一两年前就戒掉了。
People used to think that the Earth was flat.
过去人们认为地球是平的。

2) be/get/grow/become accustomed to (doing) sth 指"习惯于……",通常是某种状况或某个地方,也可以用结构 accustom sb/yourself to sth,表示"使某人习惯于……"。例如:
My eyes slowly grew accustomed to the dark.
我的眼睛慢慢适应了黑暗。
I'm not accustomed to getting up so early.
我不习惯这么早起床。
It took him a while to accustom himself to the new rules.
他花了一段时间才逐渐适应了新的规则。

3) adjust to (doing) sth 指"适应,习惯",adjust 一词有"调整,调节"之意,所以 adjust to 强调"在行为或思想上做出某些调整、改变以适应……"。例如:

It took her a while to adjust to living alone after the divorce.
她离婚以后，过了一段时间才适应了单身生活。
You'll quickly adjust yourself to student life.
你将很快适应学生生活。

29. **go on doing sth** "不停地做某事"。 go on后面接动词ing形式,则表示"不间断地继续做某事"。而短语go on之后不接其他任何成分时,则表示"(演员)出场、(设备)通电运行、(时间)流逝、继续进行、(事件)发生等"。例如：
It went on raining.
雨不停地下着。
You can't go on drinking so much—you're not doing yourself any good.
你不能再这样海量地喝酒了——你是在害自己。

相关句型：
1) go on to (do) sth 指"(完成某事后)转而做另一件事"。例如：
I think we've exhausted this subject; let's go on to the next.
我想我们已经详尽无遗地讨论了这一问题,我们接着谈下一个吧。
After her early teaching career, she went on to become a doctor.
继早年从教之后她当了一名医生。

2) go on (with) sth 指"停顿或中断之后继续(做某事)"。例如：
He paused for a sip of coffee, then went on with his story.
他停下来抿了一口咖啡,然后继续讲他的故事。

3) go on (at sb)(about sth/to do sth) 指"不停抱怨,数落(某人)"。例如：
I wish you would stop going on at me about my weight!
我希望你不要再向我唠叨我的体重。

4) go on and on 指"长时间地继续下去",常带有一种抱怨与不满的语气。例如：
The noise seemed to go on and on.
噪声似乎没完没了。

30. **go without sth** "应付做某事","没……也行"。without后面接名词或动词ing形式。例如：
Since there is no butter left, we have to go without it.
既然黄油没了,我们只能将就一下。
She went without eating for three days.
她三天没吃东西。

相关句型：
1) do without (sth/sb) 指"没有……而设法对付过去",或"情愿没有,用不着",常见于口语。例如：
He can't do without a secretary.
他不能没有秘书。

Like all teenagers there's one thing she'd rather do without — spots.
和所有十几岁的孩子一样,有一样东西她宁可没有——青春痘。

2) it goes without saying 指"不用说,不言而喻"。例如:
It goes without saying that governments have to deal with deficits.
各国政府需要解决赤字问题,这一点毫无疑问。

31. **have a lot/nothing etc. going for you**　"有(或没有)很多有利条件"。这里 going 可理解为形容词性质,后置以修饰不定代词。例如:
You're young, intelligent, attractive—you have a lot going for you!
你年轻,聪明,漂亮——有利条件可多啦!
In some respects, you have everything going for you in a recession.
从某些方面而言,在经济衰退中每件事都对你有利。

相关句型:
1) the biggest/best/nicest...going 指"当今最大的/最好的/最美好的……"。例如:
He is the biggest fool going.
他是最笨的人。
2) when the going gets tough 此谚语指"当条件变得艰苦时,当进展变得困难时",暗含有志者更勇往直前之意。例如:
When the going gets tough, the tough gets going.
道路艰难,勇者前行。
When the going gets tough, be prepared to sell your stocks.
情形不妙的话,你得做好抛售股票的准备。

32. **had better/best do (sth)**　"最好做……"。用以表示"在目前状况下最好做某事",带有提醒、催促、警告之意。had 可缩写为'd,尤其注意 do 之前不带 to。例如:
We'd better see a doctor.
我们最好找医生看看。
He'd best not tell a lie.
他最好别撒谎。

相关句型:
1) do well to do sth 指"做……明智,最好做……"。例如:
They would do well to pause and ponder upon their responsibilities.
他们最好还是停一停,好好想一想自己所负的责任。
2) may/might as well do sth 指"最好……,倒不如做……",带有"虽然真的不想做,但没办法"的语气。例如:
After sweeping the yard, we might as well clean the rooms.
我们扫完院子,不妨把房间也打扫一下。

33. **hardly/scarcely...when/before**　"一……马上就……"。强调两个动作发生的时间间隔很短,"在将做未做……之际,就……"。通常先发生的事情用过去完成时,而

后发生的动作用一般过去时。在书面语中,hardly可以出现在句首,后面跟倒装句。例如:

We had hardly started before/when it began to rain.

Hardly had we started when it began to rain.

我们刚出发,就开始下雨了。

相关句型:

1) no sooner...than 指"一……,就……",同样表示两个动作的间隔时间短,连接词than引导从句,表示"随之而发生的动作"。在书面语中,no sooner也可以置于句首,后面跟倒装句。例如:

She had no sooner closed her eyes than the infant cried loudly.

No sooner had she closed her eyes than the infant cried loudly.

她刚合上眼,小婴儿就大哭起来了。

34. **have a lot/something/nothing/little...in common with sb/sth** "与某人/某物有……共同之处"。该句型用于人时,表示在兴趣、想法等方面有相同之处;用于事物或地点时,表示有相同的特征或特色等。"have"之后可以跟a lot, something, nothing等表示相似程度的多少,指"很多、有一些或没有共同之处等"。例如:

To my surprise, I found I had a lot in common with this stranger.

令我吃惊的是,我发现自己和这个陌生人有许多共同点。

The two cultures have a lot in common.

这两种文化有很多相同之处。

We have nothing in common, and in temperament we're poles apart.

我们没有什么共性,脾气完全相反。

相关句型:

1) it is common for sth to happen 指"某事很常见"。例如:

Now, it is common for young couples to apply for a loan to buy houses.

现在,年轻夫妇申请贷款购房很普遍。

2) in common with sb/sth 介词短语,较正式,指"与某人/物一样"。例如:

In common with other companies they advertise widely.

与其他公司一样,他们也大做广告。

35. **have ...say in sth** "对……有决定权、发言权"。say在这里是名词,可用no, much, little, a修饰,表示"对某事没有、有较大、几乎没有或有发言权"。例如:

We had no say in the decision to sell the company.

在决定出售公司的问题上,我们没有发言权。

They will have a determining say in their own future.

他们有权决定自己的未来。

The people of New China all have a say in the affairs of their state.

新中国的人民对国家大事都有发言权。

The judge had the final say.
法官有最后的决定权。

相关句型：

1) there is no saying 指"说不准，很难说"。例如：

There's no saying how he'll react.
很难说他会有何种反应。

There is no saying when this war will come to an end.
天晓得这场战争何时会结束。

2) have/say one's say 指"说出要说的话，畅所欲言"。例如：

She won't be happy until she's had her say.
她要把话都说出来才舒畅。

I let her have her say, and then I laid into her.
我让她把话说完，然后就把她痛骂一顿。

3) to say your piece 指"直言不讳，说出心里话"。例如：

Ok, you've said your piece. Now shut up!
行了，你要说的话都说了——闭嘴吧！

Say your piece and pay attention to our feelings.
把你的话都讲出来，并注意我们的情绪。

4) What do you say to sth/doing sth? 用于口语中，表示征询意见。"你以为如何？"例如：

What do you say to a three-year agency agreement?
您说我们签个为期三年的代理协议如何？

What do you say to going for a walk?
去散步好吗？

36. **have/let/make sb do sth**　"让某人做某事，使某人做某事"。have/let/make是使役动词，其宾语后面必须跟动词原型。have, let通常不用被动语态，但make sb do sth句型可用于被动语态中，此时，动词原型需改成to do sth。例如：

The boss made me wait outside his office.
老板让我在他办公室外面等。

I was made to wait outside his office by my boss.
我老板让我在他办公室外面等。

The salesman made me buy that second-hand car.
销售员让我买下了那辆二手车。

I was made to buy that second-hand car by the salesman.
销售员让我买下了那辆二手车。

She didn't let her child eat fast food.
她不让孩子吃快餐。

Jim had the doctor look at his tongue.
吉姆让医生看看他的舌头。

相关句型：

1) get sb to do sth "让某人做某事"，这里的 get 也有使役意味，而作宾补的动词不定式需有 to。例如：

I got my father to repair my toy car.

我让爸爸修我的玩具车。

2) have to "不得不，必须"，表示客观上的必要。在口语中多用 have got to。例如：

You have to scale the fish before cooking it.

你在烧鱼之前得刮去鳞片。

I have got to go now.

我现在该走了。

We shall have to trim our spending down to fit our income.

我们只得削减开支以使收支平衡。

3) have got 表示"有"，更口语化，相当于 have。例如：

I have got a bad cold, running at the nose.

我感冒很重，直流鼻涕。

37. **have sb doing sth** "导致、允许、同意……做某事"。这里 have 是使役动词，可表示"引起的后果，不能容忍的情况或经历等"，多用于疑问或否定句。也可以用 get，常用于口语。例如：

With five minutes, he had us all playing hide-and-seek.

不到五分钟，他让所有人都玩起了捉迷藏。

I won't have you shouting like that at me.

我可不让你对我那样大吼大叫。

The clown soon had us all laughing.

小丑很快就逗得我们都笑了。

Be quiet! You'll have the neighbors complaining!

安静点！你会使邻居投诉的！

I'll get the car going.

我要使车发动起来。

Within minutes, he had the whole audience laughing and clapping.

短短几分钟内他就让全体观众发出阵阵笑声和掌声。

She had me doing all kinds of jobs for her.

她指使我替她做各种各样的工作。

He always has the TV going at full blast.

他总是把电视机的声音开到最大。

相关句型：

1) have(got) ... coming to sb 指"得到某人应得之物，罪有应得，活该"。常用于口语中。例如：

You had that punishment coming for a very long time.

你早该受惩罚了。

It was not surprising that his wife left him—he had it coming for years.
他妻子离开他,这毫不奇怪——他早就该到这步田地了。

38. **have sth done** "请某人做……",表示某种情况或经历。动作的执行者常常是其他人而不是自己,即某种动作或某事是他人做的。例如:

I had my watch stolen last night.
昨晚我的手表被偷了。

We had the house painted.
我们请人把房子粉刷了。

Mind you. It's easy to have your pocket picked in a crowd.
请注意,在人群中你口袋内的东西是很容易被人扒窃的。

I had my hair cut.
我请别人帮我剪了头发。

比较:

I cut my hair.
我自己剪了头发。

相关句型:

1) get sth done 指"使/让人做好;经历;做(该做的事)",更口语化。当请专业人士做某事时,倾向用have。例如:

I'll just get these dishes washed and then I'll come.
我得把盘子洗了,然后就来。

I must get the television fixed.
我必须请人修理一下这台电视机。

2) make oneself understood/heard 指"使自己被了解,被听到"。make与过去分词连用,除了过去分词具备形容词性质的场合外,仅限于这些惯用句型。例如:

I couldn't make myself understood in French.
我无法用法语沟通。

39. **How/what about doing sth?** "……如何?"用于向对方提议或推荐,about是介词,可跟名词、代词或动词ing形式。例如:

How about a cup of tea?
来一杯茶如何?

How about going shopping with me?
跟我去购物怎么样?

What about going to the movie tonight?
今晚去看电影如何?

What about eating out tonight?
今晚到外面吃饭好不好?

相关句型:

1) What do you say to sth? 字面意思是"你对……有什么要说的吗?"实际上也是询问对方意

见,"……如何?" to 是介词,后面跟名词、代词或动词 ing 形式。例如:

What do you say to renting a boat?

租一艘船怎么样?

40. **How come (that...)?** "为什么会……/……是怎么回事?"该句型表示说话人要求对所发生的事情说明理由或做出解释,尤含惊讶之意,常用于口语中,相当于"How did sb come to do...?"例如:

How come she has descended to stealing?

她怎么会堕落到偷窃的?

How come the meeting is over? Shouldn't it begin at ten o'clock?

会议怎么会结束了呢?不是应该十点开始的么?

How come he got the job?

怎么他会得到这份工作呢?

相关句型:

1) How's that? 口语中常见,既可以表示"为什么,那是怎么回事",也可用来询问对方意见,指"你认为怎么样?"例如:

"I have already been on my vacation." "How's that?"

"我已经开始休假了。""为什么?"

How's that? My collection is really rare.

怎么样?我的收藏可是很稀有的。

2) How can/could you...? 指"你怎么能……",用以表示震惊或强烈反对。例如:

How could you believe such a rumor?

你居然相信这种谣言?

How could you leave without saying goodbye?

岂能不辞而别?

How could you sell your team members out?

你怎么能这样出卖自己的队友呢?

How could you do something like that?

你怎么能做出这样的事呢?

How could you eat such a thing?

你怎么能吃这种东西呢?

41. **how/what/where/when etc. to do** "如何做、要做、要去哪里做、何时做等"。特殊疑问词加带 to 的不定式,构成名词性质,常用作动词的宾语。但是 why 不可放在不定式前面。例如:

I know where to go, but I don't know how to get there.

我知道去什么地方,但我不知道怎么走。

Would you tell me when to leave?

你能告诉我什么时候动身吗?

I don't know what to do next.
我不知道接下来要做什么。
He always knows where to go and what to do.
他总是知道要到哪里去,要做些什么。
The message tells us clearly when to leave.
信息清楚地告诉我们何时离开。
She spent several hours considering how to achieve her goals.
她花了好几个小时考虑如何达成她的目标。
She thought about whom to invite to her wedding ceremony.
她在想婚礼应该邀请谁。

42. **if it were not for/if it had not been for** "如果没有……"。该句型是虚拟语气,用来表示假设,需根据句意表达的时间来决定具体使用哪一个句型。if it were not for 表示与现在事实相反的假设,而 if it had not been for 则表示与过去事实相反的假设。该句型中的 if 可省略,were 和 had 置于句首,其后词序和疑问句一样。例如:
If it were not for love, our life would be meaningless.
Were it not for love, our life would be meaningless.
如果没有爱,人生将没有意义。
If it had not been for his seat belt, he would have been killed.
如果当时没有系安全带,他就死定了。
Were it not for their help, we would go bankrupt.
如果没有他们的帮助,我们就要破产了。
If it had not been for his sense of humor, we would be greatly embarrassed.
如果当时不是因为他的幽默感,我们就要尴尬死了。

相关句型:
1) without 可用于陈述语气中,也可用于表示假设的虚拟语气句型,指"如果没有……,要不是……",其后跟名词性短语,不可接分句。例如:
Our life would be boring without friendship.
如果没有友情,生活会很无趣。
We had to survive without light or heating for a whole month.
整个月没有照明,没有暖气,我们也得活下去。
Without your goal, we would have lost the game.
如果没有你的射门,我们原本会输掉这场比赛。

2) but for/but that 较书面化,均表示假设的虚拟语气句型,指"如果没有……,要不是……"。前者跟名词性短语,后者跟分句。例如:
But for the rain, we would have had a nice holiday.
倘若没有下雨,我们的假日会过得很愉快。
But that you had seen me in the water, I would have drowned.
要不是你看见我掉在水里,我早就淹死了。

But for your attendance, we would not have such a pleasant evening.
倘若没有你的出席,我们今晚不会过得如此开心。
But that I had taken this course, I would have been confused by your speech.
要不是我上过这门课,我真被你说迷糊了。

43. **If only...** "但愿……/要是……就好了!"该句型用虚拟语气,表示不太可能实现的愿望,多有渴望或懊悔之意,可用于直接引语,而不可用在间接引语中。动词在表示现在的希望时,用一般过去时或过去进行时;表示过去的希望时用过去完成时;表示将来的希望,常接用would, could 等。be 基本上用were,但口语中第一人称单数和第三人称单数可用was。if和only既可以连在一起用,也可以分开。例如:
He said, "If only she were here!"
他说:"要是她在这儿就好了!"
If only I had known how to do it!
我要是当初懂得怎么做就好了!
If only you would come to my help.
要是你来帮助我就好了。
If he had only remembered to send that letter.
他要是没忘记发那封信就好了。
She said, "If only I were Snow White!"
她说:"我要是白雪公主就好了!"
If only I had known how the magician did his tricks!
我要是当初懂得魔术师是怎么变戏法的就好了!

相关句型:
1) only if 指"只有"。only 是副词,起强调作用,if 引导条件状语从句。当only if 引导的句子置于句首时,后面的主句需倒装。例如:
Only if the red light comes on is there any danger to employees.
只有红灯闪亮时才有危及员工的险情。
He'll break the record only if he does his best.
他只有竭尽全力才会刷新纪录。
Only if you have been through such agony will you understand it.
你只有经历过这样的痛苦,才能真正理解。

44. **in case** "万一,以防万一……",所引导的分句有时候会用should。当句子表示"为防止某种情况发生,采取了某种预防措施"时,in case 引导的分句通常放在主句后面。例如:
I'll take an umbrella in case it rains.
我会带把伞以防下雨。
I'll buy some candles in case there should be a power failure.
我会买点蜡烛,以防停电。
In case the dress is out of stock, you must choose another one quickly.
万一那件衣服没货了,你必须很快挑选好另外一件。

I'll save some money in case I lost my job.

我会存些钱以防失业。

In case I'm late, you just set off.

万一我迟到,你们就先出发吧。

相关句型:

1) in any case 指"无论如何"。例如:

There is no point complaining now—we are leaving tomorrow in any case.

现在抱怨毫无意义,反正我们明天就离开了。

2) in case of 指"如果发生"。例如:

Just keep this number to call in case of emergency.

万一发生意外,打这个号码。

3) as the case may be 指"视具体情况而定",常用于口语中。例如:

You may pay in cash or by check as the case may be.

你可以用现金或支票支付,看着办吧。

45. in that "因为,原因是"。相当于 because,较为书面化。例如:

She was fortunate in that she had friends to help her.

她很幸运,有一些朋友帮助她。

I'm lucky in that I'm surrounded by people who love me.

我很幸运,我被爱我的人所环绕。

Men differ from animals in that they can make and use tools.

人与动物的区别在于人能制造并使用工具。

相关句型:

1) because 多用于表示直接原因,其引导的从句一般放在主句后,有时也可放在主句前。另外在回答 why 的问句时,只能用 because,不能用 for。例如:

I do it because I like it.

我做这件事是因为我喜欢。

I criticized him, not because I hate him but because I love him.

我批评他,不是因为我恨他而是因为我爱他。

2) for 可以表示原因,又可以用于提出说明,语气较轻。当表示原因时,通常是推论的结果,引导的句子只能放在后面。 for 不能跟 not...but... 这一结构连用。例如:

He felt no fear, for he was very brave.

他很勇敢,毫不畏惧。

It must have snowed last night for the ground is white.

因为地面是白色的,昨晚一定下雪了。

46. ...is to ...what...is to... "就像……一样"。what 作关系代词解,引导两个程度相当的比较,通常是 A is to B what C is to D, 也可以把 what 引导的句子置于句首构成 what C is to D, A is to B, 表示"A 对 B 的关系,犹如 C 对 D 的关系"。例如:

Air is to people what water is to fish.

空气对于人的关系犹如水对于鱼的关系。

What family members are to the Chinese, personal achievements are to the Westerners.

个人成就对于西方人的重要,就如同家人对于中国人的重要性一样。

Electricity is to modern cities what blood is to human body.

现代城市对电的依赖就像人体靠血液给氧。

相关句型:

1) (just) as...so ...指"正如……也,犹如……一样也"。例如:

Just as the Americans love hamburgers, so the Italians love pizzas.

意大利人爱吃比萨饼,就像美国人爱吃汉堡包一样。

As some people don't know how to begin a conversation, so some people don't know how to end one.

就像有的人不知如何开始谈话,有的人不知如何结束一次对话。

As some people win, so some people lose.

有人成功,就有人失败。

47. **it happens that/ it chances that** "碰巧……,恰好……"。happen 及 chance 都可以作动词,指"偶然发生……,碰巧……",后者常用于书面语。这两个动词都可以跟不定式,也可以用 it 作形式主语,接 that 从句。例如:

It happened that we spotted each other at the same time.

我们碰巧同时发现了对方。

It chanced that they were wearing the clothes of the same brand.

碰巧他们穿的是同一个品牌的服装。

It happened that she was out when we called.

我们打电话时她刚巧不在。

It chanced that they were staying at the same hotel.

碰巧他们住在同一家旅馆。

相关句型:

1) as chance would have it "不巧"。例如:

As chance would have it, every time I tried to contact you, your phone was always out of service.

真是不凑巧,我每次试图联系你,你的电话总是打不通。

2) as it happens/happened "恰恰,令人惊奇的是"。例如:

The two brothers both fulfilled their childhood dreams, as it happens.

令人惊奇的是两兄弟都实现了自己儿时的梦想。

3) these things happen 指"这类事在所难免",常用于宽慰人。例如:

Never mind. These things happen.

没关系。这种事难免发生。

48. it's (high/about) time "该是……的时候了"。后面接虚拟语气,动词通常是过去时。可加high,指"早该是……的时候了",或加about,指"差不多是……的时候了"。也可以用it's time for sb to do sth表示类似意思,但是it's (high/about) time更委婉客气。例如:

It's about time you made a plan about your future.
你该计划一下你的未来了。

It's time we discussed your performance lately.
我们该谈谈你最近的表现了。

It's high time the children went to bed.
孩子们早该上床睡觉了。

It was time you quitted smoking.
你早该戒烟了。

It's about time you had your hair cut.
你该抽时间理理发了。

It's time we were going.
我们现在该走了。

It was time you made up your mind.
你早该下决心了。

It's time for you to buy a new computer.
你该买台新电脑了。

相关句型:

1) (and) about time (too) 指"早该……",也可用"(and) not before time"表示"早就该……"。例如:

I hear Alex got promoted last week—and about time too, I'd say.
我听说阿历克斯上周晋升了——我认为他早就该升了。

"Here's Helen!" "Not before time—where has she been?"
"海伦来啦!""她早该到了——她上哪儿去了?"

2) on time "准时"。例如:

I never expected her to be on time.
我从不指望她能准时。

These buses are never on time.
这些公交车从来就不准时。

3) in time "及时",也可以用"in good time"表示"准时,提早"。例如:

We arrived in time to see the beginning of the parade.
我们到了那里正好赶上游行开始。

49. (it's) no/little/small wonder "并不奇怪……,难怪……"。表示某种情况是自然而然的,不足为奇。wonder前可以用no, little或small来做修饰词,口语中通常省略it's,用no wonder (that)... 。例如:

It's no wonder you've got a headache when you drank so much last night.

昨晚你喝了那么多酒,难怪你头痛。

It's little wonder that she survived all her family members.

她比她所有的家人都活得长久,这并不奇怪。

No wonder you suffer from heart disease, you are extremely lack of exercises.

难怪你得了心脏病,你太缺乏运动了。

相关句型:

1) it's a wonder that 指"令人惊奇的是,莫明其妙的是……",常用于口语中。例如:

It's a wonder that you recognized me after all these years.

这么多年后你还能认出我,真是令人惊奇。

2) wonders will never cease 指"真是无奇不有",用于对出乎意料的事情表示惊讶,带有幽默调侃语气。例如:

"I've cleaned my room." "Wonders will never cease!"

"我把我的房间打扫干净了。""怎么太阳从西边出来了!"

50. **it's... of sb to do sth** "某人做某事……"。该句型在 it is 后面加表示人物特质的形容词,如 kind, nice, cold-hearted 等,来形容某人的品质或对某种行为做出判断,而动作的逻辑主语是 of 后面的人。例如:

It's very kind of you to show me around the park.

你能带我逛公园,真是太好了。

It's intelligent of you to come up with such a good idea.

你能想到这个主意,真是聪明!

相关句型:

1) it's ... (for sb) to do sth 指"某人做某事……",这个句型通常不对人或物的品质做出判断,只是单纯叙述。可以用 for 来引导不定式逻辑上的主语。例如:

It's difficult (for us) to find a good job.

找个好工作并不容易。

It's necessary for you to see the doctor.

你需要去看医生。

51. **it is said/ thought/ hoped/ believed that...** "据说……/人们认为、希望、相信……"。该句型相当于中文的"据说"、"据报道"、"众所周知"等结构,其主动词通常都是表示"估计、相信"等意义的词,常见的有:assume, expect, believe, fear, know, presume, report, say, think, understand 等。例如:

It is said that she had never been away from her hometown.

据说她从未离开过故乡。

It is thought that he is a terrible driver.

大家认为他车开得很糟糕。

It is well known that this area has always been a part of China.

众所周知,这一地区向来是中国的一部分。

It was reported that the ship had been sunk.
据报道,船只已沉没。
It is feared that all the miners were buried alive.
恐怕所有矿工都已经遇难。

相关句型:

1) sb is said/ thought/ hoped/ believed to do "据说某人……"。例如"People say Mr. Lee is a smuggler."这个主动句就可以改写成以下两个被动句型:

It is said that Mr. Lee is a smuggler.
Mr. Lee is said to be a smuggler.
据说李先生是个走私者。

52. it is/was ... that/who "正是……"。该句型是强调句式,也称为分裂句,可用来强调充当主语、宾语、补语的名词或代词,也可以强调状语,但不可以强调动词或形容词。通常将强调的成分置于it is 和that之间。另外,当强调主语时可用who取代that。在口语中可省略it is...that当中的that。当强调代词时,原则上代词为主语要用主格,但也有用宾格的情况。例如:

It was Mary who bought a lamp in this shop yesterday.
昨天在这家商店买了一盏灯的是玛丽。
It was a lamp that Mary bought in this shop yesterday.
昨天玛丽在这家商店买的是一盏灯。
It was in this shop that Mary bought a lamp yesterday.
昨天玛丽是在这家商店买的一盏灯。
It was yesterday (that) Mary bought a lamp in this shop.
玛丽就是在昨天在这家商店买的一盏灯。
It is I who am in charge of this firm.
负责这家事务所的是我。
It's me who's in charge of this firm.
负责这家事务所的是我。
It is because peacocks look beautiful that we adore them so much.
我们那么喜欢孔雀是因为它们看起来很美。

相关句型:

1) what...is/was...可以用关系代词what来强调主语或宾语。例如:

What I like is his kindness.
我喜欢的是他的善良。

2) all you/we have to do is 省略了all后面的关系代词that, 指"只要……就行了",这种用法在be动词后面可直接加动词原形。例如:

All we have to do is (to) work hard.
我们只要努力就行了。
All you have to do is (to) change your approach.
你只要改变你处理事情的方式就行了。

53. **it is the first time that...** "这是第一次……"。该句型的主句动词为 is/will be 时,that 引导的分句动词一律用现在完成时,that 可以省略;主句动词为 was 时,分句动词通常用过去完成时,偶尔用一般过去时;如果有明确的时间状语,且说话时这一时间尚未成为过去,甚至可以用现在完成时。主句的主语还可以用 this, this evening, yesterday 等,这种句型中的 first 也可用其他序数词,如 second, third 等。"time" 位置也可以是其他名词。例如:

It's the first time I've been here.
这是我第一次来这儿。

It was the first time she had been at a camp site and she thoroughly enjoyed it.
这是她第一次参加野营,她非常开心。

It was the first time this year he hasn't worked on a Saturday.
这是他今年第一次星期六休息。(言下之意,说话的时候仍是星期六,还没有结束。)

This is the tenth time that she has asked me to join her company.
这是她第十次请求我加入她公司了。

This evening will be the first time that we have played volleyball on the beach.
今晚将是我们第一次在沙滩上打排球。

It's the first month that I've been a visiting scholar.
这是我做访问学者的第一个月。

54. **it is urgent/essential/imperative etc. that** "某人做某事……就是……"。在这一句型中,充当表语的形容词多表示说话人惊讶、厌恶、紧张等情感、判断或表示事情的必要、紧急程度等。that 从句常用 should 式的虚拟语气,should 可省略。若是叙述客观事实时,也可用陈述语气。例如:

It's natural that babies cry.
婴儿天性会哭。

It is important that you be sincere.
真诚是重要的。

It is surprising that he should insist in his original plan.
他竟然坚持自己最初的计划,真令人惊讶。

It was strange she should help you after your fight.
你们争吵后她还会帮你的忙,真奇怪。

It's essential that he (should) justify his absence.
他现在解释他为何缺席是有必要的。

相关句型:

1) suggest, advise, decide, demand, insist, order, propose, recommend, request, etc. that (should) 在这一类表示建议、提议、要求等的动词所接的从句需用 should 式的虚拟语气,should 可省略。例如:

He insisted that I (should) give him my number.
他坚持要我给他我的电话号码。

2) suggestion, advice, etc. is that (should) 这些表示"建议、提议、要求"的动词派生词相关的从

句中,需用should式的虚拟语气,should可省略。例如:
My suggestion was that she play for our team.
我的建议是她替我们队打比赛。

55. **it seems (to sb) that**　"在某人看来……"。seem是系动词,不用于进行时,后面可接不定式或从句,表示某人的看法或推测。it seems that或it would seem that可用来缓和语气,表示一种不确切或客气。例如:
It seems to me (that) you don't have much choice.
在我看来,你好像没有多少选择的余地。
It seems that they know what they are doing.
看来,他们知道自己在干什么。
It would seem that we all agree.
我们大家似乎都同意。

相关句型:
1) seem like 指"好像,似乎",相当于look like,更侧重于感觉,而不是视觉。例如:
Well, it seemed like a good idea at the time.
哦,这主意当时好像还不错。
It seems like only yesterday that Mike was born.
迈克出生仿佛是昨天的事。

56. **it takes/took sb...to do sth**　"花费某人……做……"。take在这里指"为做成某事而需要时间、金钱、努力或某种特殊品质等",其中it是形式主语,后面的不定式是真正主语。该句型也可直接用sth take sb...,表示某物需要某人的时间、金钱、努力等。例如:
It took us half an hour to get there.
我们花了半个小时到达那里。
It took a lot of courage to admit that you were wrong.
要承认自己错了,需要很大的勇气。
It took us the whole day to trek across the rocky terrain.
我们花了一整天的时间艰难地穿过那片遍布岩石的地带。
It took him a long time to get over his cold.
很久之后他的感冒才好。
It took me nearly a thousand dollars to buy the horse.
买这匹马花了我快一千美元。
The journey takes three weeks.
这旅程要花三周时间。

相关句型:
1) sth cost(s); it cost(s) sb...to do sth 指"某物或做某事的价钱为……,需付费……",付出的多为金钱而非时间,有时也用工作、生命、婚姻等为付出的代价。例如:
Tickets cost ten dollars each.
每张票价为十美元。

The scenery for the play must have cost too much.
那出戏的舞台布景一定很费钱。
We'd like to send the children to a private school but it would cost us an arm and a leg.
我们想把孩子送到私立学校去,但是学费非常昂贵。
It costs a fortune to fly first class.
乘坐飞机头等舱要花一大笔钱。
His brave action cost him his life.
他的勇敢行为使他牺牲了生命。

2) sb spend(s) ...on sth/doing sth 指"某人花费……在某物或做事上",与take和cost不同,句子的主语通常是人。例如:
More money should be spent on health and education.
应该把更多的钱花在医疗保健和教育上面。
I spend too much time watching television.
我看电视花的时间太多。
She spent 100 pounds on a new bike.
她花了100英镑买了一辆新自行车。

57. **I wish...** "我希望……"。从句用虚拟语气,wish后所接的内容,多为无法实现的愿望。当从句动词表示与现在事实相反的愿望时,用一般过去时;在表示与过去事实相反的愿望时则用过去完成时;表示将来不太可能实现的希望,多用would, could等动词。究竟用何时态,和wish本身用现在时或过去时无关,而在于是否和"期望的当时"同步,或是比它更早。当同步时用过去时,比它更早时则用过去完成时。主句主语可用于所有人称,be动词基本上用were形式。例如:
I wish I were a king.
我真希望是个国王。
We wish that the problem could be solved.
我们希望这个问题能得到解决。
He wishes that I would stay with him.
他希望我能和他在一起。
I wish she had been at home when I called.
我真希望我打电话给她的时候她在家。

相关句型:
1) would rather/sooner (that) you/he/they... 指"宁可,宁愿……"。该句型也用于虚拟语气,其后跟的结构用法和wish后面的分句一样。例如:
I would rather (that) they came tomorrow.
我宁愿他们明天来。
I could go myself but I would sooner you went.
我自己也能去,但我宁愿你去。
I'm sure he is keeping something back. I'd rather he told me the truth.
我肯定他有事瞒着我。我倒希望他对我讲真话。

He didn't attend the meeting. I would rather he had been present.
他没有参加会议,我倒宁愿他出席了会议。

2) I hope... 也表示"希望",但并不表示假设意义,随后的动词形式除表示婉转口气外,很少用过去时形式。例如:

I hope you're coming to our party.
我希望你来参加我们的派对。

We hope the weather would be favorable.
我们希望天气有利。

58. **I wonder if...**   "我在想……"。if之后的谓语动词可用过去时,常为could,表示较为礼貌地"自己想做"或"想要对方做",也可以用I was wondering if...表示委婉地请求帮忙。这些表达虽然形为过去时态,但指的则是现在的事情。wonder 还可以用 think 或 hope 替代。例如:

I wonder if you could help me.
不知您能否帮我的忙?

I wonder if some time I could have a word with you.
我在想可不可以找个时间跟你谈一谈?

I was wondering if I could use your phone.
我是不是可以借用一下你的电话呢?

I was wondering if you could let me stay for a few days.
我在想,不知你能不能让我住上几天?

相关句型:

1) would 希望对方帮忙或是请求对方许可时,可以使用虚拟语气,含礼貌之意。例如:

It would be nice if you could help me with my task.
如果你能帮我做这项任务,那就太好了。

2) would/do you mind doing... 指"做某事你介意吗"。如果动作由说话人完成,可在动词ing前加上逻辑主语。例如:

Would you mind opening the window?
请你把窗户打开好吗?

Do you mind me smoking?
你介意我吸烟吗?

Would you mind my sitting here?
你介意我坐在这里吗?

59. **lest...(should)**   "以免……"。lest后所连接的从句中常用should,表示"以免,生怕,唯恐"。should 常被省略。这一句型为书面语。例如:

He gripped his brother's arm lest he be trampled by the mob.
他紧抓着他兄弟的胳膊,怕他被暴民踩着。

Close the window quickly lest the raindrops (should) slant in.
快关窗户,别让雨点潲进来。

I obeyed her lest she should be angry.

我得顺着她,免得她生气。

Be careful lest you fall from that tree.

要当心,以免从树上摔下来。

相关句型:

1) for fear that/of 指"以防……,唯恐……"。多表示对于未来的不安,所以常加入 will 或 would,口语中 that 可省略。for fear 也可以跟 of 介词短语。例如:

We climbed onto the top floor of the building for fear that the flood would surge inside.

我们爬上了楼的顶层,唯恐洪水涌入室内。

We spoke in whispers for fear that we might wake the baby.

我们轻声说话,以免吵醒婴儿。

I had to run away for fear that he might one day kill me.

我只好逃走,生怕他有一天把我杀了。

A lot of people won't go out at night for fear of being mugged.

因害怕遭到行凶抢劫,许多人在晚上不出门。

60. **look forward to (doing) sth** "期盼(做)某事"。to 在这里是介词,因此后面跟名词或动名词结构,表示"高兴地盼望某事"。该结构常表示一种愉快的期盼心情。例如:

I look forward to hearing from you in the near future.

我盼望着不久收到你的信。

We look forward to your comments on the above-mentioned proposal.

对上述建议,希望听取贵方的意见。

I'm really looking forward to our vacation.

我真心盼着假期的到来。

We're really looking forward to seeing you again.

我们非常盼望能再见到你。

相关句型:

1) be looking to do sth 指"正打算做某事,期待做某事"。例如:

We're looking to buy a new car early next year.

我们正打算明年初买辆新车。

Companies are looking to make technology in the home more friendly.

各公司正打算将家庭中的科技产品变得更为友好。

61. **make some sense** "有些道理"。sense 义为"(明确而容易理解的)意义",make sense 即"有意义,讲得通""明智的,合乎情理的"。该词前可加上表示不同程度的限定词,如 some, little, no 等,以表示合乎情理的程度如何。例如:

Peter wasn't making much sense on the phone.

彼得在电话上话说得不大清楚。

It just makes no sense—why would she do a thing like that?

这真是没法解释——她为什么会做出那样的事情?

This story doesn't make sense.

这个故事不合乎情理。

It makes sense to buy a second-hand bike.

买二手的自行车是明智的。

相关句型：

1) make sense of sth 指"理解、弄懂（通常不易理解的事）"。例如：

I can't make sense of that painting.

我看不懂那幅画。

It brought life, energy and pace to proceedings and made sense of the term musical performance.

它为音乐注入生命力、能量，并层层推进，表现出更丰富的音乐感。

2) there is no sense (in) doing sth 指"做某事是不明智的"，常用于口语中。例如：

There is no sense in beating around the bush.

拐弯抹角说话没有意义。

There's no sense in getting upset about it now.

现在大可不必为这件事苦恼。

3) in a sense/in one sense/in some sense 指"在某种意义上"。例如：

In a sense, I think he likes being responsible for everything.

从某种意义上来说，我认为他喜欢包揽一切。

In some sense, you could say that the caterpillar dies.

从某种意义上来说，你也可以说，毛虫死了。

62. may sb do sth "祝你……"。may 加主语，再加动词原型，用以表示祝愿的场合，这种用法较书面化。例如：

May you be happy forever!

祝你永远开心！

May your fortune be as boundless as the East Sea and may you live a long and happy life!

福如东海，寿比南山！

May you two live together till old and grey.

愿你们两口儿白头偕老。

May you go from strength to strength for the next ten years!

祝你在今后的十年里越来越飞黄腾达！

相关句型：

1) wish 其动词表示"祝，祝愿"时，后接复合宾语。例如：

He wished her good night.

他向她道晚安。

I wish them luck.

我祝他们好运。

I wish you the life of happiness and prosperity.
我祝你生活幸福、万事如意。
I wish you well and happy.
我祝愿你健康愉快。

63. **neither...nor** "两者都不……;既不……也不……"。主句谓语的数通常与最近一个名词或代词相一致。neither 多用于表示"不是这个也不是另一个"。要指"多个中一个也没有"时最好用 none。可将 neither 置于句首,后面句子倒装。例如:
Neither threats nor promises could change his inflexible determination.
威胁与利诱均不能改变他坚定的决心。
She seemed neither surprised nor worried.
她似乎既不惊讶也不担心。
She lives in retirement, neither making nor receiving visits.
她过着隐退的生活,既不访客,也不见客。
She neither called nor wrote.
她既没打电话也没写信来。
None of the three candidates impressed me greatly.
这三位候选人中没一位给我留下深刻印象。
Neither could theory do without practice, nor could practice do without theory.
理论没有实践不行,实践没有理论也不行。
Neither you nor I, nor anybody else knows the answer.
你,我,其他任何人都不知道这答案。

相关句型:
1) either...or... 指"不是……就是……"。例如:
Either my father or my brothers are coming.
不是我父亲就是我兄弟要来。
Either be there on time, or don't go at all.
要去就别迟到,不然就甭去了。
Either dye or paints are used to color cloth.
不论是染料还是颜料都是用来染布的。
I'm considering buying my niece a Christmas present, either a dictionary or an encyclopedia.
我在考虑给我侄女买一样圣诞礼物,不是词典就是百科全书。

64. **no matter how/who/where/what** "不管(怎样、谁、哪里、什么等)"。no matter 后面接特殊疑问词,引导让步状语从句,表示"不管,无论",特殊疑问词包括 how, who, where, what, which, when。例如:
No matter where you go, I will follow you.
不管你去哪里,我都跟你走。
No matter what happens, they are ready to face it.
无论发生什么,他们都准备好了去面对。

All stories seemed dreadfully alike, no matter who told them.
看来,无论谁讲,这些故事都是千篇一律的。
No matter how busy he is, he is ready to help others.
不管他多忙,他总是乐意帮助别人。
He will jump on every little mistake you make, no matter how trivial.
他对你的每一点差错都要斥责一番,不管是什么鸡毛蒜皮的事。

相关句型:
1) however/whoever/ wherever/ whatever 这些复合关系词在表示"让步"意味时,可以用来替代 no matter 结构,且更常见。例如上述例句可以改写成:
However tired he is, he always looks happy.
无论他多累,他总是看起来乐呵呵的。
Wherever you go, I will follow you.
不管你去哪里,我都跟你走。
Whatever happens, they are ready to face it.
无论发生什么,他们都准备好了去面对。
Whoever passes here would stop to admire the scenery.
但凡过路的人,都要停下一览这儿的风光。

65. no more...than
"同……一样不……"。相当于"not ...any more than",表示比较的两者"都不……"。在语序上,no more 通常放在名词、动词、形容词之前,而 any more 则有所不同,比较以下例句:

He is no more a winner than I am.
He is not a winner any more than I am.
他和我都不是赢家。
He can no more speak Chinese than I can.
He cannot speak Chinese any more than I can.
他和我都不会说中文。
Eating too little is no more healthy than sleeping too little.
Eating too little is not any more healthy than sleeping too little.
吃太少和睡太少一样不健康。

相关句型:
1) no less than 指"不少于……,和……相同",比较的双方都是肯定意义。例如:
She is no less beautiful than her mother.
她和她妈妈一样美丽。
2) no more than 后面接数词时,表示"只有……,不过……",强调数量少。例如:
I need no more than 2000 dollars.
我只需要两千美元。
There are no more than five students in the classroom.
教室里只有五个学生。

3) not more than 指"至多……",表示数量的上限,相当于 at most。例如:
There were not more than ten lemons in the box.
箱子里至多有十个柠檬。

66. **not any longer/no longer** "不再"。强调现在与以前不同。例如:
He no longer smokes.
他不再吸烟了。
Vegetarians are no longer dismissed as cranks.
素食者不再被视为有怪癖的人。
He was so down that he didn't want to live any longer.
他情绪低落以至于不想活了。
You mustn't put it off any longer, remember, tomorrow never comes.
你不得再拖延了,记住切莫依赖明天。

相关句型:
1) not long for 指"不大可能在……中存在很久"。例如:
The dog is merely 12 years old and not long for this world.
这只狗才活12年却快要死了。
He was not long for this world. He had made that clear in his letter.
他活不了多久了。这一点他在信中已写得一清二楚了。
2) before long 指"很快"。例如:
It looks like it's going to snow before long.
看来马上就要下雨了。
Before long, the moon rose to follow the stars.
不久,月儿随着星星出来了。

67. **not only...but (also)...** "不仅……,而且……"。该句型引导并列结构,其中 not only 与 but also 之后的词性应一致。当 not only 置于句首时,句子可以倒装成疑问句的语序。also 也可以省略。例如:
They not only saved my life, but (also) taught me how to make a living.
他们不仅救了我,还教会我如何谋生。
People are not only complex but also highly variable.
人不仅是复杂的,而且也是多变的。
Not only did he make a promise, but also he kept it.
他不仅做出了许诺,而且履行了诺言。
Not only are housewives not paid, but also most of their boring work is unnoticed.
家庭主妇不仅得不到报酬,而且她们单调的工作大多数不会被人注意。

相关句型:
1) not...but... "不是……,而是……"。所接的可以是短语,也可以是分句。例如:
The question is not how she did it, but why she did it.
问题不在于她是如何做的,而在于她为何做这件事。

68. not so much...as

"与其说(是)……不如说(是)……"。not so much 之后的短语和 as 之后的短语在结构上处于对称位置，词性也应保持一致。例如：

She is not so much a singer as an actress.
她与其说是位歌手，不如说是位演员。

He is not so much a journalist as a writer.
与其说他是个新闻工作者，不如说他是个作家。

In many cases nursing is not so much a job as a way of life.
在许多情况下，护理与其说是一件工作倒不如说是一种生活方式。

The oceans do not so much divide the world as unite it.
海洋与其说分割不如说连接了整个世界。

He is not so much foolish as careless with friends.
他与其说是愚蠢，倒不如说是交友不当。

相关句型：

1) more...than "比……更……"。
2) less...than "不及……"。
3) rather than "而不是……"。

以上句型都可表示"与其说(是)……不如说(是)……"，例如"她与其说是位歌手，不如说是位演员。"可改写为：

She is more an actress than a singer.
She is less a singer than an actress.
She is an actress rather than a singer.

69. not to mention

"更不用说，且不说"。表示一种递进关系，多为插入语。例如：

He has two big houses in USA, not to mention his villa in France.
他在美国有两栋大房子，更不用提他在法国的别墅了。

They have three dogs to look after, not to mention the cat and the bird.
他们有三只狗要照顾，更别提那只猫和鸟了。

相关句型：

1) to say nothing of 指"更不用说，而且还"。例如：

It was too expensive, to say nothing of the time it wasted.
这太贵了，更不用说它浪费的时间了。

2) not to speak of 指"更不用说，何况"。例如：

His friends felt sad at his death, not to speak of his family.
他的过世让朋友们伤心，更不用提家人了。

3) let alone 指"更不用提，更别说"。例如：

There isn't enough room for us, let alone our guests.
连我们都没有足够的空间，更不用说客人了。

70. not...until

"直到……才……"。用于表示"……之前，都没有……"，书面语中可以将 not until 置于句首，后面句子倒装。例如：

I didn't leave the office until it was 11 p.m.

我到夜里十一点才离开办公室。

Not until you told me had I heard the news.

在你告诉我之后,我才知道这个消息。

It's not until midnight did I finish the homework.

我到半夜才做完作业。

相关句型:

1) only 指"只有……才……",后面可以跟短语或句子。当 only 位于句首时,后面句子倒装。例如:

Only in this peaceful village have I seen such a beautiful landscape.

只有在这个宁静的小山村,我才见到如此美丽的景致。

Only when a tiger is hungry will it attack a human being.

老虎只有当饥饿时才攻击人。

I received my mother's call at noon, only then did I remember it was my birthday today.

我中午接到妈妈电话,那时才想起来今天是我的生日。

2) it is not long before 指"不久前才……,很快……",即做某事前没有花很长时间。例如:

It was not long before he started to smoke.

他不久前才开始抽烟。

It will not be long before she comes to see you.

她很快就会来看你了。

71. **now that** "既然"。引导状语从句,语调较为缓和,相当于 seeing that,在口语中,that 可以省略。now that 后面的从句只能是现在时态。例如:

It's good to fling off heavy clothing now that spring is here.

春天到了,脱去笨重的冬装真让人高兴。

They are hoping for a return to normality now that the war is over.

既然战争结束了,他们希望一切都恢复常态。

Now that we are all here, the meeting can begin.

既然大家都在场,会议可以开始了。

I do remember, now (that) you mention it.

你这一提,我倒确实想起来了。

相关句型:

1) since "既然"。从句通常表示已知的原因。例如:

Since that is so, there is no more to be said.

既然如此,再没什么可说的了。

72. **one moment..., and now...** "刚才还……,现在却……"。该句型引导两个并列动作,带有一定转折意味。通常前面的动作用过去时态,后面的动作用进行时。例如:

One moment it was fine, and now it is raining.

刚才天还晴着,现在却下起雨来。

One moment the two boys were playing, and now they are fighting.
刚才两个男孩还玩得好好的,现在却打了起来。

相关句型:

1) on the one hand...,on the other hand... 指"一方面……,另一方面……",通常用于引出不同的,尤其是对立的观点或思想。例如:

On the one hand they'd love to have kids, but on the other (hand), they don't want to give up their freedom.
一方面,他们想要孩子;另一方面,他们又不想放弃自由自在的生活。

On the one hand I admire his gifts, but on the other I distrust his judgment.
一方面我羡慕他的才华,而另一方面我却怀疑他的判断力。

On the one hand I want to sell the house, but on the other hand I can't bear the thought of moving.
一方面我想把房子卖掉,另一方面,我又不想搬家。

73. or/otherwise

"否则……"。该句型的前半部分是祈使句或表示意愿、建议的句子,接or, or else 或 otherwise 引导的句子表示后果。祈使句接 or 的结构,也可以改成用 if 引导的句子。例如:

Turn the heat down or your cake will burn.
把热度调低吧,要不蛋糕就要糊了。

Work hard, or you will fall behind.
努力点,否则你会落后的。

If you don't work hard, you will fall behind.
如果你不努力,你会落后的。

You had better take a taxi, or you can't catch the train.
你最好乘计程车去,否则你就赶不上火车了。

相关句型:

1) 祈使句 + and "如此一来,就……"。这一祈使句加 and 的句型相当于条件句。例如:

Think it over, and you will find the answer.
再想想,你会找到答案的。

Follow the instructions and you can install this software.
按照指令操作,你就可以安装这个软件了。

74. prefer to do...rather than do

"(两者相比)宁做前者而不做后者"。该句型相当于 would rather do sth than do sth,但不能用于进行时。例如:

I prefer to stay at home rather than go to the park in such weather.
这种天气我宁愿待在家里,而不是去公园。

Rather than ride on a crowded bus, he always prefers to ride a bicycle.
比起乘坐拥挤的公交车,他总是愿意骑自行车。

相关句型:

1) prefer...to "宁可是前者,而非后者"。用于对两者偏好性的比较,这里的to是介词。例如:

I prefer cooking at home to eating out.

我宁愿在家下厨,而不是在外面吃饭。

I prefer cats to dogs.

比起狗,我更喜欢猫。

2) prefer (sb) to do sth/doing sth 指"更倾向做"。prefer之后可跟不定式或动词ing形式。例如:

Would you prefer me to stay?

你愿意我留下来么?

I prefer not to think about it.

我不想考虑此事。

Many people prefer traveling by train.

许多人更喜欢乘火车旅行。

75. **prevent sb from doing** "阻止,制止,妨碍"。from是介词,接名词或动词ing形式。例如:

We were prevented by heavy smog from seeing anything.

浓雾使我们看不到任何东西。

What prevented you from joining us last night?

昨天晚上什么事使你不能参加我们的晚会?

My only idea was to prevent the woman from speaking.

我唯一的想法就是不让那女人讲话。

相关句型:

1) keep sb from doing "阻止;避开;克制"。例如:

I kept the children from going out.

我不让孩子们出去。

He couldn't keep from laughing.

他忍不住大笑。

2) prohibit sb from doing "禁止,阻止"。例如:

Federal law prohibits foreign airlines from owning more than 25% of any U.S. airline.

联邦法律禁止外国航空公司拥有任何一家美国航空公司超过25%的股权份额。

They prohibited him from going there.

他们禁止他去那里。

3) forbid sb to do sth(or forbid sb's doing sth) "禁止,阻止"。例如:

They forbid any ships to enter the water.

他们禁止任何船舶进入这片水域。

The teacher forbade us to leave our seats. = The teacher forbade our leaving seats.

老师不准我们离开座位。

76. **protect sb from** "保护……，使……免于受到损坏或攻击"。例如：
   Clothes protect us from cold.
   衣服可帮我们御寒。
   She protected her eyes from the sun with her hand.
   她用手遮住太阳以保护她的眼睛。
   You should protect the children from catching cold.
   你应该防备孩子们受凉。

相关句型：

1) shelter sb/sth from sth "隐蔽；为……提供外壳或保护"。例如：
   Here, a myriad of tall buildings shelter the streets from the sun, while lawns and parks dot the city.
   这里高楼林立，夹道成荫，草坪花圃，点缀其间。
   They huddled in the shop doorway to shelter from the rain.
   他们挤在商店门口躲雨。

77. **provided/providing** "假若，倘若，倘使"。可以用来表示条件。例如：
   You may keep the book a further week provided (that) no one else requires it.
   倘若这本书没有其他人想借的话，你可以再续借一个星期。
   I will go, provided you go too.
   如果你去，我才去。
   Provided they are fit I see no reason why they shouldn't go on playing for another four or five years.
   只要他们身体强健，我看不出他们有什么理由不继续再打四五年比赛。
   You can go to the party providing/provided (that) you promise to return by 10:00.
   如果你答应十点前回来，你可以去参加派对。
   I do believe in people being able to do what they want to do, providing they're not hurting someone else.
   我真的认为人们只要不伤害别人，自己想做什么就可以做什么。

相关句型：

1) suppose/supposing (that) "假设"。在口语中可作为连词，引导条件从句。例如：
   Suppose/ Supposing he is absent, what shall we do?
   假使他不在，我们该怎么办呢？

78. **so/such...that** "如此……以至于……"。so后接形容词或副词，当遇到以冠词加形容词再加名词构成的句子成分时，需将形容词提到冠词之前，变成so加形容词加冠词；such后接名词，也可以用"...be such that..."表示"事情非常……以至于……"。在强调so/such结构时，也可以将其置于句首，后面跟与疑问句相同语序的倒装句。例如：
   The movie was so touching that many people were moved to tears.
   电影如此感人，以至于很多人留下了感动的泪水。

It was so interesting a book that the little girl wouldn't put it down.
So interesting was the book that the little girl wouldn't put it down.
这本书如此有趣,小女孩看得爱不释手。

She was in such a hurry that she forgot to lock the windows.
她是如此匆忙以至于忘记关窗了。

His anger was such that he nearly shouted.
他气愤过度以至于大吼大叫。

He was so bedazzled by her looks that he couldn't speak.
她的美貌令他惊讶得说不出话来。

She was so sleepy that she ran into a lamppost.
她如此困倦,以致撞到路灯杆上。

He told such funny stories that we all laughed.
他讲了这样滑稽的故事,把我们都逗笑了。

相关句型:

1) so (that) 指"所以……",表示结果;也可以指"为了……",表示目的。在口语中that可省略。例如:

I got up early, so that I did some reading.
我起床早了,所以我读了会儿书。

He tried to hide himself so that nobody would notice him.
他为了不被人注意,尽量把自己躲藏起来。

I stepped aside so that she might come in.
我往旁边走一步,以便她能进来。

Shine the torch on so that we can read the labels.
用手电筒照这个标签,我们好看得见。

2) in order to/that "为了……"。引导目的状语,较为正式,分句常用may或might。例如:

I closed the door in order that we might continue our conversation undisturbed.
我关上了门以便我们不受干扰地继续谈话。

Arrive two days early in order to acclimatize.
提前两天到达以便适应新环境。

They flew there in order that they might be in time to attend the opening ceremony.
他们飞往那里以便能及时参加开幕典礼。

79. **so/neither/ nor do/have sb** "前者……,后者也……"。该句型表示"另一者也如此",即前者的情况也适用于后者。用so, neither/ nor引导的倒装句应与前面的分句保持一致,即前面分句中的谓语动词是肯定形式时用so,否定形式时用neither/nor。助动词的选择依据前句的谓语动词。若前句的谓语动词既有肯定又有否定形式,或谓语动词不属于一类时,用it is /was the same with sb或so it is/ was with sb。例如:

He has finished his homework, so have I.
他写完作业了,我也是。

My wife prefers coffee, so do I.

我妻子偏好咖啡,我也是。
John can't ride a bicycle, neither/ nor can I.
约翰不会骑自行车,我也不会。
If he buys the book, so will his classmates.
他要是买这本书,他的同学也会买。
He is a worker and he works hard, so it is with John.
他是个工人,工作很努力,约翰也是。

相关句型:

1) so sb do/have 这一句型用于的场合是,若后一句是对前一句所说的内容表示赞同或认可,没有增添新的信息,则so放句首,后面主语和谓语不倒装。例如:
"It is cold today." "Yes. So it is."
"今天天冷。""是的,的确如此。"
"He visited Tokyo last week." "Yes. So he did."
"他上周去东京了。""是的,他是去了"。

80. **that sb should/could do sth!** "某人竟然/多么希望……"。该句型用于表示感慨、愿望或遗憾,属于虚拟语气,多用于书面语。例如:
That she should shout at us!
她竟然对我们大吼大叫!
Oh, that I could fly!
要是我能飞就好了!
That they were here now!
他们要是在这里就好了!

相关句型:

1) that clause+V... that引导的名词性从句可以做主语,置于句首。例如:
That he loved her deeply soon became widely known.
他深爱着她,这件事很快人尽皆知。
That such a young child should win the chess game was spurring.
这么小的孩子赢得了象棋比赛,真令人惊讶。

2) the fact, thought, idea etc. that... 这里that引导的名词性从句作同位语,与前面的名词同位。例如:
The fact that fruit is good for health is obvious.
水果有益健康是显而易见的。

81. **that is (to say)** "换言之,也就是说"。该副词分句常用做插入语。to say有时可省略。例如:
He was found innocent in the court, that is to say, the court could not convict him legally.
他被法庭判为无罪,那就是说,法庭依法律不能定他的罪。
That is to say, men rule the world, but their mothers and wives rule them.
这就是说,男人统治世界,但男人们的母亲和妻子统治着他们。

You'll find her very helpful—if she is not too busy, that is.
你会觉得她很愿意帮忙,也就是说,如果她不太忙的话。

I'll see you in a week's time—that is to say, next Monday.
我们见面时间安排在一星期后,也就是说在下周一。

He is keeping goal, that is to say, he is the goalkeeper.
他是守球的,换言之,他是守门员。

The poor man has lost the lawsuit, that is to say, money talks.
那个可怜的男人输了官司,也就是说,钱说了算。

相关句型:

1) i.e. 是拉丁文 id est 的缩略形式,表示"即,就是"。例如:
The best pupil in the class, i.e. Peter, won the prize.
班上最好的学生,就是彼得,他得了奖。
This is a process of recursion, i.e. the metempsychosis.
这是一个回归的过程,即轮回。

2) namely 指"即,就是,换句话说"。namely 为副词,相当于 that is to say。例如:
There are three major advantages of the design, namely cheapness, simplicity and availability.
这种设计有三大优点,即价廉、简便、实用。
This novel is translated into three foreign languages, namely, English, German and French.
这本小说译成了三种外文,即英、德和法文。

82. the moment/minute/second/instant "一……就……"。表示短暂时间的名词 moment, minute 等,加上定冠词 the,可以作为连词短语使用引导从句,表示"一……,就……",两个动作时间间隔短。见 as soon as。例如:

I recognized her the instant (that) I saw her.
我一眼就认出她了。

She ran off the minute she heard the steps.
她一听到脚步声就跑开了。

The moment they met, he was completely smitten by her.
从一见面的那一刻起,他就完全被她迷住了。

The moment the clown appeared on stage, the audience folded up.
小丑一出现在舞台上,观众们个个笑得前俯后仰。

The instant she caught his eye she looked away again.
刚碰到他的目光,她便把眼睛转了开去。

The instant they heard the alarm, they fell in for action.
他们一听到警报,就立即集合准备战斗。

相关句型:

1) on doing sth 指"一……,就……;在……后立即",较为正式。例如:
On arriving home I discovered they had gone.
我一到家就发现他们已经离开了。

On hearing the news, he burst into tears.
一听到那个消息,他泪流满面。

2) instantly/immediately/directly... 指"一……,就……",这些词也可以作为连词,引导时间状语从句。例如:

I went home directly I had finished work.
我一干完活就回家了。

He put the lunch on immediately he came home.
一回到家他就开始做饭。

83. **there be** "有……"。该结构表示"……存在,有……"。其后如果接多个并列主语,be动词的选择要取决于第一个主语,即就近原则。在there be句型中,be动词还有其他变化形式,常见的有:There seem to be/There happen to be/There used to be/ There is likely to be/There have been/has been 等。例如:

There is a pen and two books on the desk.
书桌上有一支笔和两本书。

There are two books and a pen on the desk.
书桌上有两本书和一支笔。

There seems/ appears to be much hope of our team winning the match.
看起来我们队有很大可能赢得比赛。

There happened to be nobody in the room when I came in.
我进房间的时候,恰好房间里一个人也没有。

There used to be a bus station at the corner of the street.
在街角处原本是有一个公交站台的。

There are likely to be more difficulties than expected while we are carrying out the plan.
当我们实施计划的时候,可能会遇上比预计更多的困难。

There is an acute shortage of water.
水严重短缺。

Our trips are all-inclusive—there are no hidden costs.
我们的旅行费用全包——没有任何隐含性费用。

I find it hard to work at home because there are too many distractions.
我发觉在家里工作很难,因为使人分心的事太多。

There are calls for more punitive measures against people who drink and drive.
有人呼吁对酒后驾车的人要有更具处罚性的措施。

There are no places available right now but I'll put you on a waiting list.
现时没有空位,但我会把你列入等候者名单的。

相关句型:

1) There is (no) hope/ chance / possibility of doing... 指"(没)有可能性"。例如:

Is there any chance of us/ our winning the game?
我们有可能赢得比赛么?

There is no chance of doing business if you insist on that offer.

如果你们坚持那个报价,就不可能做成生意。

There is no hope of bumper harvest this summer because of a serious drought.
由于严重干旱,今年夏季大丰收的希望不大。

2) There is (no) difficulty/ trouble/ point/ delay/use (in) doing 指"做某事(没)有难度、困难、意义、耽误、用处等"。例如:

There is no point in discussing the problem again.
再讨论这个问题没有意义了。

There is no use arguing with him.
跟他争辩是没用的。

There is no use in complaining. They can't do anything to help you.
抱怨于事无补;他们没办法帮助你。

There is no point in mentioning dull events in the past.
这些陈芝麻烂谷子的往年事,就不要再提了。

3) There is no doubt that 指"毫无疑问……"。例如:

There is no doubt that our educational system leaves something to be perfected.
毫无疑问,我们的教育体系还有可改进之处。

There is no doubt that she loves him all heart.
毫无疑问,她是全心全意地爱他。

There is no doubt that mobile phone and the Internet are important means of communication.
毫无疑问,手机和网络是信息交流的重要工具。

84. **the last thing/person** "最不……"。last 表示"最后的",这个句型表示"最不可能,最不愿意……",有强烈的否定意味。例如:

She is the last person to tell a lie.
她不可能说谎。

Singing is the last thing I would do.
我最不会唱歌。

That is the last thing I want to do.
我才不愿那样做呢。

A plane crash was the last thing that we had expected.
我们绝对没有想到飞机会出事。

I wouldn't marry you if you were the last person on earth.
即使世上就剩下你一个人,我也不会和你结婚。

相关句型:

1) the least 在 least 后面接形容词或副词,表示"最不……",即程度上最轻的。例如:

This is the least expensive phone in the store.
这是店里最便宜的电话机了。

Of two evils, the least should be taken.
两害相权取其轻。

2) than any other 比较级接 than any other，再接单数名词，表示的是最高级含义。例如：

He is taller than any other boy in the class.

他在班上个子最高。

Shanghai is bigger than any other city in China.

上海是中国最大的城市。

Autumn is better for reading than any other season.

秋天比任何季节都适合读书。

This year's crop is better than any other year's.

今年的收成比以往哪一年都好。

85. **the more..., the more...** "越……,就越……"。该句型的基本构成成分是定冠词+比较级+主语1+谓语动词1,定冠词+比较级+主语2+谓语动词2。该句型用以表示两个相关的动作或状态以一定的比例增加或减少。例如：

The more you study the more you know.

学得越多,你知道得也越多。

The more time you have, the more things you can do.

你拥有的时间越多,能做的事情也就越多。

The more one has, the more one wants.

越有越贪心。

The elder I am, the fatter I become.

我年纪越大越胖。

More haste less speed.

欲速则不达。

相关句型：

1) more and more 指"越来越……",表示一种程度的加深。例如：

I was becoming more and more upset.

我越来越沮丧。

More and more people are believing in vegetarianism and diet for health.

越来越多的人相信素食和节食有利于身体健康。

2) more or less 指"或多或少,某种程度上"。例如：

We came to more or less the same conclusion.

我们大致达成一致结论。

Today, there are more or less fifteen hundred languages in the world.

今天,全世界大约有1500种语言。

86. **thus** "因此,从而,于是"。用于正式文体中。例如：

She studied hard; thus she got high marks.

她用功读书,因此获得高分。

There has been no rain — thus, the crops are dying.

天没下雨,因此庄稼要枯死了。

They abused their power and bullied the people, thus arousing intense discontent among the masses.

他们仗势欺人，引起群众强烈的不满。

相关句型：

1) so "因此"，口语中多用。例如：

I don't use the language much, so I tend to forget it.

那门语言我用的不多，所以往往会遗忘。

I shall get back late, so don't sit up for me.

我回来晚，所以别熬夜等我。

2) therefore "因此"，在正式语体和书面语中常用。例如：

The country was beautiful. I therefore decided to return the next year.

那个国家很美丽，因此我决定第二年再去。

He's only 17 and therefore not eligible to vote.

他只有17岁，因此没有投票选举的资格。

3) consequently/as a result/for this reason "因此，因为这个缘故"。常用于句子开头。例如：

I missed the train. Consequently /As a result/For this reason I was late for work.

我没有赶上火车，结果上班迟到了。

4) hence 是副词，指"因此，所以"，较正式。例如：

It is very late; hence you must go to bed.

时间已经很晚了，因此你必须睡觉去。

This piece is from a famous designer; hence it's expensive.

这件衣服出自一位著名设计师，所以很昂贵。

87. **to tell the truth/to be frank** "说实话，坦白说"。这两个短语是不定式构成的惯用语，常在句中充当插入语。类似的还有 so to speak, to be brief, to make matter worse, to be sure, to cite a few, to sum up, to begin with 等。例如：

To tell (you) the truth, the dress doesn't match your shoes.

说老实话，这裙子和你的鞋子不配。

To be brief, you need to rearrange the shop.

简而言之，你需要重新安排店里的摆设了。

To make matter worse, her mother fell ill all of a sudden.

更糟糕的是，她妈妈突然病了。

To be sure, you have done a great job.

确定的是，你做得非常出色。

To tell the truth, I am rather pessimistic about that.

说实话，我对此相当悲观。

To be frank, this mission is beyond my might.

说实话，这一使命非我能力所及。

To be brief, the students should be independent and the teachers should be sincere.
一句话,学生要自强,老师要真诚。

To make the matter worse, it began to rain.
更糟糕的是,天开始下雨了。

To be sure, it is no longer winter; neverthless, it is quite cold.
现在固然已不是冬天了,可是天气还是相当冷。

相关句型:

1) generally speaking 这是由分词构成的惯用语,分词主语是不特定的人或是说话人。类似的还有:frankly speaking, judging from, considering 等。例如:

Generally speaking the women are more sensitive.
一般而言,女性要更敏感。

Frankly speaking, I think the movie is quite boring.
坦白说,我觉得这电影相当无聊。

Judging from his appearance, no one can tell he is a millionaire.
从外表看,没人看得出他是位百万富翁。

Generally speaking, tourists should first visit cities like Beijing, Shanghai and Xi'an.
一般地说,第一次到中国应当先到北京、上海、西安等地。

Frankly speaking, at home I only play computer games day and night.
坦白说,我在家里只是日夜不停地玩电脑。

Judging from the look of the sky, it may clear up.
由天色看来,可能会放晴。

Considering the strength of the opposition, we did very well to score two goals.
就对方的实力而论,我们能进两个球就很不错了。

88. **too...to** "太……而不能……"。too 加形容词或副词再加不定式可用来表示"太……以至于不能"。不定式之前可以用 for sb 引导出不定式的逻辑主语。不定式的逻辑宾语是句子主语时,不定式不需接宾语。例如:

The hot pot is too spicy for me to eat.
火锅太辣了,我吃不下。

He's far too young to go on his own.
他年纪太小,不能独自一人去。

It's too late to do anything about it now.
现在进行任何补救都为时太晚。

I was too nervous to eat.
我紧张得饭都吃不下。

The offer was too enticing to refuse.
这提议太有诱惑力,使人难以拒绝。

相关句型:

1) so...that... 当 that 后面用否定句时,可表示"如此……以至于不能……"。例如:

He was so fat that he had a double chin.

他胖得有双下巴了。

2) enough to "足以……"。enough 必须放在形容词和副词的后面。常可用 so...that... 句型来改写。例如：

She is old enough to decide for herself.
她已到自己做决定的年龄。
You may be joking but she's simple enough to believe you.
你也许是在开玩笑,但她却傻得信以为真。
The house was big enough for us to live.
这房子很大,足够我们住了。
The house was so big that we could live in it.
这房子如此之大,足够我们住了。
Our yard is spacious enough for a swimming pool.
我们的院子很宽敞,足够建一座游泳池。
Our yard is so spacious that we can build a swimming pool.
我们的院子这么宽敞,可以建一座游泳池了。

89. **twice/three times etc. as ...as** "两/三倍……"。当两个人或事物作比较,且差异为倍数关系时,可以在as...as前面加上倍数或是分数来表示,如 twice, three times, half, a quarter 等。例如：

The ship is twice as large as that one.
这艘船是那艘船的两倍大。
The ship is half as large as that one.
这艘船是那艘船的一半大。
She has four times as much money as I have.
她有我四倍的钱。
This car can run two and a half times as fast as the old model.
这辆车的速度是旧款车速度的两倍半。
The output is twice as much as that of ten years ago.
产量是十年前的两倍。
He has collected more than three times as many stamps as I (have).
他收集的邮票是我的三倍还不止。

相关句型：

1) length, size, height, width, weight, depth 等名词都可以用倍数来表示差异。例如：

The ship is twice the size of that one.
这艘船是那艘船的两倍大。
This movie is a quarter the length of that one.
这部电影是那部电影的四分之一长。
This street is three times wider than that one.
这条街比那条街宽三倍。

90. **unless** "除非,如果不"。该连词表示"除了在……的条件下,除非……",否则主句的情况将发生,即unless的后面连接让主句成立的唯一例外,语气较为强烈。它也可以做介词用,表示"除……之外"。例如:

Unless he studies hard, he will never pass the examination.
他如果不努力学习,就永远不能考及格。

I shall go unless it rains.
如果不下雨我就去。

This baby seldom cries unless he is tired.
除非在疲倦时,这个婴儿很少哭。

Talent is worthless unless you persevere in developing it.
除非你坚持不懈地发展天赋,否则它是没有价值的。

She will burn herself out unless she gets more sleep.
她要是再不休息的话,身体就要垮了。

I will not believe it unless and until he tells me so.
除非他亲口对我说,否则我决不相信。

Don't borrow unless you intend to repay.
除非你打算还,要不你别借钱。

相关句型:

1) if ...not 指"如果没有……的话",大多数情况下可以替代unless。如上面的例句可以改写成:

He will never pass the examination if he doesn't study hard.
他如果不努力学习,就永远不能考及格。

Silk dresses are easy to crumple up if not carefully handled.
真丝衣服若不能正确处理,很容易起皱。

91. **up to** 词义较多,可表示以下含义:

1) "是某人的责任或职责,由某人决定"。例如:

It's not up to you to tell me how to do my job.
还轮不到你来告诉我怎么做我的事。

It is up to the courts to rule on this matter.
这得靠法院对这事做出裁决。

2) "多达,直至"。例如:

His work isn't up to much.
他的活儿做得不怎么样。

The little boy can count up to a thousand.
这个小男孩能够数到一千。

His new book did not come up to expectation.
他的新作没有达到预期水平。

3) up to doing sth指"(体力或智力上)胜任某工作,有资格做"。例如:

He's not up to the job.

他无法胜任这项工作。

I'm not up to going to work today.

今天我不能去上班。

4) 在口语中表示偷偷地干(坏事),常见up to no good这一短语。例如:

I'm sure he's up to no good.

我敢说他在打什么坏主意。

Those kids are always up to no good.

那些孩子尽会恶作剧。

相关句型:

1) be up against 在口语中指"面临问题或困境"。例如:

Remember that you will be up against a more experienced player.

记住,你将碰上的是一位经验丰富的选手。

2) be (well) up on/in/with 口语中指"非常熟悉,精通……"。例如:

Jim is well up with baseball.

吉姆棒球打得不错。

By the age of three babies will be well on their way to communicative competence.

三岁时孩子们就开始发展交流能力了。

3) it's sb's turn to 指"轮到某人做某事了,该某人做某事",强调的是次序上的先后。例如:

It's your turn to serve the ball.

轮到你发球了。

92. **want/need/require doing sth** "需要(被)……"。want, need, require等动词的ing形式可表示被动的意义,want/need/require的主语是动词ing的宾语。同样的内容可用不定式的被动语态来表达,但较少见。例如:

The carpet really wants cleaning.

The carpet really wants to be cleaned.

这块地毯真的需要清洗了。

All cars require servicing regularly.

All cars require to be serviced regularly.

所有汽车都需要定期检修。

This shirt needs ironing.

This shirt needs to be ironed.

这件衬衫需要熨一熨。

The plants want watering daily.

The plants want to be watered daily.

这些花草得天天浇水。

His leather shoes need mending.

His leather shoes need to be mended.

他的皮鞋需要修补。

相关句型：

1) 有些动词如 wash, write, sell, iron 等形式上用主动，但表示的是被动意义。这些词通常用于一般现在时，多描述物体的某些内在属性。例如：

This kind of cloth washes very well.

这种布很耐洗。

Your pen writes quite smoothly.

你的笔写起来很流畅。

A good book does not necessarily sell well.

好书未必畅销。

2) 少数动词的进行时有被动意义，如 do, owe, cook, print, build 等，常见于口语中。例如：

The book is printing.

书在印刷中。

The meat is cooking.

肉正在煮。

93. **what...** "多么……"。以 what 开头的感叹句，后面加冠词，再依次加形容词、名词、主语和动词，强调形容词加名词的意思，表达强烈的语气。当名词为不可数或是复数形式时，不需要加冠词。主语和动词常省略。有时不需要形容词。例如：

What a big house this is!

这是座多么大的房子！

What pretty flowers!

多漂亮的花儿！

What awe weather!

天气糟透了！

What a dreadful idea!

多么可怕的想法！

What a harsh life!

生活不容易啊！

What a considerate kid!

多么体贴的孩子！

What an unexpected surprise!

真让人意想不到的惊喜！

相关句型：

1) how... 以 how 开头的感叹句强调副词或形容词所表示的意思。词序为 how 加形容词或副词，再加主语和动词。主语和动词也常省略。例如：

How fast you eat!

你吃得好快啊！

How well you look!

你看起来多么健康啊！

How kind of you!
你真客气!
How they cried!
他们哭得多伤心啊!
How time flies!
光阴似箭!
How marvelous the performance is!
演出真精彩啊!
How sensational the news was!
爆炸性新闻啊!
How severe the competition was!
竞争真激烈啊!
How stimulating the college life is!
大学生活真精彩啊!

94. **what...for?** "为了什么目的……?"口语中用来询问理由,还可以单用 What for? 表示"为什么?"例如:

What's this gadget for?
这个小玩意是干什么用的?
What did you do that for?
你为何做那件事啊?
What is Microblog for?
为什么有微博?
"I need to see a doctor." "What for?"
"我得去看医生。""为什么?"
Can I have the day off tomorrow? "What for?"
"明天我可以请假吗?""那为什么?"

相关句型:

1) give sb. what for 可以指"责备或严厉的训斥"。例如:

The teacher gave the lazy student what for.
老师痛斥了懒惰的学生。
The teacher gave me what for because I was late.
老师因我迟到批评了我。

2) So what? "那又怎么样呢? 那有什么了不起?"常用于口语中。

I know he is rich. So what?
我知道他富有,那又如何?
She is a well-acknowledged beauty. So what?
她是个公认的大美女。那又怎样?

95. **when it comes to...** "当涉及,谈到……"。这里的 to 是介词,后面可以是名词或是动词 ing 形式。例如:

When it comes to politics, I know very little.
谈到政治,我几乎一窍不通。

When it comes to relationships, everyone makes mistakes.
在处理人际关系上,人人都会犯错。

I can use a computer, but when it comes to repairing them, I'm useless.
我会用电脑,但要说修电脑,我就不行了。

No one matches him when it comes to swimming.
谈到游泳,没有人比得过他。

When it comes to the crunch they will support us.
到紧要关头他们会支持我们的。

When it comes to dancing, I'm all thumbs.
谈到跳舞,我真是一窍不通。

相关句型:

1) sth comes to sb 指"某人突然想起或是意识到……",相当于 occur to,不用于被动态。例如:

The solution came to him in a flash.
他灵机一动,计上心来。

The idea occurred to him in a dream.
这个主意是他在梦中想到的。

The title just won't come to mind.
那个标题就是想不起来。

It didn't occur to him that she would refuse his invitation.
他没有想到她会拒绝他的邀请。

2) come to sth 还可以指"(数额上)共计,总共",以及"达到某状况,落到某种田地",尤其是较坏的局面。口语中还常用 "What's it all coming to? What's the world coming to?"("这是怎么回事?")表示震惊或失望。例如:

The bill came to 17 dollars.
账单共计17美元。

The doctors will operate if it proves necessary—but it may not come to that.
必要时医生会实施手术——但也许还不致如此。

All these years, and in the end it came to nothing.
那么多年了,最后却一事无成。

If it comes to a fight, you can depend on me!
如果要打架的话,你可以放心,有我呢!

He comes to the fore as a physicist at an early age.
他在早年就成了杰出的物理学家。

Those who fly too high may come to grief.
野心勃勃的人可能遭惨败。

All his little schemes for making money seem to come to grief.
他为赚钱而耍的花招看来都会失败。

96. **whether ...or** "不论是(前者)……还是(后者)……"。表示让步。
如果后者用not替代,就变成了whether ...or not,指"无论是不是(前者)的情形"。例如:
He doesn't care whether he wins or loses.
他不在乎是赢还是输。
I shall go, whether you come with me or stay at home.
不论你来还是留在家中,我都要去。
Whether we help him or not, he will fail.
不论我们帮助他与否,他都将失败。
We don't know whether he's alive or dead.
我们不知道他是死是活。
He seemed undecided whether to go or stay.
他似乎还没有决定去留。
Whether the game will be played depends on the weather.
比赛是否举行要看天气而定。

相关句型:
1) whether to do "是否做某事",具有名词性质。例如:
I can't decide whether to believe his words.
我无法决定要不要相信他的话。
I spent days agonizing over whether to take the job or not.
我用了好些天苦苦思考是否接受这份工作。
It's up to you to decide whether you go or not.
去还是不去,任你决定。

2) whether or no 指"不管任何情形"。例如:
We must stick to our promise whether or no.
不管怎样,我们心须遵守诺言。

97. **why not do sth?** "为什么不做……?"用于向对方提议或推荐,not后面接动词原型。例如:
Why not just forget his comment?
你为什么不忘了他的评论呢?
Bob is a man of the world; why not go to him for advice?
鲍勃是个通晓世故的人,干吗不去听听他的意见呢?
You need a break. Why not take a fortnight off from work?
你需要休息,为什么不休假两周呢?
Why not enjoy oneself while one could?
何不得乐且乐呢?

相关句型：
1) why don't you do sth? 指"你为什么不……?" 例如：
   Why don't you work out?
   你为什么不锻炼一下身体呢？
   You don't like your job. In this case why don't you leave?
   你不喜欢这份工作,为什么不辞掉它呢？
2) why not? 指"当然好啊",用于回答对方的请求帮忙或提议。例如：
   "Let's go to Guilin together." "Why not?"
   "我们一起去桂林吧!""好啊。"

98. **with...** 用法较多,可表示以下含义。
   1) 可用来指"和,同,对着,因为"等。例如：
   How are you getting on with him?
   你和他相处得如何？
   At the news the children jumped with joy.
   听到这消息,孩子们高兴得蹦了起来。
   She handled the problem with calmness.
   她镇定地处理这个问题。
   I can't abide people with no sense of humor.
   我讨厌和没有幽默感的人打交道。
   They accepted the offer with alacrity.
   他们欣然接受了建议。
   Serve hot, with pasta or rice and French beans.
   趁热和意大利面或米饭以及四季豆一起端上桌。
   2) 也可以引导分词结构作状语,表示原因、伴随状况等,通常是用with加代词或名词再加分词结构。当代词或名词是分词动作的逻辑主语时,分词用现在分词形式;当代词或名词是分词动作的逻辑宾语时,分词用过去分词形式。例如：
   The dog sat there with his tongue hanging out.
   这只狗伸长了舌头坐在那里。
   She walked back to the bus stop, with him following her.
   她走回公交车站时,他紧跟在她后面。
   He was sitting in the chair with his eyes closed.
   他坐在椅子上,闭着眼睛。
   He escaped with only a broken arm.
   他得以逃生,只是断了一只胳膊。
   3) 用with 表示伴随状况时,常用形容词、副词、介词短语或是不定式来取代分词,构成"with加代词/名词再加形容词/副词/介词短语/不定式结构"。例如：
   Some people sleep with their eyes open.
   有些人睁着眼睛睡觉。
   With Jim away, there's no laughter in the house.

吉姆搬走了，房子里没有了欢声笑语。
With a rose in his hand, he entered the room.
手拿一支玫瑰，他走进了房间。
They are highly mechanized farms, with machinery to do all the work.
它们是高度机械化的农场，所有工作都由机器完成。
Michelle had fallen asleep with her head against his shoulder.
米歇尔睡着了，头靠在他的肩上。
She stood with her hands on the sink, staring out the window.
她站着，两手放在水槽上，眼睛凝视着窗外。
He always plays his stereo with the bass turned right up.
他放立体声音响时总把低音调得很大。

99. **would like/love sth/to do sth** "愿意，想要……，选择……"。该句型用于表示礼貌性的请求或建议，like/love 后面可以跟不定式或分句。例如：
Would you like milk or tea?
你要喝牛奶还是喝茶？
We'd really like a holiday in Italy, but it's so expensive.
我们真想去意大利度假，但是太贵了。
I'd like to join your club.
我想加入你们俱乐部。
I'd just like to comment on a few things that were said.
我想就说过的一些事发表一些意见。
We would like to have your custom.
我们欢迎您的惠顾。
The director would like you to play the sister as a sympathetic character.
导演要你把姐姐演成一个富于同情心的人物。
I am not materialistic, but I would love to own a Ferrari.
我不是一个物质享乐主义者，不过我想拥有一辆法拉利。

相关句型：
1) be willing to do sth "乐于做某事，愿意做某事"，通常指没有理由不去做某件事情，心甘情愿做某件事情。例如：
I'm perfect willing to discuss the problem.
我十分乐意讨论这个问题。
He cherishes friendship and is willing to do anything for his friends.
他珍视友谊，为朋友他什么事情都肯做。
He was willing to do, without question, any favor we might ask him.
毫无疑问，他很乐意对我们可能提出的要求尽力帮忙。
2) be ready to do sth 指"愿意做某事"，通常是迅速的，急于行动的。也可将不定式短语换成介词短语 with sth。例如：
Don't be so ready to believe the worst about people.

不要总把人往坏处想。
He's always ready with an excuse.
他总是爱给自己找借口。
Mr. Green is always ready to help.
格林先生很乐于助人。
He burned his boats and was ready to do it to the end.
他破釜沉舟,决心做到底。
He was feeling black and ready to quit the job.
他感到悲观绝望,随时都会辞职。

3) can't wait /can hardly wait to do sth 指"迫不及待做某事",也可用介词短语 for sth 来替代不定式。例如:
I can't wait for my vacation.
我迫不及待要休假。
She can hardly wait to see him again.
她迫不及待想再见到他。
I am tired after all that walking and I can't wait to get between the sheets.
走了那么远的路我累了,我要马上睡觉。
I can't wait to get my payroll check.
我真等不及拿到我的工资单了。

100. **would rather...(than)** "宁可……(而不);宁愿"。rather...than...表示"宁可……也不……",多与 would 连用;rather 也可单独使用,后面跟不带 to 的不定式,而不需 than,表示"宁愿,宁可"。当 would rather 后面跟从句表示"宁可"时,从句用虚拟语气,通常是动词用过去时。例如:
She would rather die than ask for his favor.
她宁死也不愿求他帮忙。
Which job would you rather take?
你愿意做哪份工作呢?
Sorry, I'd rather not discuss it in public.
抱歉,我不愿公开讨论此事。
I'd rather know that now than afterwards.
我宁可现在就知道这件事,而不是以后。
I would rather remain poor than get money by dishonest means.
我宁可安于贫穷,也不愿用不当手段赚钱。
I would rather die than live in disgrace.
我宁可死,也不愿忍辱偷生。
I would rather stay at home than go to the theater.
我宁可待在家,也不想去剧院。
I'd rather you didn't lie to children.
我看你最好不要对孩子们说谎。

Would you rather I helped you with your task?
你愿意我来帮你完成任务么?

相关句型:

(would)...rather than 指"与其……(不如);不是……(而是)",这里的 rather than 前后所连接的成分在词性、结构上都比较对称;rather than 后面跟不带 to 的不定式或动词 ing 形式。例如:

The problem is mental rather than physical.
这与其说是生理上的问题,不如说是精神上的问题。

Rather than making your own cake, have you tried buying some cake at the bakery?
你是否试过在蛋糕房买点蛋糕,而不是自己做?

The teachers should be blamed rather than the students.
应该受到责备的是教师,而不是学生。

We tend to be traditional rather than fashion-forward in our designs.
我们的设计往往流于传统而没有超前意识。

Her speech was memorable for its polemic rather than its substance.
她的演说之所以令人难忘,不是因其内容而是因其辩论方法。

He is a man who will spoil rather than accomplish things.
他这个人成事不足,败事有余。

His love had been woven of sentiment rather than passion.
他的爱是以情感而不是以情欲为其经纬的。

阅读技能与训练

一、阅读意义

英国作家理查德·斯梯尔说:"Reading is to the mind what exercise is to the body. (读书之于心灵,犹如运动之于身体。)"可见,读书是人类不可或缺的一种生活方式。

读书就是阅读,是从书面材料中获取信息的过程。Gibson 和 Levin 认为:"阅读乃是从篇章中提取意义的过程。"Anderson 认为:"阅读是一个积极主动的过程,意义的产生需要阅读者和阅读文本的共同参与。"为此,阅读是一个复杂的把书上的字词与阅读者的背景知识和经历结合起来的过程。德国诗人歌德曾说过:"The experienced reader reads with two eyes: one looks at the front page, and the other the back page."(经验丰富的人读书用两只眼睛,一只眼睛看到纸面上的话,另一只眼睛看到纸的背后。)这就是说,阅读有两类,一类阅读是要求读者看纸面上的话语,譬如读报纸、广告、说明书等。对于这类阅读,读者一般使用的是一目十行的速读,即眼睛像电子扫描一样地在文字间快速浏览,及时捕捉自己所需内容,舍弃无关的部分。另一些阅读则要求读者放慢速度,发挥另一只眼睛看到纸的背后的能力。读者的眼睛时常离开书本,对书中的一字一句都细加思索,去捕捉作者的真正用意,从而理解其中的深奥的哲理。

古往今来很多名人大家都对阅读的意义作过感性的阐述,培根曾说:"读书使人充实。"笛卡尔也说过:"读好书,如同与先哲们交谈。"概而言之,阅读可以使人类变得富有、强大,可以提高生命质量,可以修身养性。与此同时,阅读也是获取智慧和经验,认识世界和改造世界的重要途径。

作为世界上使用最广泛的语言之一,英语已成为世界通用语言。当今,全球85%的信息可以从英语书籍资料中获得。为此,广泛阅读英文的科技、历史、政治、经济、社会学等方面的文章及文学作品,可以拓宽视野、增强跨文化方面的知识、不断提升自身的文化素养,以达到了解世界、认识世界的目的。

二、阅读技巧

1. 设定积极的目标主动阅读(Setting up a positive goal to read initiatively)

在信息时代,阅读成为你获取信息、与人沟通及产生共鸣的重要途径之一。而有效的阅读会受各种因素制约,例如你的身体状态、心理状态、阅读技能技巧、语言知识水平,还有阅读材料、阅读时间、外界环境等。所以为了提高自己的阅读效果,包括理解与速度,你首先要设定积极的目标,主动地阅读。积极的阅读目标是指你对阅读材料产生更多的认知,希望从阅读中获取所需的较为全面的信息交流,扩大你的知识面,开拓自己的视野。主动地阅读是要求你在阅读时主动地思考,例如,作者的意图、文章或书的用途、与你的联系等等。比起填鸭式的被动接受信息,由你主动地分析消化阅读内容是更行之有效的方法。

下面是一种常见的鱼骨头分析法(fishbone analysis):鱼头是你需要达到的目标(设定积极目标主动阅读),主干鱼骨是可能阻碍目标实现的因素(阅读时没有目标,没有动机,没有关联性,阅读中没有重点,没有认知,没有集中注意力),副鱼骨列举了具体情况,请对照主、副鱼骨分析你的阅读状态。(你的鱼骨头越多,你就越需要改进阅读态度和方法了!)

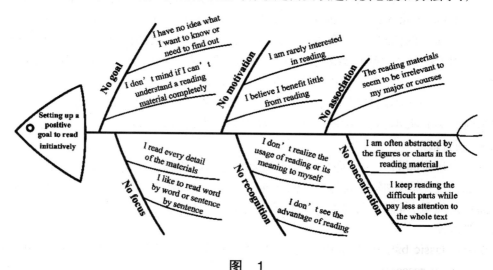

图 1

Reading Simulation 阅读仿真

阅读仿真将为你模拟两种特定的阅读过程,其中阅读材料A和B在信息的类型、字数和难度上十分接近,请你依照仿真步骤的顺序(step1, 2, 3等)和要求进行阅读并完成仿真中的练习,从中体验设定积极的目标主动阅读所带给你的不同阅读效果:

Step 1: 阅读A部分。

A

Quantum computers that can perform vast numbers of calculations simultaneously may be closer to science fiction than reality, but previously unpublished documents indicate the U.S. National Security Agency is working hard to build a real quantum supercomputer, powerful enough to decode virtually every form of encryption(加密) now known.

Such a computer, many times faster than today's fastest machines, could easily solve codes now considered "unbreakable"—the type of ciphers(密码) currently used worldwide by scientific and financial institutions and governments to protect their data.

The basic principle of quantum computing is a physical phenomenon that is not yet fully understood: certain subatomic(亚原子的) particles can simultaneously exist in two different states. A conventional computer works with "bits" of information that are represented as either zero or one; quantum bits could be both zero and one simultaneously. In theory, that coincidence of physics will allow quantum computers to skip through much of the elaborate mathematical computations necessary to solve complex encryption keys.

The U.S. government is said to be competing against quantum-computer research efforts by the European Union and Switzerland, but experts in the field say practical exploitation of such systems is years if not decades in the future.

Step 2: 覆盖原文A，列举quantum computer的工作原理和特点。

How does a quantum computer work: _____;
What is the feature of this computer: _____;
What is its current research status: _____.

Step 3: 模拟自己是一名计算机专业人员，你对下一篇介绍quantum computer的文章有积极的兴趣：它是与自己的职业领域相关，很可能给工作带来好处，将来会大幅提高工作效率等。请你在阅读B部分前设定几个问题并在阅读中留意它们，如：

Question 1: What is the working procedure of a quantum computer?
Answer: _____
Question 2: How will its feature or processing speed be like if it is produced?
Answer: _____
Question 3: How far have the researchers reached in creating such a computer?
Answer: _____

Step 4: 阅读B部分。

B

When classic bits are transformed into quantum bits it increases a computer's processing power. German researchers are among those who've succeeded in doing this, but so far only under laboratory conditions. It was 22 years ago that quantum computing would be predicted to be possible. In 2012, it was put it into practice by a German laboratory scientist with the help of his colleagues from Grenoble and Tokyo.

When computers process data, the two bit states are encoded, resulting in a series of zeros and ones. They describe the so-called bit state of an electrical charge—its voltage level. Electrons also have other properties that researchers can exploit in order to create so-called quantum bits, that process allows a person to define more than just two possible states.

The transformation into a quantum bit works as follows: Normally, the stimulated electrons move through the metal or semiconductor along defined, parallel paths. But researchers interrupted this pattern by sending an additional wave of electricity. Thereafter, the researchers harnessed the electron's surf path into two channels lying very close together. The electron can actually only move itself into one of the two channels, causing it to take on the state coded either as zeros or ones. But by coupling the two channels, the electron exists in both simultaneously. Its overlapping bit states become a quantum bit. The extent to which quantum computing has already been developed remains unknown. The "Washington Post" cited that the NSA is developing a quantum supercomputer. Thus far, quantum computers have been viewed as a theoretical concept being tested out in laboratories.

Step 5: 覆盖原文B,回答上面3个问题。

Step 6: 总结仿真。请你对两次阅读效果及完成问题做个比较,相信可以体验到在阅读过程中带有积极的目标主动阅读的好处了。

2. 测试阅读速度和理解力(Measuring reading rate and comprehension)

了解设定积极的目标主动地阅读的好处后,你也许会问:"到底我的阅读速度和理解能力如何呢?"现在就开始测试一下吧!

下面的练习将帮你测量目前的阅读速度和理解力,所以请你做到以一贯的速度去阅读材料。阅读时要读懂文章主旨并掌握其细节,读完后回答随后的问题,同时尽可能不回看文章。练习时你需要记录下阅读的起始和结束时间(即开始时××分××秒,结束时××分××秒,两项相减后再换算成××分钟,就是你的阅读时间,例如15分15秒换算成15.25分),所以请准备手表一类的工具,保证时间可精确到秒。

● 开始时间: _____ 分 _____ 秒

Diagnosing Disease with the Touch of a Button

They might not have electricity or running water, but some of the world's poorest communities might soon have a way of quickly diagnosing diseases on the spot.

With a drop of blood, iPad-sized Gene-RADAR can detect deadly diseases such as HIV/AIDS and tuberculosis in less than an hour, its creator, Dr. Anita Goel, told *Newsweek*. The device is about to be field-tested in Africa.

Gene-RADAR, which recently emerged from the laboratories of Nanobiosym, a Cambridge, Mass-based technology incubator, uses a computer chip to scan bodily fluids for specific strips of genetic code that signify the presence of an infection.

The device's software then analyzes the data providing a near-instant yet perfect diagnosis. Gene-RADAR is so easy to use its operation does not require trained medical personnel. And it will cost far less than conventional lab tests, said Goel.

The rapid turnaround from a sample to diagnosis is especially important in countries like Rwanda, where less-effective, cheap AIDS tests abound. These "quick and dirty" tests, Goel adds, still require final confirmation from a lab. In these countries, which have so few medical facilities, the process can take up to six months.

"What we're doing is bringing that gold standard capability outside of a lab infrastructure into a mobile device," she said. "The idea is to really empower people to take control over their own health and manage their own health in a timely way."

Goel said Gene-RADAR not only has implications for the approximately 4 billion people who don't have access to basic health care. At some point it could also be tailored to perform DIY triage at home that will save general health-care costs. Worried parents, for example, could test to see whether their child's high fever is from a cold or whether it's something far worse before rushing for treatment at a hospital emergency room.

Gene-RADAR and similar devices also have tremendous preventive potential, said Dr. Sara Brenner, who serves as assistant vice president for nanohealth initiatives and is assistant professor of nanobioscience at the State University of New York, Albany.

Making diagnosis easier, she said, allows patients to treat diseases before they have "gone haywire." Brenner does not think Gene-RADAR or similar devices have the same risks as other direct-to-consumer diagnostic devices such as 23andMe, an at-home gene screening product. The FDA recently ordered Google-backed 23andMe to stop selling its services, saying it was being marketed as a diagnostic tool without proper approval—which geneticists worried would spur patients to seek out invasive, costly medical treatments that may prove unnecessary.

"Unlike 23andMe, which provides a lot of genetic information [that] we do not know how to interpret, this type of diagnostic test would simply be a faster and more accurate way to do what we already do within the laboratory," she says. "The benefit of a rapid diagnostic that's accurate will outweigh the risks."

News of the forthcoming field tests comes amid other initiatives to bring impoverished communities cheap and effective medical tools, such as a Portland, Oregon company's recent testing of a portable, battery-powered device that screens for cervical cancer.

(513 Words)

- 结束时间：_____分_____秒

现在计算阅读花了多长时间,换算成以分钟为单位。用本篇文章的字数除以时间,即得到你的阅读速度_____ wpm (每分钟阅读字数)

- 接着完成理解能力的测试,请回答下面10道选择题(尽量不要回看文章)：

1. According to the new research, people can diagnose disease, such as HIV, on the spot by____.

   A) using an iPad application

   B) following leisure habits

   C) using a drop of blood

   D) following working habits

2. Gene-RADAR creator Dr. Anita Goel explained this new device will be used in ____.

   A) the work places of the rich

   B) the field- tested in Africa

   C) the poor communities

D) the research laboratories

3. Which of the following is not true about Gene-RADAR?

   A) Gene-RADAR has been recently emerged.

   B) Gene-RADAR can provide a delayed but perfect diagnosis.

   C) Gene-RADAR has been developed from a technological incubator.

   D) Gene-RADAR can scan bodily fluids to tell the presence of an infection.

4. The creator of Gene-RADAR have believed that

   A) Gene-RADAR does not require experienced doctor or nurse to operate.

   B) Gene-RADAR cost far more than traditional lab check.

   C) Gene-RADAR is especially important in Roma.

   D) Gene-RADAR diagnosis sample blood in the lab infrastructure.

5. What is the reason for people to create Gene-RADAR?

   A) It can be used in important countries.

   B) It can be developed into slow device.

   C) It can bring the gold standard outside of the hospital.

   D) It can remind people to manage their body condition.

6. Who will be the largest target Gene-RADAR serves?

   A) Tailored customer.

   B) Worried parents.

   C) Poor people without basic health treatment.

   D) Emergent patients.

7. What does the word "haywire" mean?

   A) Crazy.   B) Impatient.
   C) Panic.   D) Scared.

8. What can't be known about Gene-RADAR?

   A) Gene-RADAR has similar devices.

   B) Gene-RADAR doesn't have the same risks as 23andMe.

   C) Gene-RADAR have tremendous predictive potential.

   D) Gene-RADAR is a diagnosis tool.

9. Which of the following statements is true?

   A) The FDA recently ordered Google-backed 23andMe to stop improving its services.

   B) The FDA recently ordered Google-backed 23andMe to stop selling its services.

   C) 23andMe's diagnostic test would simply be a faster and more accurate way.

   D) 23andMe's diagnostic test would simply be interpreted.

10. What is the main idea of this article?

    A) Gene-RADAR improves the rate of curing the cancer patients.

    B) Gene-RADAR is needed in countries of large population.

    C) Gene-RADAR is an easy but cheap tool to fast test an infection.

    D) Gene-RADAR will replace other similar devices soon.

正确答案：
1. C 2. B 3. B 4. A 5. D 6. C 7. A 8. C 9. B 10. C
● 计算你的理解正确率 Test Score: _____%

现在，你该知道自己的阅读速度和理解力情况了，以下的章节将从不同方面进一步介绍英语阅读，帮助你提高阅读的速度和理解能力。

3. 不良的阅读习惯(Bad reading habits)

不良的阅读习惯往往让你的阅读效果事倍功半，因此应该找出它们并尽量克服：

（1）发音(vocalization)

很多人错误地认为阅读是由眼睛的"阅"和嘴巴的"读"组成的，常常边看文章边读出来。其实，发音阅读会大大地降低阅读的理解和速度。为了配合嘴巴出声，眼睛不能完全发挥其扫视的运动，因而速度也会变慢。对于任何读者来说都应克服边看边读出声的不良习惯。

（2）潜在发音(sub-vocalization)

在心里默读文章是一种潜在发音，你也许会自然而然产生这种不良倾向。潜在发音使你注意力分散，表面上像是正常的阅读，但是你可能不自觉地在默读某个单词、某句话等，这样就破坏了阅读的速度和效果。在分析自己的阅读习惯时，你要判断是不是有这种潜在发音的做法，提醒自己不要在心里默读材料。

（3）头部摆动(head movement)

中国古代的读书人读起书来常摇头晃脑。现在有些人在阅读英语材料时也喜欢随视线的移动而摆动头部。这是一个常见却又不必要的小动作，它同样会影响你的阅读速度和效果。所以，在阅读时只运动你的眼睛就够了。

（4）复读(regression reading)

当遇到陌生的单词和有难度的句子、段落时，很多读者爱把它们重复读一遍或两遍，甚至多遍，打断了正常的阅读节奏。阅读时过分地关注一些难懂的语言知识同样会阻碍你的阅读速度和效果。语言在语境中能产生细微的差异，脱离整体的语境单独地理解语言中各个字、词、句、段不是有效阅读所应该提倡的方法。当你遇到不熟悉的语言知识时，可以暂时跳过，继续读下面的内容。阅读中可运用推断、比较、分析等方法从上下文中获得帮助，从而增强你的理解能力。

（5）潜在翻译(sub-translating)

潜在翻译是指读者在阅读时把读到的外语文字翻译成母语以帮助理解。实际上，英语和汉语属于不同的语系，它们在文化习俗、生活习惯以及语言表达上存在着很大差距。因此，要把一篇英语阅读材料在短时间内对等地翻译成中文对你来说是一件出力不讨好的事。假如你把读到的每个句子都翻译成中文来理解的话，阅读速度一定会变慢。

（6）频繁停顿(frequent intervals)

在阅读时你应该保持注意力的集中，一气呵成完成整个阅读过程。有些读者做些习惯性的小动作分散了注意力，有些读者喜欢中断阅读过程，过多地分析段落、句子、语法等，还有些读者阅读的时候不时地去查阅词典，这些频繁停顿都让阅读无法连贯地进行下去及达到最好的效果。

为了达到良好的阅读效果,你可以分析自己的阅读习惯,对照如上列出的不良习惯加以改正。

4. 训练眼睛的移动(Training eye movement)

一般的阅读过程是由眼睛摄取到信息,通过大脑对摄入的信息进行解码和整理,最后获得信息的细节和意义。那么,能有效地使用眼睛来摄入信息就是你实现良好阅读效果的关键。

眼睛摄入信息时,最佳的移动方式是由上到下垂直型(请参照图2)。这种移动方式不论在眼睛移动的速度上还是灵活度上都很好。由上到下垂直地阅读就是扩大眼睛扫视的范围,把目光主要停留在中间部分,由上到下垂直移动进行阅读,每行文字的左右两端可以各留出2至3厘米,利用余光快速地扫视它们。眼睛移动的能力可以训练,加快自己的阅读速度。一开始可以选择较窄短的材料(如报纸、杂志中非整幅的文章)训练自己眼睛从上到下垂直扫视的感觉,培养这样阅读的习惯,最大限度地发挥垂直和水平边缘视觉能力,使看清的字数和行数逐渐增多,速度增快。

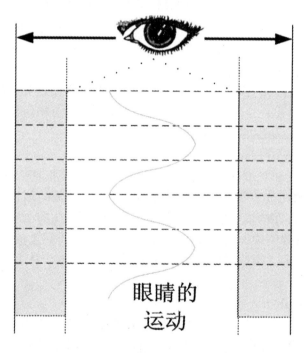

图 2

Exercise:

请用由上到下垂直型眼睛移动方式快速阅读下文,其中左、右两侧2厘米的阴影部分用眼睛的余光扫视,然后完成问题。

We can not feel speed. But our senses let us know that we are moving. We see things moving past us and feel that we are being shaken.

We can feel acceleration, an increase in speed. But we notice it for only a short time. For instance, we feel it during the takeoff run of an airliner.

We feel the plane's acceleration because our bodies do not gain speed as fast as the plane does. It seems that something is pushing us back against the seat.

Actually, our bodies are trying to stay in the same places, while the plane is carrying us forward.

Soon the plane reaches a steady speed. Then, because there is no longer any change in speed, the feeling of forward motion stops.

眼睛的运动

Question 1: We can tell that we are moving by _____.
    A) watching things moving past   B) feeling the speed
    C) feeling ourselves being shaken   D) both A and C

Question 2: Acceleration means _____.
    A) an increase in speed   B) a steady speed
    C) any kind of movement   D) the movement of a plane

Question 3: We feel the plane's acceleration because our bodies gain speed _____.
    A) just as fast as the plane   B) faster than the plane
    C) more slowly than the plane   D) before the plane

Key: 1. D 2. A 3. C

5. 协调的注视节奏(Harmonious fixation)

优秀的阅读者可以像个演奏家演奏音乐一样,有节奏、有重心地阅读。前面说过的眼睛扫视范围是眼睛的识别幅(eye span),识别幅越宽,阅读速度就越快,反之亦然。而和识别幅关系紧密的是眼睛的注视点(fixation)——眼睛在摄入信息时最终聚焦的位置。你可以确定一定长度以内的由3至4个词组成的语言意群作为一个识别幅,像词组 in the afternoon, write in English, be widely accepted, people all support that;同时把眼睛的注视点放在当中某一个关键词上(如 afternoon, English, accepted, support)。下面以一个长句为例:

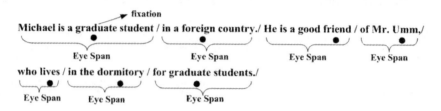

Exercise:

请你划分短文意群,尝试确定每个意群的关键词,即注视点(fixation)。

Michael is a graduate student in a foreign country. He is a good friend of Mr. Umm, who lives in the dormitory for graduate students. They share a similar sense of humor and enjoy many activities together. Since Michael is interested in architecture, Mr. Umm decides that it would be a good idea for Michael to meet his older friend Mr. Smith, a professor of design at the university. First he tells Michael all about Mr. Smith's architectural research. As it turns out, Mr. Smith's research is exactly what Michael needs for his thesis. Michael is so excited that the next day he goes directly to Mr. Smith's office, introduces himself, and briefly mentions Mr. Umm's name. The two men spend several hours discussing their research ideas. That evening Michael tells Mr. Umm how much he enjoyed meeting Mr. Smith. Mr. Umm reacts very coldly. His serious tone tells Michael that something is wrong, but Michael has no idea what the problem might be.

Reference Key:

Michael is a graduate student/ in a foreign country. / He is a good friend / of Mr. Umm, / who lives / in the dormitory / for graduate students. / They share / a similar sense of humor / and enjoy / many activities together. / Since Michael is interested / in architecture, / Mr. Umm decides / that it would be a good idea / for Michael to meet / his older friend Mr. Smith, / a professor of design / at the university. / First he tells Michael / all about Mr. Smith's / architectural research. / As it turns out, / Mr. Smith's research is / exactly what Michael needs / for his thesis. / Michael is so excited / that the next day / he goes directly / to Mr. Smith's office, / introduces himself, / and briefly mentions / Mr. Umm's name. / The two men / spend several hours / discussing their research ideas. / That evening / Michael tells Mr. Umm / how much he enjoyed / meeting Mr. Smith. / Mr. Umm reacts very coldly. / His serious tone tells Michael / that something is wrong, / but Michael has no idea / what the problem might be.

6. 确定文章的体裁 (Types of writing)

　　文章的体裁不同,其结构特点就会各异。同时,不同文体阅读要求与方法不尽相同。因此,读者准确、快速定位要找的信息最有效的方法之一就是首先确定文章的体裁。一旦确定了文章的体裁,读者就能根据相关的体裁知识,预测文章的行文趋势。

　　英语文章的体裁主要有三类:记叙文、说明文和议论文。本单元首先介绍如何通过略读确定文章的体裁。

　　文章的标题一定程度上能够反映文章的体裁,因此通过标题,读者可以分析判断出文章的体裁。

　　请看下面几篇文章的标题:

(1) Four Goals in Our Life
(2) Ageism
(3) Drink Water, Lose Weight
(4) Words Can Give You Power
(5) My First Job
(6) A Miserable College Day

　　标题(1)和(2)不仅给出了文章的关键词,而且表明了文章的体裁是说明文。标题(3)和(4)是具有典型的议论文的标题特点,同时也表明了文章的论点。标题(5)和(6)分别是

"我的第一份工作"和"大学生活中某日悲惨的故事",因此文章的体裁属于记叙文。

Exercise:根据标题,请判断下列文章属于哪类体裁:

(1) The Diversity of My University Life

(2) Thinking: A Neglected Art

(3) Double Seventh Festival

(4) A Difficult Interview

(5) Intelligent Children Should Be Taught Separately and Given Special Treatment

(6) My Childhood in an Indian Village

(7) The United Nations: The World in One Building

(8) A Brave Man

(9) Human's Seven Gifts Given by Nature

(10) Honesty: Is It Going to Be Out of Style

答案:(1)、(3)、(7)和(9)是说明文;(2)、(5)和(10)是议论文;(4)、(6)和(8)是记叙文。

除了根据标题判断文章的体裁外,读者还可以根据首段原则和首尾句原则来了解作者的思路、确定文章的体裁。通常文章开头段大致包含了文章的大意、背景情况、作者的文章风格、口吻或语气等。另外,据统计,大约有80%的主题句是段落的首句,其余20%左右的是尾句,所以,读者还可以通过阅读文章开头段以及中间段的首句或尾句来确定文章的体裁。

请看下文:

The age of gilded youth is over. Today's under-thirties are the first generation for a century who can expect a lower living standard than their parents.

Research into the lifestyles and prospects of people who were born since 1970 shows that they are likely to face a lifetime of longer working hours, lower job security and higher taxes than the previous generation.

When they leave work late in the evening, they will be more likely to return to a small rented flat than to a house of their own. When, eventually, they retire, their pensions are far lower in real terms than those of their immediate forebears.

These findings are revealed in a study of the way the ageing of Britain's population is affecting different generations.

Anthea Tinker, professor of social gerontology(老人学)at King's College London, who carried out much of the work, said the growth of the proportion of people over 50 had reversed the traditional flow of wealth from older to younger generations.

"Today's older middle-aged and elderly are becoming the new winners," she said. "They made relatively small contributions in tax but now make relatively big claims on the welfare system. Generations born in the last three to four decades face the prospect of handing over more than a third of their lifetime's earnings to care for them."

The surging number of older people, many living alone, has also increased demand for property and pushed up house prices. While previous generations found it easy to raise a mortgage, today's under-thirties have to live with their parents or rent. If they can afford to buy a home it is more likely to be a flat than a house.

Laura Lenox-Conyngham, 28, grew up in a large house and her mother did not need to work. Unlike her wealthy parents, she graduated with student and postgraduate loan debts of £13,000. She now earns about £20,000 a year, preparing food to be photographed for magazines. Her home is a one-bedroom flat in central London and she sublets(转租)the lunge sofa-bed to her brother.

"My father took pity and paid off my student debts," she said. "But I still have no pension and no chance of buying a property for at least a couple of years—and then it will be something small in a bad area. My only hope is the traditional one of meeting a rich man."

Tinker's research reveals Lenox-Conyngham is representative of many young professionals, especially in London, Manchester, Edinburgh and Bristol.

在文章的首段,作者明确表明了自己的观点: "The age of gilded youth is over. Today's under-thirties are the first generation for a century who can expect a lower living standard than their parents."之后段落中,作者运用大量实例,论及现在的中老年人可以享受较好的社会福利系统,这却对年轻人产生了压力,以此论证了他的观点。在文章的结尾作者运用Lenox-Conyngham的实例,说明当代年轻人无法享受相应的社会福利和舒适生活。根据文章的首尾段和中间段的首句或尾句,读者就可以判断出这篇文章的体裁为议论文。

练习一:根据给出的文章首段和中间段的首句或尾句判断文章的体裁

The case for college has been accepted without question for more than a generation. All high school graduates ought to go, says conventional wisdom and statistical evidence, because college will help them earn more money, become "better" people, and learn to be more responsible citizens than those who don't go.

But college has never been able to work its magic for everyone. And now that close to half our high school graduates are attending, those who don't fit the pattern are becoming more numerous, and more obvious. College graduates are selling shoes and driving taxis; college students interfere with each other's experiments and write false letters of recommendation in the intense competition for admission to graduate school. Others find no stimulation in their studies, and drop-out often encouraged by college administrators.

Some observers say the fault is with the young people themselves—they are spoiled and they are expecting too much. But that's a condemnation of the students as a whole, and doesn't explain all campus unhappiness. Others blame the state of the world, and they are partly right.

We've been told that young people have to go to college because our economy can't absorb an army of untrained eighteen-year-olds. But disappointed graduates are learning that it can no longer absorb an army of trained twenty-two-year-olds, either.

Some adventuresome educators and campus watchers have openly begun to suggest that college may not be the best, the proper, the only place for every young person after the completion of high school. We may have been looking at all those surveys and statistics upside down. Perhaps college doesn't make people intelligent, ambitious, happy, liberal, or quick to learn things—maybe it's just the other way around, and intelligent, ambitious, happy, liberal, quick-learning people are merely the ones who have been attracted to college in the first place. And perhaps all those successful college graduates would have been successful whether they had gone to college or not.

This is heresy(异端邪说) to those of us who have been brought up to believe that if a little schooling is good, more has to be much better. But contrary evidence is beginning to mount up.

答案:这是一篇议论文。在文章第二段的首句,作者明确地表明了自己的观点"But college has never been able to work its magic for everyone."即上过高校的人未必比没有上过高校的人更会挣钱、更具有责任感。之后段落分别讨论了原因,有人归结于年轻人娇生惯养,对未来期待太多;经济无法接纳缺乏经验的年轻人。第五段首句"Some adventuresome educators and campus watchers have openly begun to suggest that college may not be the best, the proper, the only place for every young person after the completion of high school."说明了大学不一定是高中毕业生的唯一出路。最后一段作者再次重申观点"But contrary evidence is beginning to mount up."说明上学不是越上越好。

练习二:根据给出的文章首尾段和中间段的首尾句判断文章的体裁

From the moment that an animal is born it has to make decisions. It has to decide which of the things around it are for eating, and which are to be avoided when to attack and when to run away. The animal is, in effect, playing a complicated and potentially very dangerous game with its environment, discomfort or destruction.

This is a difficult and unpleasant business and few animals would survive if they had to start from the beginning and learn about the world wholly by trial and error, for there are the have possible decisions which would prove fatal. So we find, in practice, that the game is always arranged in favor of the young animal in one way or another. Either the animal is protected during the early stages of its learning about the world around it, or the knowledge of which way to respond is built into its nervous system from the start.

The fact that animals behave sensibly can be attributed partly to what we might call genetic (遗传的) learning, to distinguish it from the individual learning that an animal does in the course of its own life time. Genetic learning is learning by a species as a whole, and it is achieved by selection of those members of each generation that happen to behave in the right way. However, genetic learning depends upon a prediction that the future will more or less exactly resemble the past. The more variable individual experience is likely to be, the less efficient is genetic learning as a means of getting over the problems of the survival game. It is not surprising to find that very few species indeed depend wholly upon genetic learning. In the great majority of animals, behavior is a compound of individual experience and genetic learning to behave in particular ways.

答案:这是一篇典型的说明文。作者在首段指出了所要说明的话题"The animal is, in effect, playing a complicated and potentially very dangerous game with its environment, discomfort or destruction."即动物与环境、不适和灭亡的抗争既复杂又危险。文章的第二、三段介绍了动物行为是由个体经验和遗传因素决定的。

7. 体裁：确定阅读的重点 (The focus of reading of different types)

不同体裁的文章，其结构特点各异，因此，确定了文章的体裁，读者就可以根据文章的体裁预测文章的结构以及略读的重点，从而快速理解通篇文章。

（1）记叙文的结构模式 (The basic structure of narration)

记叙文(Narration)就是记叙一件事或一连串事件。大学英语记叙文的阅读模式即围绕六个要素——概要、定位、叠合事件、评议、解决和结局以及尾声展开。

概要是记叙文叙述开始前叙述者提供的对故事的摘要。定位是记叙文的基本组成部分，帮助读者识别时间、地点、人物、人物活动或者情境。定位的标记主要是动词的过去进行时以及时间、方式和地点状语。叠合事件包含着一系列叙事句。叙事句采用一般过去时和一般现在时，是叙事结构中的最小单位，并以时间为顺序排列。评议是叙事结构非常重要的元素，是叙事者或他人对某种情况的看法、观点和态度，包括对故事的起因、要点、影响和人物等所做的评议。评议分为直接评议和间接评议。解决、结局是指事件是怎么解决的。尾声用来体现故事的完整性，标志着事情已经结束，并把故事讲述者和读者带回到故事的起点。

由于英语记叙文的阅读模式主要是围绕上述六个要素而展开并按一定时间顺序发展的，因此阅读时一定要注意表示时间顺序的词，如then, next, later, soon, eventually 等。

记叙文的基本结构模式是：

在文章的开头部分，作者引入要叙述的经历。

在文章的中间部分，作者叙述经历。

在文章结尾部分，作者做出总结、感悟或发现。

请看下文：

As she walked round the huge department store, Edith reflected how difficult it was to choose a suitable Christmas present for her father. She wished that he was as easy to please as her mother, who was always delighted with perfume.

Besides, shopping at this time of the year was a most disagreeable experience: people trod on your toes, poked you with their elbows and almost knocked you over in their haste to get to a bargain ahead of you.

Partly to have a rest, Edith paused in front of a counter where some attractive ties were on display. "They are real silk," the assistant assured her, trying to tempt her. "Worth doubles the price." But Edith knew from past experience that her choice of ties hardly ever pleased her father.

She moved on reluctantly and then quite by chance, stopped where a small crowd of men had gathered round a counter. She found some good quality pipes on sale—and the prices were very reasonable. Edith did not hesitate for long: although her father only smoked a pipe occasionally, she knew that this was a present which was bound to please him.

When she got home, with her small well-chosen present concealed in her handbag, her parents were already at the supper table. Her mother was in an especially cheerful mood, "Your father has at last decided to stop smoking." She informed her daughter.

在文章的开头部分，作者通过女儿为父亲挑选圣诞礼物这件事引出了文章的话题：为父亲挑个合意的礼物真不容易。在文章的中间部分，作者叙述了挑选礼物的过程。在文章的结尾部分，作者通过父亲戒烟的决心，突出了文章的戏剧性效果。

练习一：

  The rain was pounding against my window as I awoke at the "ungodly" hour of seven thirty. It was bad enough that I had to be there for 9 AM. I felt so secure and warm wrapped up in my winter duvet. It was the best feeling in the world. As I finally dragged myself out of the comfort and security of my bed, I felt the cold as I rushed to get a shower.

  I didn't really want to go, but something inside me told me I should, it would be for the best. Today wasn't just my first day at college; it was the start of a journey. I arrived early, about eight thirty. I'll always remember that I totally lost feeling. I felt as though I was in a jungle, a concrete jungle. The buildings were like the trees and the people were like the wild animals. The jungle seemed to be full of monkeys and other wild animals. All the wild animals seemed to know each other; I felt like I was invading their private space, like on one of those wildlife programs, where the monkeys just stare at the camera, as if to say, "Get out of my space."

  I was scared. Somehow I found my way through the maze, which I knew at XXX College/University. Reception seemed like a busy place, full of all the wild animals; everyone was standing away from the main desk. I asked the lady behind the desk where my classroom was. I was given directions to the drama hall. As I walked into the classroom, I was nervous. These were the jungle animals I would spend the year with. I would have to make friends with them.

  I was only in college for about an hour, filling in forms and answering questions. We only used the computers for the last fifteen minutes, when we were setting up our student account, which involved setting our user name and password. We were given our timetable. I was in the next morning at nine. So I went home, that was my first day of the journey through the jungle.

  I started walking home; by this time it had stopped raining. I felt good about myself; I had survived my first day at the jungle known as college. I thought to myself, one down only another three years to go!

Select the best choice for each of the following questions or unfinished statements.

1. As I walked into the classroom, I was _____.
  A) excited   B) delighted
  C) nervous   D) scared
2. "I asked the lady behind the desk where my classroom was." In the line, the word "lady" can be best replaced by _____.
  A) the waitress   B) the professor
  C) the receptionist   D) the bell-ringer
3. "These were the jungle animals I would spend the year with." In the line, the term "jungle animals" actually means
  A) wild animals   B) wild animals living in the jungle
  C) domestic animals   D) college students

Key: 1. C 2. C 3. D

练习二：

I don't ever want to talk about being a woman scientist again. There was a time in my life when people asked constantly for stories about what it's like to work in a field dominated by men. I was never very good at telling those stories because truthfully I never found them interesting. What I do find interesting is the origin of the universe, the shape of space-time and the nature of black holes.

At 19, when I began studying astrophysics, it did not bother me in the least to be the only woman in the classroom. But while earning my Ph.D. at MIT and then as a post-doctor doing space research, the issue started to bother me. My every achievement—jobs, research papers, awards—was viewed through the lens of gender (性别) politics. So were my failures. Sometimes, when I was pushed into an argument on left brain versus (相对于) right brain, or nature versus nurture (培育), I would instantly fight fiercely on my behalf and all womankind.

Then one day a few years ago, out of my mouth came a sentence that would eventually become my reply to any and all provocations: I don't talk about that anymore. It took me 10 years to get back the confidence I had at 19 and to realize that I didn't want to deal with gender issues. Why should curing sexism be yet another terrible burden on every female scientist? After all, I don't study sociology or political theory.

Today I research and teach at Barnard, a women's college in New York City. Recently, someone asked me how many students in my class were women. You cannot imagine my satisfaction at being able to answer, 45. I know some of my students worry how they will manage their scientific research and a desire for children. And I don't dismiss those concerns. Still, I don't tell them "war" stories. Instead, I have given them this: the visual of their physics professor heavily pregnant doing physics experiments. And in turn they have given me the image of 45 women driven by a love of science. And that's a sight worth talking about.

Select the best choice for each of the following questions or unfinished statements.

1. Why doesn't the author want to talk about being a woman scientist again?

   A) She feels unhappy working in male-dominated fields.

   B) She is fed up with the issue of gender discrimination.

   C) She is not good at telling stories of the kind.

   D) She finds space research more important.

2. From Paragraph 2, we can infer that people would attribute the author's failures to _____.

   A) the very fact that she is a woman

   B) her involvement in gender politics

   C) her over-confidence as a female astrophysicist

   D) the burden she bears in a male-dominated society

3. What did the author constantly fight against while doing her Ph.D. and post-doctoral research?
   A) Lack of confidence in succeeding in space science.
   B) Unfair accusations from both inside and outside her circle.
   C) People's stereotyped attitude toward female scientists.
   D) Widespread misconceptions about nature and nurtured.
4. Why does the author feel great satisfaction when talking about her class?
   A) Female students no longer have to bother about gender issues.
   B) Her students' performance has brought back her confidence.
   C) Her female students can do just as well as male students.
   D) More female students are pursuing science than before.
5. What does the image the author presents to her students suggest?
   A) Women students needn't have the concerns of her generation.
   B) Women have more barriers on their way to academic success.
   C) Women can balance a career in science and having a family.
   D) Women now have fewer problems pursuing a science career.

Key: 1.B 2.A 3.C 4.D 5.C

（2）说明文的结构模式 (The basic structure of description)

说明文 (Description) 是就某个人、某个地方、某件物体或某个场景用文字进行描绘。大学英语说明文的阅读模式可见下图：

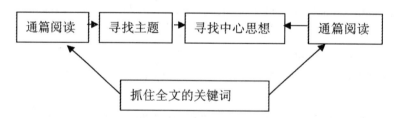

① 寻找主题。英语说明文的主题一般涉及这样一些问题，即文章是有关何人、何事物的，文章所谈论或描述的是什么。文章的标题又是怎样的。

文中多次出现的一些具有鲜明特点的词语、名称、专用语被作者采用层层推进的手法反复论证，读者则完全可以据此断定文章的主题就是这些多次出现的语言成分。有的文章对某些词语进行定义性解释、描述，读者也可断定被解释和描述的对象即为文章的主题。

找到了文章的主题之后，读者接下来应带着这样一些问题继续阅读，即文章是如何谈论主题的？文中所谈的主题的内容又是什么？文章本身又是如何围绕着主题展开的？而能够回答这些问题的答案就恰好构成了文章的中心思路。

② 寻找中心思想。中心思想是每篇文章、每个段落甚至每个句子中最重要的部分。通常各段文字的中心是该段落的开头句，它对整段文字起着定性的作用。但有的中心思想恰好是段落的结尾语或隐含在字里行间，读这样的材料就需要读者对文字多加关注，特别注意文中重要的事实、例证，并以此为线索，从中揣摩出支持的观点。

不过有些词语还是可给读者一些启发的,常见的这类词语有:perhaps, apparently, presumably 等,best, greatest, successful, worst, interesting, effective 等形容词也常用来表示作者对某个事物的评价和断。此外像 finally, in conclusion 等词语都是用于引出作者的结论的。

总体而言,可参考以下的基本结构模式:

在文章的开头部分,作者提出问题(或以一个事例引出问题)。

在文章的中间部分,作者发现直接原因或分析深层原因。

在文章的结尾部分,作者进行总结或做出结论。

请看文章:

One of the greatest changes in family life nowadays is that many couples decide not to have any children because they think that children bring more misery than joy. To my mind, these couples are not only short-sighted but also selfish. It is an undeniable fact that a married couple without children have more opportunities to get jobs, enjoy the freedom from the troubles and worries caused by children, and can spend all the money they earn for their own pleasure and comforts, but they should not forget that there are also three outweighing advantages in having children.

  Firstly, ...

  Secondly, ...

  Thirdly, ...

In short, from a long point of view, the advantages of having children overweigh those of having no children. From a social point of view, those who choose to be childless are selfish and irresponsible. Human society needs to carry on and its members should give birth to babies, bring them up, and educate them according to the requirements of society. If everybody escapes from these responsibilities out of selfish considerations, there will be no human beings on the planet of earth. This view of mine, however, does not mean that we should have as many children as possible. If we are responsible members of the human society, we should also limit the number of our children according to the social requirements.

阅读了这篇说明文以后,首先明白作者采用演绎法对全文进行说明,随后在寻找主题的时候发现第一段就表达了作者观点,形成主题句。主题句起统领下文的作用,然后作者在肯定不要孩子的好处的同时指出了生小孩的三个优点,并逐一说明。第三段围绕第一段的主题句,从社会角度说明不要孩子是自私和不负责任的表现。文章最后说明作者赞同要小孩,但主张对孩子的数量进行控制。这样写,观点容易被接受。

练习一:

There's simple premise behind what Larry Myers does for a living: If you can smell it, you can find it.

Myers is the founder of Auburn University's Institute for Biological Detection Systems, the main task of which is to chase the ultimate in detection devices—an artificial nose.

For now, the subject of their research is little more than a stack of gleaming chips tucked away in a laboratory drawer. But soon, such a tool could be hanging from the belts of police, arson (纵火) investigators and food-safety inspectors.

The technology that they are working in would suggest quite reasonably that, within three to five years, we'll have some workable sensors ready to use. Such devices might find wide use in places that attract terrorists. Police could detect drugs, bodies and bombs hidden in cars, while food inspectors could easily test food and water for contamination.

The implications for revolutionary advances in public safety and the food industry are astonishing. But so, too, are the possibilities for abuse; Such machines could determine whether a woman is ovulating (排卵), without a physical exam or even her knowledge.

One of the traditional protectors of American liberty is that is has been impossible to search everyone. That's getting not to be the case.

Artificial biosensors created at Auburn work totally differently from anything ever seen before. Aroma Scan, for example, is a desktop machine based on a bank of chips sensitive to specific chemicals that evaporate into the air. As air is sucked into the machine, chemicals pass over the sensor surfaces and produce changes in the electrical current flowing through them. Those current changes are logged into a computer that sorts out odors based on their electrical signatures.

Myers says they expect to load a single fingernail-size chip with thousands of odor receptors (感受器), enough to create a sensor that's nearly as sensitive as a dog's nose.

Select the best choice for each of the following questions or unfinished statements.

1. Which of the following is within the capacity of the artificial nose being developed?
    A) Performing physical examinations.
    B) Locating places which attract terrorists.
    C) Detecting drugs and water contamination.
    D) Monitoring food processing.
2. A potential problem which might be caused by the use of an artificial nose is _____.
    A) negligence of public safety
    B) an abuse of personal freedom
    C) a hazard to physical health
    D) a threat to individual privacy
3. The word "logged" (Line 5, Para. 7) most probably means "_____."
    A) preset   B) entered
    C) processed   D) simulated
4. To produce artificial noses for practical use, it is essential _____.
    A) to develop microchips with thousands of odor receptors
    B) to invent chips sensitive to various chemicals
    C) to design a computer program to sort out smells
    D) to find chemicals that can alter the electrical current passing through

5. The author's attitude towards Larry Myers' works is _____.
   A) cautious   B) approving
   C) suspicious   D) over-enthusiastic

Key: 1. C 2. D 3. B 4. A 5. B

练习二：

In our culture, the sources of what we call a sense of "mastery"—feeling important and worth-while and the sources of what we call a sense "pleasure"—finding life enjoyable—are not always identical. Women often are told "You can't have it all." Sometimes what the speaker really is saying is: "You chose a career, so you can't expect to have closer relationships or a happy family life." or "You have a wonderful husband and children—What's all this about wanting a career?" But women need to understand and develop both aspects of well-being, if they are to feel good about themselves.

Our study shows that, for women, well-being has two dimensions. One is mastery, which includes self-esteem (自尊), a sense of control over your life, and low levels of anxiety and depression. Mastery is closely related to the "doing" side of life, to work and activity. Pleasure is the other dimensions, and it is composed of happiness, satisfaction and optimism (乐观). It is tied more closely to the "feeling" side of life. The two are independent of each other. A woman could be high in mastery and low in pleasure, and vice versa. For example, a woman who has a good job, but whose mother has just died, might be feeling very good about herself and in control of her work life, but the pleasure side could be damaged for a time.

The concepts of mastery and pleasure can help us identify the sources of well-being for women, and remedy past mistakes. In the past, women were encouraged to look only at the feeling side of life as the source of all well-being. But we know that both mastery and pleasure are critical. And mastery seems to be achieved largely through work. In our study, all the groups of employed women rated significantly higher in mastery than did women who were not employed.

A woman's well-being is enhanced (增进) when she takes on multiple roles. At least by middle adulthood, the women who were involved in a combination of roles-marriages, motherhood, and employment were the highest in well-being, despite warnings about stress and strain.

Select the best choice for each of the following questions or unfinished statements.
1. It can be inferred from the first paragraph that _____.
   A) for women, a sense of "mastery" is more important than a sense of "pleasure"
   B) for women, a sense of "pleasure" is more important than a sense of "mastery"
   C) women can't have a sense of "mastery" and a sense of "pleasure" at the same time
   D) a sense of "mastery" and a sense of "pleasure" are both indispensable to women
2. The author's attitude towards women having a career is _____.
   A) critical   B) positive
   C) neutral   D) realistic

3. One can conclude from the passage that if a woman takes on several social roles, _____.
   A) it will be easier for her to overcome stress and strain
   B) she will be more successful in her career
   C) her chances of getting promoted will be greater
   D) her life will be richer and more meaningful
4. Which of the following can be identified as a source of "pleasure" for women?
   A) Family life.   B) Regular employment.
   C) Multiple roles in society.   D) Freedom from anxiety.
5. The most appropriate title for the passage would be _____.
   A) The Well-being of Career Women
   B) Sources of Mastery and Pleasure
   C) Two Aspects of Women's Well-Being
   D) Freedom Roles Women in Society

Key: 1.D 2.B 3.D 4.A 5.C

（3）议论文的结构模式 (The basic structure of argumentation)

议论文(Argumentation)是作者用以说服读者接受自己的立场和观点的一种文体。在大学英语议论文阅读的过程中，根据英语议论文的特性，以语篇阅读及其综合技巧应用为基础，采用"自上而下"和"自下而上"的阅读方式，重视语篇、语义和观点关联和衔接关系，特别是文章的主题思想和观点的发展。英语议论文谋篇布局通常采用"问题—问题的解决"模式(Problem-solving)以及"主张—反主张"的形式，通常以综述或提出问题，评述观点，阐述自己的观点和态度的形式展开。要学会基本的篇章分析法，在抓住文章的主题的基础上，归纳每段的中心思想或段落大意。

另外，还要注意充分利用语篇中的标识语或逻辑信号词语，增强条理性和逻辑性，准确理解文本信息。做到重视文章所表达的意义，从而改变不良阅读习惯和方法，尽量减少不必要的回缩，减低由于过多细节化的内容容易带来的对文章意思理解的干扰。

议论文的基本结构模式：

在文章的开头部分，读者一般能够直接找到作者的观点或推断出作者的观点。有时候作者的观点也会出现在结尾部分。

文章的中间部分是作者的论证过程。

在文章的结尾部分，作者通常会重新阐述自己的观点或者提出建议或解决问题的方法。

请看下文：

Here is one of the most familiar forms of the vicious circle of poverty. The poor get sick more than anyone else in the society, which is because they live in slums, jammed together under unhygienic condition; they have inadequate diets, and cannot get decent medical care. When they become sick, they are sick longer than other groups in society. Because they are sick more often and longer than anyone else, they lose wages and work, and find it difficult to hold a steady job. And Because of this, they cannot pay for good housing, for a nutritious diet, for doctors. At any given point in the circle, particularly when there is a major illness, their prospect is to move to an even lower level and to begin the cycle, round and round, toward even more sufferings.

　　因果互证,是通过揭示论点和论据之间的因果关系,来证明论点的一种论证方法。换言之,它是用原因来证明结果,即以"原因"作为论据来证明作为论点的"结果"。这篇英语议论文中指出:贫穷是导致某些人经常患病、失业和痛苦的根本原因。文章先谈原因,后谈结果,以原因的必然性来证实结果的必然性。当然有些大学英语的议论文还使用结果作证据,证明作为论点的原因,即先谈结果,后谈原因,以结果的必然性来证明原因的必然性。可见,文章的论点和论据之间有着必然的因果关系。

　　议论文还有另外一种较为普遍的模式,即"主张—反主张"模式。在这类模式中,作者首先陈述一种社会上普遍认可的观点,然后批驳这种观点,最后提出自己的主张或者观点。

　　请看下文:

　　Recent stories in the newspapers and magazines suggest that teaching and research contradict each other, that research plays too prominent a part in academic promotions, and that teaching is badly underemphasized. There is an element of truth in these statements, but they also ignore deeper and more important relationships.

　　Research experience is an essential element of hiring and promotion at a research university because it is the emphasis on research that distinguishes such a university from an arts college. Some professors, however, neglect teaching for research and that presents a problem.

　　Most research universities reward outstanding teaching, but the greatest recognition is usually given for achievements in research. Part of the reason is the difficulty of judging teaching. A highly responsible and tough professor is usually appreciated by top students who want to be challenged, but disliked by those whose records are less impressive. The mild professor gets overall ratings that are usually high, but there is a sense of disappointment in the part of the best students, exactly those for whom the system should present the greatest challenges. Thus, a university trying to promote professors primarily on the teaching qualities would have to confront this confusion.

　　As modern science moves faster, two forces are exerted on professor: one is the time needed to keep on with the profession; the other is the time needed to teach. The training of new scientists requires outstanding teaching at the research university as well as the arts college. Although scientists are usually "made" in the elementary schools, scientists can be "lost" by poor teaching at the college and graduate school levels. The solution is not to separate teaching and research, but to recognize that the combination is difficult but vital. The title of professor should be given only to those who profess, and it is perhaps time for universities to reserve it for those willing to be an earnest part of the community of scholars. Professor unwilling to teach can be called "distinguished research investigators" or something else.

　　The pace of modern science makes it increasingly difficult to be a great researcher and a great teacher. Yet many are described in just those terms. Those who say we can separate teaching and research simply do not understand the system, but those who say the problem will disappear are not fulfilling their responsibilities.

　　本文作者采用了"主张—反主张"的模式。在文章的开头部分,作者陈述了报纸、期刊的普遍的观点,即教学与科研相互抵触。在提拔中过多重视科研,而低估了教学(teaching and research contradict each other, that research plays too prominent a part in academic promotions, and that teaching is badly underemphasized)。作者在后面的三段里对杂志的观点进行了反驳,提出科研是高校与其他学院区分的标志,而教学优劣很难判定。最后一段再次强调,教学科研问题不可片面而论,这个问题将长期存在。(Those who say we can separate teaching and research simply do not understand the system, but those who say the problem will disappear are not fulfilling their responsibilities.)。

通过研究不同体裁文章的结构模式,不难发现,对文章结构特点的把握有助于读者在阅读中快速定位,准确答题。

练习一:

The earliest controversies about the relationship between photography and art centered on whether photograph's fidelity to appearances and dependence on a machine allowed it to be a fine art as distinct from merely a practical art. Throughout the nineteenth century, the defence of photography was identical with the struggle to establish it as a fine art. Against the charge that photography was a soulless, mechanical copying of reality, photographers asserted that it was instead a privileged way of seeing, a revolt against commonplace vision, and no less worthy an art than painting.

Ironically, now that photography is securely established as a fine art, many photographers find it pretentious or irrelevant to label it as such. Serious photographers variously claim to be finding, recording, impartially observing, witnessing events, exploring themselves—anything but making works of art. They are no longer willing to debate whether photography is or is not a fine art, except to proclaim that their own work is not involved with art. It shows the extent to which they simply take for granted the concept of art imposed by the triumph of Modernism: the better the art, the more subversive it is of the traditional aims of art.

Photographers' disclaimers of any interest in making art tell us more about the harried status of the contemporary notion of art than about whether photography is or is not art. For example, those photographers who suppose that, by taking pictures, they are getting away from the pretensions of art as exemplified by painting remind us of those Abstract Expressionist painters who imagined they were getting away from the intellectual austerity of classical Modernist painting by concentrating on the physical act of painting. Much of photography's prestige today derives from the convergence of its aims with those of recent art, particularly with the dismissal of abstract art implicit in the phenomenon of Pop painting during the 1960's. Appreciating photographs is a relief to sensibilities tired of the mental exertions demanded by abstract art. Classical Modernist painting—that is, abstract art as developed in different ways by Picasso, Kandinsky, and Matisse—presupposes highly developed skills of looking and a familiarity with other paintings and the history of art. Photography, like Pop painting, reassures viewers that art is not hard; photography seems to be more about its subjects than about art.

Photography, however, has developed all the anxieties and self-consciousness of a classic Modernist art. Many professionals privately have begun to worry that the promotion of photography as an activity subversive of the traditional pretensions of art has gone so far that the public will forget that photography is a distinctive and exalted activity—in short, an art.

Select the best choice for each of the following questions or unfinished statements.

1. The author is mainly concerned with _____.
   A) defining the Modernist attitude toward art
   B) explaining how photography emerged as a fine art
   C) explaining the attitude of serious contemporary photographers toward photography as art and placing those attitudes in their historical context
   D) defining the various approaches that serious contemporary photographers take toward their art and assessing the value of each of those approaches

2. Which of the following adjectives best describes "the concept of art imposed by the triumph of Modernism" as the author represents it in lines 12—13?
   A) Objective.   B) Mechanical.
   C) Superficial.   D) Paradoxical.

3. Why does the author introduce Abstract Expressionist painter?
   A) He wants to provide an example of artists who, like serious contemporary photographers, disavowed traditionally accepted aims of modern art.
   B) He wants to set forth an analogy between the Abstract Expressionist painters and classical Modernist painters.
   C) He wants to provide a contrast to Pop artist and others.
   D) He wants to provide an explanation of why serious photography, like other contemporary visual forms, is not and should not pretend to be an art.

4. How did the nineteenth-century defenders of photography stress photography?
   A) They stressed photography was a means of making people happy.
   B) It was art for recording the world.
   C) It was a device for observing the world impartially.
   D) It was an art comparable to painting.

Key: 1.C 2.D 3.A 4.D

练习二：

As Dr. Samuel Johnson said in a different era about ladies preaching, the surprising thing about computer is not that they think less well than a man, but that they think at all. The early electronic computer did not have much going for it except a marvelous memory and some good math skills. But today the best models can be wired up to learn by experience, follow an argument, ask proper questions and write poetry and music. They can also carry on somewhat puzzling conversations.

Computers imitate life. As computer get more complex, the imitation gets better. Finally, the line between the original and the copy becomes unclear. In another 15 years or so, we will see the computer as a new form of life.

The opinion seems ridiculous because, for one thing, computers lack the drives and emotions of living creatures. But drives can be programmed into the computer's brain just as nature programmed them into our human brains as a part of the equipment for survival.

Computers match people in some roles, and when fast decisions are needed in a crisis, they often surpass them. Having evolved when the pace of life was slower, the human brain has an inherent defect that prevents it from absorbing several streams of information simultaneously and acting on them quickly. Throw too many things at the brain one time and it freezes up.

We are still in control, but the capabilities of computers are increasing at a fantastic rate, while raw human intelligence is changing slowly, if at all. Computer power has increased ten times every eight years since 1946. In the 1990s, when the sixth generation appears, the reasoning power of an intelligence built out of silicon will begin to match that of the human brain.

That does not mean the evolution of intelligence has ended on the earth. Judging by the past, we can expect that a new species will arise out of man, surpassing his achievements. Only a carbon chemistry enthusiast would assume that the new species must be man's flesh-and-blood descendants. The new kind of intelligent life is more likely to be made of silicon.

Select the best choice for each of the following questions or unfinished statements.

1. What do you suppose is the attitude of Dr. Samuel Johnson towards ladies preaching?
    A) He believed that ladies were born worse preachers than men.
    B) He was pleased that ladies could though not as well as men.
    C) He disapproved of ladies preaching.
    D) He encouraged ladies to preach.
2. Today, computer are still inferior to man in terms of _____.
    A) decision making   B) drives and feelings
    C) growth of reasoning power D) information absorption
3. In terms of making quick decisions, the human brain cannot be compared with the computer because _____.
    A) in the long process of evolution slow pace of life didn't require such ability for the human brain
    B) the human brain is influenced by other factors such as motivation and emotion
    C) the human brain may freeze up when dealing with too many things at the same time
    D) computers imitate life while the human brain does not imitate computers
4. Though he thinks highly of the development of computer science, the author doesn't mean that _____.
    A) computers are likely to become a new form of intelligent life
    B) human beings have lost control of computers
    C) the intelligence of computers will eventually surpass that of human beings
    D) the evolution of intelligence will probably depend on that of electronic brains

5. According to the passage, which of the following statements is TRUE?
   A) Future man will be made of silicon instead of flesh and blood.
   B) Some day it will be difficult to tell a computer from a man.
   C) The reasoning power of computers has already surpassed that of man.
   D) Future intelligent life may not necessarily be made of organic matter.

Key: 1.A 2.B 3.C 4.B 5.D

8. 区分事实和看法 (Distinguishing facts and opinions)

区分事实和看法是阅读理解能力最为重要的一环。事实一般是陈述发生过的事件。文章中事实细节往往带有明显的标志,例如, for example, for instance, as a matter of fact, in fact 等。这类文章提供的诸如数据等往往是事实细节的标志。看法则是作者的观点、判断和感受。通常能够体现作者观点的词语包括三类:第一类是引出作者观点的词语,例如 I believe, I think, I guess, in my opinion, I'm convinced 等;第二类是表达作者个人感情色彩的一些形容词,如 excellent, clever, pompous, stupid 等;第三类是表达作者判断性话语的一些词,如 must, probable, maybe, perhaps 等。同时,有一些句子既包含事实,同时还有作者的观点,读者可能很难做出正确的判断,尤其是当读者的观点和作者的观点一致时,读者就会把作者的观点当做事实。因此,读者在阅读时一定要注意一些暗示性的词语。

下面我们来判断下列各句是事实还是看法:

1. Automation refers to the introduction of electronic control and automatic operation of productive machinery.

2. Present production is running at 51 per cent above pre-war levels, and the government has called for an expansion to 60 per cent by 1956.

3. Though science has little studied how habitual air-conditioning affects mind and body, some medical experts suggest that, like other technical avoidance of natural variations in climate, air-conditioning can damage the human capacity to adapt to stress.

4. This may sound like a fantastic proposal, but so, I think, our insurance system would have sounded to people a hundred years ago.

5. Trained and tamed for many generations, domestic animals are not accustomed to roaming (到处走动) in search of food and shelter.

6. Consumers are being confused and misled by the hodge-podge (大杂烩) of environmental claims made by household products, according to a "green labeling" study published by Consumers International Friday.

根据各句的标志词语,如 2 句中的数据,3 句中表达判断性话语的 can, 4 句中的 I think 以及 5 句对家禽特点的描述,我们可以判定 3、4 是看法,而 1、2、5 为事实。6 句既是看法又可理解为事实。它是引用别人的话,因此可以理解为事实。同时,这句话又表明了说话者的个人观点,也可理解为观点。

练习:判断下列各句是看法(O)还是事实(F)。

1. Scientists, like other human beings, have their hopes and fears, their passions and disappoint-

ments, and their strong emotions may sometimes interrupt the course of clear thinking and sound practice.

2. My father's reaction to the bank building at 43rd Street and Fifth Avenue in New York City was immediate and definite: "You won't catch me putting my money in there!" he declared. "Not in that glass box!"

3. Brazil's population growth rate has dropped, for instance, from 2.99% a year between 1951 and 1960 to 1.93% a year between 1981 and 1990, and Brazilian women now have only 2.7 children on average.

4. The story is the tale of a little girl with a wild imagination taking her first music lesson.

5. I have had just about enough of being treated like a second-class citizen, simply because I happened to be that put upon member of society—a customer.

6. Love, in my opinion, is a pleasant sensation, which to experience is a matter of chance, something one "falls into" if one is lucky.

7. It is a curious paradox that we think of the physical sciences as "hard," the social sciences as "soft," and the biological sciences as somewhere in between.

8. Protests at the use of animals in research have taken a new and fearful character in Britain with the attempted murder of two British scientists by the terrorist technique of the pre-planted car-bomb.

9. The overall incidence of cancer, counting up all the cases, is probable roughly the same everywhere.

10. Thierry Daniel Henry (Born 17 August 1977) is a French football striker currently playing for Spanish La Liga club FC Barcelona and the French national team.

Key: 1.O 2.O 3.F 4.F 5.O 6.O 7.O 8.O 9.O 10.F

练习一：

Some children, like some adults, have chronic, unexplainable pain. They have backaches every day or their legs and feet hurt every day or their necks tremble constantly — and no one is sure why. Doctors call this pain idiopathic, a medical term for "being born with." Idiopathic pain arises spontaneously and without a known cause.

How best to treat idiopathic pain is one of medicine's great mysteries. You can help patients with painkillers, but that's not a great long-term solution, since patients become habituated (and in some cases addicted) to pain meds. In children, the situation is even more terrible, since they may face decades of swallowing drugs. That's why a study just published in the journal *Pain* is so encouraging.

According to the study, clinicians who used a particular form of behavior therapy called Acceptance and Commitment Therapy (ACT) with a group of 16 chronic-pain patients aged 10 to 18 saw remarkable results: after just 10 weeks of ACT sessions, during which patients were taught strategies for accepting chronic pain so they could pursue important goals, those kids suffered less intensely and functioned significantly better day to day than did a control group of 16 chronic-pain kids who had been treated the way kids with persistent aches are normally treated — with drugs and standard talk therapy. Both groups improved, but the children in the ACT group, who got no drugs, improved more than those who took pills.

In ACT, therapists, unlike psychotherapists who often try to change negative thoughts by asking probing questions (does everyone at the office *really* hate you, or are you just indulging in your own self-doubt?), take the position that's trying really hard to make you accept negative thoughts. ACT promotes not only the acceptance of negative thoughts, but also emotions and bodily sensations (like chronic pain) that a patient may have struggled with for a long time. In short, ACT therapists encourage engagement with life even when it hurts.（324 words）

1. Some children suffer from the idiopathic pain, which is caused _____.
   A) through a chronic illness   B) without any specific hints
   C) by taking lots of medicines   D) along with the backache, etc
2. What is the reason that taking pills is not the solution to idiopathic pain?
   A) It will bring more expenses on patients.
   B) The patients have to wait for a long time.
   C) The effect of the pills is pending still.
   D) It will cause patients to be addictive.
3. According to the passage, which of the following statements is true?
   A) In this study, Acceptance and Commitment Therapy is a general form of therapy.
   B) The ACT is proved to be a therapy to release patients from pains.
   C) The ACT group of children could get rid of the pains after the treatment.
   D) The ACT group of children suffered less than the group taking pains killing medicines only.
4. What is the method of Acceptance and Commitment Therapy?
   A) ACT therapist follows the psychotherapist way of positive thinking.
   B) ACT therapist combines the positive and negative thinking together.
   C) ACT therapist guides patients to take the negative thinking in.
   D) ACT therapist discourages patients to overcome their pains.
5. What is the main idea of this passage?
   A) Pain is something that anyone cannot escape from.
   B) Humans may depend on medicines to kill their pains.
   C) Ignorance of the pain is a better way to reduce pains.
   D) People can adjust their life style to fight against pains.

Key: 1.B 2.D 3.D 4.C 5.C

练习二：

Smith College's career office sent its job-hunting seniors a letter last month with a reassuring message: "There ARE jobs and you can find employment." Unfortunately, there are far fewer jobs than anticipated, according to a report today from the National Association for Colleges and Employers (NACE).

The companies surveyed are planning to hire 22% fewer grads from the class of 2009 than they hired from the class of 2008. Some 44% of companies in the survey, conducted last month, said they plan to hire fewer new grads, and another 22%, more than double last year's figure, said they do not plan to hire at all this spring. "If you were a student and would graduate in the fall," says Edwin Koc, director of strategic and foundation research at NACE, "frankly speaking, the spring does not look good."

Job prospects for college grads dropped in virtually every sector this year. The most dramatic decline was, not surprisingly, in finance, which is cut off 71% expected job openings. Less expected but equally troubling is the 37% decline in hiring for professional services, which include accounting and engineering. "Poor hiring estimates from this area speak to the depth of the recession in the college labor market for the class of 2009," the report says. Government is essentially the only industry planning to hire more new grads this year than last.

Meanwhile, schools are pulling out the stops to help students beat out the competition. Counselors everywhere are encouraging students to turn to their alumni networks for help. The University of Maryland has conducted workshops with an emphasis on networking. The career office shared by Haverford and Bryn Mawr recently gave each senior 50 business cards listing their name and major. "In this economy, we don't even use the terminology 'sewn up' anymore," says Roseborough. More like coming apart at the seams.

(309 words)

1. Which of the following is the best title of this passage?
   A) Graduate Students' Job-Hunting.
   B) Companies Suffer in the Economic Crisis.
   C) University Career Office's Letter.
   D) Job Scarce in the Economic Crisis.
2. Which statement about the job market is false?
   A) In 2009, new graduates will suffer from a shrinking employment market.
   B) 11% of companies hired no new employees last year.
   C) The current condition in this year's job market influence certain fields of graduates.
   D) Experts suggest delaying the graduation date from spring to autumn.
3. What does Edwin Koc mean by saying "frankly speaking, the spring does not look good"?
   A) Spring season shall experience a cold weather.
   B) This year's economic condition does harm to graduate students' employment.
   C) People should not expect a bright timing to go out.
   D) Everything looks gloomy in the season of spring.
4. Among all, ____ is the only industry which has better employment prospect.
   A) accounting   B) engineering
   C) government   D) business

5. Which of the following phrases properly explains "beat out" in the last paragraph?
   A) fight against   B) knock down
   C) make clear   D) get rid of

Key: 1.D 2.D 3.B 4.C 5.A

练习三：

Nicolo Machiavelli was born at Florence (佛罗伦萨) on 3rd May 1469. Though it is useless to protest against the world-wide and evil signification of his name, it may be pointed out that what this evil reputation implies was unknown to his own day, and that the researches of recent times have enabled us to understand him more reasonably.

He was undoubtedly a man of great observation, acuteness and industry; noting with appreciative eye whatever passed before him, and with his excellent literary gift turning it to account in his enforced retirement from affairs. He does not describe himself, nor is he depicted by his contemporaries, as a type of that rare combination, the successful statesman and author. He was misled by Catherina Sforza, ignored by Louis XII, overawed by Cesare Borgia; several of his periods of embassy were quite barren of results; his attempts to fortify (增强) Florence failed. In the conduct of his own affairs he was timid; he dared not appear by the side of Soderini, to whom he owed so much, for fear of *compromising* himself; his connection with Medici was open to suspicion, and Giuliano appears to have recognized his real talent when he set him to write the "History of Florence," rather than employ him in the state. And it is on the literary side of his character, and there alone, that we find no weakness and no failure.

Although the light of almost four centuries has been focused on "The Prince," its problems are still debatable and interesting, because they are the eternal problems between the ruled and their rulers. Such as they are, its ethics are those of Machiavelli's contemporaries; yet they cannot be said out of date so long as the governments of Europe rely on material rather than on moral forces. Its historical incidents and personages become interesting by reason of the uses which Machiavelli makes of them to illustrate his theories of government and conduct.

(322 words)

1. What is the main idea of paragraph 1?
   A) Nicolo Machiavelli deserves his infamy.
   B) People misunderstand Nicolo Machiavelli totally.
   C) Our opinion on Nicolo Machiavelli has been long prejudiced.
   D) People could never do justice to Nicolo Machiavelli.
2. What does the word *compromising* in paragraph 2 mean?
   A) Confronting.   B) Endangering.
   C) Elevating.   D) Confusing.

3. According to paragraph 2, what can be inferred about Nicolo Machiavelli?

    A) He is successful in a variety of fields.

    B) His deeds are of more significance than his works.

    C) He seemed to be only highly prosperous on the literary side.

    D) None of his contemporaries appreciated him.

4. What is the attitude of the author toward "The Prince"?

    A) Outdated.   B) Undervalued.

    C) Overrated.   D) Significant.

5. What can be inferred from the last paragraph?

    A) People have reached an agreement on the problems of "The Prince" after four centuries' discussion.

    B) The theory in "The Prince" should be amended, or else it will be out of date.

    C) In "The Prince," Nicolo Machiavelli cited many incidents and personages.

    D) The governments of Europe, unfortunately, have changed little since the time of Nicolo Machiavelli.

Key: 1. C 2. B 3. C 4. D 5. C

练习四：

Drinking hot tea may cause throat cancer, Iranian researchers said Friday, suggesting people should let steaming drinks cool before consuming them. Previous studies have linked tobacco and alcohol with cancer of the esophagus (食道), and the research published in the *British Medical Journal* suggests that scalding beverages may also somehow pave the way for such tumors (瘤).

Drinking very hot tea at a temperature of greater than 70 degrees Celsius was associated with an eight-fold increased risk of throat cancer compared to sipping warm or lukewarm tea at less than 65 degrees, the researchers said.

Reza Malekzadeh of Tehran University of Medical Sciences and colleagues studied the tea-drinking habits of 300 people with esophageal cancer and another 571 healthy men and women from the same area in Golestan Province in northern Iran. That region has one of the highest rates of throat cancer in the world but smoking rates and alcohol consumption are low, the researchers said. Nearly all the volunteers drank black tea regularly, consuming on average more than a liter each day.

People who regularly drank tea less than two minutes after pouring were five times more likely to develop the cancer compared to those who waited four or more minutes, the researchers said. British studies have reported people prefer their tea at an average temperature of 56 degrees to 60 degrees, they noted.

It is not clear how hot tea might cause cancer but one idea is that repeated thermal injury to the lining of the throat somehow initiates it, researchers said. Cancers of the esophagus kill more than 500,000 people worldwide each year, with the bulk of the disease occurring in discrete populations in Asia, Africa, and South America. The tumors are especially deadly, with five-year survival rates of 12 to 31 percent.

(302 words)

1. In paragraph 1, what does the "scalding beverages" indicate according to the author?
   A) Scathing alcohol.　　　　B) Ice water.
   C) Extremely hot drinks.　　D) Dangerous juice.
2. "An eight-fold increased risk of throat cancer" means _____.
   A) there are another seven increased risks of developing throat cancer
   B) there is an eight times higher risk of developing throat cancer
   C) there is a way to increase the risk of throat cancer eight times
   D) there are eight ways to increase the risk of throat cancer
3. According to the passage, how should people drink in order to prevent throat cancer?
   A) People should avoid drinking higher than 70 degree Celsius.
   B) People should wait at least four minutes before drinking.
   C) People should drink without thermal injuring their throats.
   D) Through A, B, and C.
4. Which of the following statements is false?
   A) Researchers in Tehran University drew the conclusion from studying 300 people of esophageal cancer and 571 healthy ones.
   B) People who regularly drank tea less than four minutes after pouring were four or more times likely to catch esophageal cancer.
   C) British researchers found that people like the tea to be between 56 degrees to 60 degrees Celsius.
   D) Tumors of esophageal cancer are dangerous causing 69 to 88 percent of people dying within five years.
5. Which can be the best title of this passage?
   A) Don't Smoke Tobacco.　　B) Don't Drink Alcohol.
   C) Caution: HOT.　　　　　D) Caution: DANGER.

Key: 1.C 2.B 3.D 4.B 5.C

练习五：

Some writers have so *confounded* feeling about the relation of society with government, as to leave little or no distinction between them. Society is produced by our wants, and government by our wickedness; the former promotes our happiness positively by uniting our affections, the latter negatively by restraining our vices (不道德行为).

Society in every state is a blessing, but government even in its best state is a necessary evil; for when we suffer, we might expect in a country without government. However, our misfortune is heightened at the moment we suffer! Government, like dress, is the symbol of lost innocence.

For when the impulses of conscience (良心) is clear, uniform, and irresistibly obeyed, man would need no other lawgiver; but that not being the case, he finds it necessary to surrender up a part of his property to furnish means for the protection of the rest; and this he is encouraged to do by the same *prudence* which in every other case advises him out of two evils to choose the least. Therefore, security being the true design and aim of government, and whatever form of it appears most likely to ensure it to us, with the least expense and greatest benefit, is preferable to all others.

In order to gain a clear and just idea of the design and end of government, let us suppose a small number of persons settled in some remote part of the earth, unconnected with the rest, they will then represent the first peopling of any country. In this state of natural liberty, society will be their first thought. A thousand motives will excite them, the strength of one man is so unequal to his wants, and his mind so unfitted for perpetual solitude, that he is soon obliged to seek assistance and relief of another, who in his turn requires the same. Four or five united would be able to raise a tolerable dwelling in the midst of a wilderness, but no one man might labor out the common period of life without any others' facilitation.

(346 words)

1. What does the word *confounded* in paragraph 1 mean?
   A) Substitute. B) Compared.
   C) Mixed. D) Distinguished.
2. What does the author infer by "our misfortune is heightened only... suffer" in paragraph 2?
   A) The government even in its best state is but a necessary evil.
   B) The miseries are heightened in a country without government.
   C) The misfortune is due to our own intention.
   D) We failed to furnish the suitable means.
3. The word *prudence* in paragraph 2 can be replaced by _____.
   A) courage B) intelligence
   C) purpose D) advice
4. What is the relationship between paragraph 2 and paragraph 3?
   A) The statement in paragraph 2 is contradicted in paragraph 3.
   B) Their opinions are independent of each other.
   C) In paragraph 3, a new conclusion is reached based on paragraph 2.
   D) The opinion in paragraph 2 is illustrated in paragraph 3.
5. It can be inferred, after the last paragraph, the author would say _____.
   A) the emigrants will begin to relax in their duty and attachment to each other
   B) the society the arrived emigrants formed would remain perfect
   C) the necessity of law and government thus rendered unnecessary
   D) the design and end of government is still mysterious

Key: 1. C 2. C 3. B 4. D 5. A

练习六：

Are we alone in the universe? It is a question that has perplexed mankind for centuries — and now two Yale scientists are part of the latest NASA search for the elusive (难以捉摸) answer.

Earlier this month, NASA launched the Kepler Mission — a robotic probe capable of finding Earth-sized and smaller planets around other stars in the Milky Way that may support extraterrestrial (地球外的) life. Among those involved in the NASA project, which is the first of its kind, are two Yale Astronomy professors, Sarbani Basu and Pierre Demarque.

The Kepler Mission's probe, a spacecraft that weighs one ton, will spend three and a half years surveying our region of the universe in hopes of locating terrestrial planets — hotspots with optimal temperatures to host liquid water and therefore potentially support life. In addition, the mission also aims to lay the groundwork for future exploration by mapping out new areas of exploration and identifying planetary bodies most likely to contain life.

The probe consists of a 55-inch diameter telescope, which also acts as a 95-million-pixel digital camera. Over the course of its mission, it will record the luminosity (发光度) of 100,000 stars in the constellations Cygnus and Lyra every half hour, searching for signals that suggest a planet has crossed in front of its star.

"Pulsations (震动) of a star produce light variations too, so data from Kepler can be used not only to detect planets, but also to determine stellar pulsation frequencies." Basu said. Demarque, the Munson Professor Emeritus of Natural Philosophy and Astronomy, will use the data generated by the space probe to further his own research on the theory of stellar evolution. The Kepler Mission will offer Demarque a rare opportunity to apply his hypotheses.

While the Kepler Mission was launched less than three weeks ago, there are already high expectations about its possible outcomes. Basu said she hopes the data collected by the mission's probe will shed light on current theories of stellar evolution. Demarque said the mission has the potential to be "truly historic" should Earth-like planets orbiting other stars be located.

(360 words)

1. What is the possible explanation of "perplex" in the first paragraph?
   A) Seduce.   B) Mislead.
   C) Fool.   D) Bewilder.
2. What is the feature NOT belonging to the robotic probe in Kepler Mission?
   A) It is a spacecraft which weighs one ton.
   B) It can work as long as three and a half months.
   C) It consists of a 55-inch diameter telescope.
   D) Its telescope works as a 95-million-pixel digital camera.
3. Which of the following is the information detected by the Kepler probe?
   A) Luminosity.   B) Pulsations.
   C) Pulsation frequency.   D) All of A, B and C.

4. How can the last sentence be paraphrased into?
   A) If there is another planet similar to Earth to be located in the project, then Kepler Mission shall be of significant value in the history.
   B) There is certainty of some planets like Earth in the stars' orbits waiting for human's discovery.
   C) Humans will create another miracle by enlarging their living space into some Earth-like planets.
   D) If man truly discovers a planet possessing suitable living condition, then this Kepler Mission shall be awarded hugely.
5. What is true of the Kepler Mission according to the passage?
   A) The Kepler Mission will provide Basu with a rare opportunity to apply her hypotheses.
   B) The Kepler Mission will be launched in less than three weeks.
   C) The Kepler Mission contains a robotic probe capable of finding Earth-like planets in the Milky Way that may support extraterrestrial life.
   D) The Kepler Mission aims to prepare for the new areas of exploration and stimulation of planetary life.

Key: 1. D 2. B 3. D 4. A 5. C

练习七：

The Apache Indians have always been characterized as fierce warriors with an <u>indomitable</u> will. It is not surprising that the last armed resistance by Native Americans came from this proud tribe of American Indians. As the Civil War ended the U. S. Government brought its military to bear against the natives out west. They continued a policy of containment(围堵政策) and restriction(限制政策) to reservations.

In 1875, the restrictive reservation policy had limited the Apaches to 7200 square miles. By the 1880's the Apache had been limited to 2600 square miles. This policy of restriction angered many Native Americans and led to confrontation between the military and bands of Apache. The famous Chiricahua Apache Geronimo led one such band.

Born in 1829, Geronimo lived in western New Mexico when this region was still a part of Mexico. Geronimo was a Bedonkohe Apache that married into the Chiricahuas. The murder of his mother, wife and children by soldiers from Mexico in 1858 forever changed his life and the settlers of the southwest. He vowed at this point to kill as many white men as possible and spent the next thirty years making good on that promise.

Surprisingly, Geronimo was a medicine man and not a chief of the Apache. However, his visions made him indispensable to the Apache chiefs and gave him a position of prominence with the Apache. In the mid 1870's the government moved Native Americans onto reservations, and Geronimo took exception to this forced removal and fled with a band of followers. He spent the next 10 years on reservations and raiding with his band. His exploits became highly chronicled by the press and he became the most feared Apache. Unfortunately, Geronimo and his band were eventually captured at Skeleton Canyon in 1886. The proud Geronimo had been reduced to a sideshow spectacle. He lived the rest of his days as a prisoner and died in 1909 at Fort Sill, Oklahoma.

(331 words)

1. What does the underlined word "indomitable" mean in the context?
   A) Determined.　　　　　　B) Unconquerable.
   C) Aggressive.　　　　　　 D) Arbitrary.
2. Why did the U.S. government adopt containment and restriction after the Civil War?
   A) They wanted the natives to obey to their orders.
   B) They wanted the natives to remain the low status quo.
   C) They wanted the natives to move to the west.
   D) They wanted the natives to be extinct forever.
3. How old was the hero Geronimo when he sweared to kill the white as many as possible?
   A) At the age of 27.　　　　B) At the age of 28.
   C) At the age of 29.　　　　D) At the age of 30.
4. What did Geronimo do originally in the Apache ?.
   A) As a medicine man.　　　B) As a chef.
   C) As a soldier.　　　　　　D) As a farmer.
5. What is the main idea of the passage?
   A) Geronimo's bravery acts and his guide of the Apache band in the restrictive age.
   B) Geronimo's growth history in the restrictive age.
   C) Why the U. S. government implemented the restriction policy.
   D) Why the Apache people never surrender to the unfair treatment.

Key: 1.B 2.C 3.C 4.A 5.A

练习八：

The transition from forest to treeless tundra (苔原) on a mountain slope is often a dramatic one. Within a vertical distance of just a few tens of meters, trees disappear as a life-form and are replaced by low shrubs, herbs, and grasses. This rapid zone of transition is called the upper timberline or tree line. In many semiarid areas there is also a lower timberline where the forest passes into steppe or desert at its lower edge, usually because of a lack of moisture.

The upper timberline, like the snow line, is highest in the tropics and lowest in the Polar Regions. It ranges from sea level in the Polar Regions to 4,500 meters in the dry subtropics and 3,500—4,500 meters in the moist tropics. Timberline trees are normally evergreens, suggesting that these have some advantage over deciduous tree in the extreme environments of the upper timberline. There are some areas, however, where broadleaf deciduous trees form the timberline. Species of birch, for example, may occur at the timberline in parts of the Himalayas.

At the upper timberline the trees begin to become twisted and deformed. This is particularly true for trees in the middle and upper latitudes, which tend to attain greater heights on ridges, whereas in the tropics the trees reach their greater heights in the valleys. This is because middle- and upper-latitude timberlines are strongly influenced by the duration and depth of the snow cover. As the snow is deeper and lasts longer in the valleys, trees tend to attain greater heights on the ridges, even though they are more exposed to high-velocity winds and poor, thin soils there. In the tropics, the valleys appear to be more favorable because they are less prone to dry out, they have less frost, and they have deeper soils.

(303 words)

1. The word "dramatic" in the passage is closest in meaning to _____.
   A) gradual   B) complex
   C) visible   D) striking
2. Which of the following can be inferred from paragraph 1 about both the upper and lower timberlines?
   A) Both are treeless zones.
   B) Both mark forest boundaries.
   C) Both are surrounded by desert areas.
   D) Both suffer from a lack of moisture.
3. Paragraph 2 supports which of the following statements about deciduous trees?
   A) They cannot grow in cold climates.
   B) They do not exist at the upper timberline.
   C) They are less likely than evergreens to survive at the upper timberline.
   D) They do not require as much moisture as evergreens do.
4. The word "they" in the last sentence in paragraph 3 refers to _____.
   A) valleys   B) trees
   C) heights   D) ridges
5. According to paragraph 3, which of the following is true of trees in the middle and upper latitudes?
   A) Tree growth is negatively affected by the snow cover in valleys.
   B) Tree growth is greater in valleys than on ridges.
   C) Tree growth on ridges is not affected by high-velocity winds.
   D) Tree growth lasts longer in those latitudes than it does in the tropics.

Key: 1.D 2.B 3.C 4.A 5.A

练习九：

The floodlit (泛灯光照明的) cream shells of the famed Opera House dimmed Saturday as Sydney became the world's first major city to plunge itself into darkness for the second worldwide Earth Hour, a global campaign to highlight the threat of climate change. From the

Great Pyramids to the Acropolis, the London Eye to the Las Vegas strip, nearly 4,000 cities and towns in 88 countries planned to join in the World Wildlife Fund-sponsored event, a time zone-by-time zone plan to dim nonessential lights between 8:30 p.m. and 9:30 p.m.

Involvement in the effort has exploded since last year's Earth Hour, which drew participation from 400 cities after Sydney held a solo event in 2007. Interest has spiked ahead of planned negotiations on a new global warming treaty in Copenhagen, Denmark, this December. The last global accord, the Kyoto Protocol (京都协议), is set to expire in 2012.

Despite the boost in interest from the Copenhagen negotiations, organizers initially worried enthusiasm for this year's event would wane with the world's attention focused largely on the global economic crisis, Earth Hour executive director Andy Ridley said. "Earth Hour has always been a positive campaign; it's always around street parties, not street protests, it's the idea of hope not despair," he continued.

In Australia, people attended candlelit speed-dating events and gathered at outdoor concerts as the hour of darkness rolled through the country. Earlier Saturday, the Chatham Islands officially kicked off Earth Hour by switching off its diesel generators. China was participating in the campaign for the first time, with Beijing turning off the lights at its Bird's Nest Stadium and Water Cube, the most prominent venues for the Olympics, according to WWF. Shanghai was also cutting lights in all government buildings and other structures on its waterfront. In Hong Kong, the government planned to suspend its nightly "Symphony of Lights," which beams lasers and lights into the sky from 44 buildings on the city's famed Victoria Harbor. Later Saturday, Thailand's Prime Minister Abhisit Vejjajiva planned to press a button to turn off the lights at Khao San Road, a famous haven for budget travelers in Bangkok that is packed with bars and outdoor cafes.

Earth Hour organizers say there's no uniform way to measure how much energy is saved worldwide. However, Earth Hour 2009 has garnered support from global corporations, nonprofit groups, schools, scientists and celebrities. McDonald's Corp. planned to dim its arches at 500 locations in the United States. The Marriott, Ritz-Carlton and Fairmont hotel chains and Coca-Cola Co. also planned to participate.

(430 words)

1. What is the main idea of this passage?
   A) To state Earth Hour's goal and its current achievements worldwide.
   B) To arouse people's attention to the environment pollution.
   C) To appeal to the public to use less non-recycled resources, such as water, wood.
   D) To promote the idea of a better world without energy-consuming facilities.
2. Which country first launched the event to alert the climate change?
   A) Thailand.　　　　B) Australia.　　　　C) United States.　　　　D) Britain.
3. Where will be the next warming treaty after the expiration of Kyoto Protocol?
   A) At Acropolis.　　　　B) At Sydney.
   C) At Copenhagen.　　　　D) At Chatham Islands.

4. What does the underlined word "wane" mean in the 3rd paragraph?
   A) Increase.　　　B) Enlarge.　　　C) Disappear.　　D) Decrease.
5. Which of the following statements is not false about Earth Hour 2009?
   A) In Australia, people attended candlelit speed-dating events and gathered at outdoor camping as the hour of darkness rolled through the country.
   B) Thailand's Prime Minister planned to turn off the lights at a road in Bangkok that is crowded with bars and outdoor cafes.
   C) Earth Hour organizers say there should not be a uniform way to measure how much energy is saved worldwide.
   D) Earth Hour 2009 has received support from global corporations, nonprofit groups, schools, scientists and representatives.

Key: 1.A 2.B 3.C 4.D 5.B

练习十：

The subject of this essay is not Liberty of the Will, but Civil, or Social Liberty: the nature and limits of the power which can be legitimately *exercised* by society over the individual. A question seldom stated, and hardly ever discussed, in general terms, but which profoundly influences the practical controversies of the age by its latent presence, and is likely soon to make itself recognized as the vital question of the future. It is so far from being new, that, in a certain sense, it has divided mankind, almost from the remotest ages; but in the stage of progress into which the more civilized portions of the species have now entered, it shows itself under new conditions, and requires a different and more fundamental treatment.

The struggle between Liberty and Authority is the most obvious feature in the portions of history with which we are earliest familiar, particularly in that of Greece, Rome, and England. But in old times this contest was between subjects, or some classes of subjects, and the Government. By liberty, was meant protection against the tyranny of the political rulers. The rulers were conceived as in a necessarily opposed position to the people whom they ruled. Their power was regarded as necessary, but also as highly dangerous; as a weapon which they would attempt to use against their subjects, no less than against external enemies. To prevent the weaker members of the community from being preyed on by numberless vultures, it was needful that there should be an animal of prey stronger than the rest, commissioned to keep them down. But as the king of the vultures would be no less bent upon preying upon the flock than any of the minor harpies, it was *indispensable* to be in a perpetual attitude of defense against his beak (喙) and claws. The aim, therefore, of patriots was to set limits to the power which the ruler should be allowed to exercise over the community; and this limitation was what they meant by liberty.

(340 words)

1. The word *exercised* in paragraph 1 is closest in meaning to _____.
   A) trained   B) used   C) imagined   D) acquired
2. According to paragraph 1, which of the following is true?
   A) Because the question of liberty is seldom stated, and hardly ever discussed, its influence could be ignored.
   B) The question of liberty would remain important and latent.
   C) As the more civilized portions of us entered into the stage of progress, the question of liberty would be bound to be solved.
   D) The question of liberty has long been controversial.
3. According to paragraph 2, what does the author think of the political or governing rulers?
   A) They are typified by the popular governments of Greece.
   B) Their authority from inheritance or conquest are doubtful.
   C) People are always overawed by them.
   D) They discriminate their subjects from external enemies when exercising power.
4. What does the word *indispensable* in paragraph 2 mean?
   A) Essential.   B) Independent.
   C) Reasonable.   D) Convenient.
5. In this passage, the author's attitude toward the rulers is _____.
   A) fearful   B) alert   C) appreciative   D) amiable

Key: 1. B 2. D 3. C 4. A 5. B

三、图式理论在阅读理解中的应用

图式理论(schema theory)运用到英语阅读理解中标志着第二语言阅读理论的一个新的发展方向。图式的概念首先由德国哲学家康德提出。他指出,图式是想象力的产物。英国心理语言学家巴特利特将图式描述为一种先前反应或经验的积极组织,由过去的经验组成。应用语言学和心理语言学定义图式为人们大脑中存储的认知架构,它使信息有条不紊地储存在长期记忆中,由于人们大脑中的知识是按内容分门别类的,它组合成一个互相联系的图式网。概言之,图式理论指的是学习者利用大脑中储存的信息图式内化新信息时的过程,也就是说人们在理解新知识时,头脑中相关的旧图式会被激活,帮助他们加工、阐释和储存新知识。以"船舶命名图式"(Anderson, Pearson; 1984)为例(图1)。

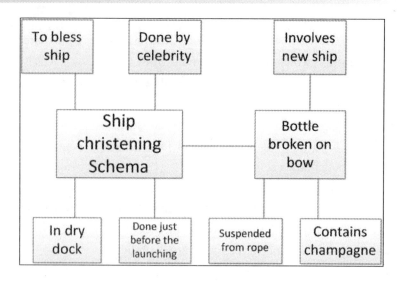

图 1(Anderson &Pearson, 1984)

人们对船舶命名的认知有"祝福新船""栈桥""名人剪彩""船头打破香槟庆祝""船长""鸣汽笛"等图式。阅读材料中出现有关这类图式的词语表达,大脑中的"船舶命名图式"便会启用,人们即会开始理解文章。请看下面一段文章:

Captain Draper gestured to a button on a console and asked Kate if she would like to sound the liner's whistle. After a window was opened the Duchess pressed the control and a long low sound reverberated around the dock. The Duchess laughed and smiled and described the experience as "brilliant" adding: "I was expecting something high pitched."

文章中 Kate 和 The Duchess 与"名人剪彩"相符,dock 与"栈桥"一致,whistle 即"鸣汽笛"。尽管文章中没有提到打破香槟庆祝,但是从图式网络中可以了解到,这段话讲的就是新船下水,庆祝首航。

不难发现,大脑中的旧图式对人们更快更好地学习新知识起到了决定性的作用。读者运用图式理论理解阅读材料时,与阅读话题有关的图式会被积极激活,读者利用它们来预测、推断和做出决定,并把新材料关联到原有图式之中去,从而完成阅读理解的一系列活动。图式一般分为三种类型:语言图式(linguistic schema)、内容图式(content schema)和修辞图式(rhetorical schema)。阅读理解过程中的语言图式系指读者已有的语言知识,即语音、词汇和句法等方面知识的掌握程度;内容图式指读者对阅读材料所涉及的主题(内容范畴)的了解程度;修辞图式指读者对阅读文章的体裁、语篇结构的熟悉程度。

阅读材料中所包含的知识信息来自于词汇、语法、语义、语用和语篇等逐步从低向高层次的信息。从认知心理学和信息处理的角度来看,人们在处理这些语言信息时运用两种方法:一种是自上而下模式(top-down processing),处理高层次信息;另一种是自下而上模式(bottom-up processing),处理低层次信息,如图2。读者在使用这些模式处理信息时,他们头脑中不同的图式结构发挥着不同的作用,以下将分别举例说明。

图 2

  在自上而下处理阅读信息的模式中,读者头脑中的内容图式和修辞图式会被激活,包括先前存在的关于世界的知识、文化和道德价值、组织文章和话语的潜在结构、脚本(它是与特定环境有关的事件和行动,如"玛丽饿了,她进了一家餐厅,9点钟她结账然后离开",其中与餐厅有关的事情可能是餐桌、点菜、吃等包含在"餐厅"这一脚本中)和文体类型等。以一篇题为"Can a Sleep Disorder Predict Parkinson?"的阅读材料为例。当读者看到 predict, disorder, Parkinson 等字眼时,首先他们会激活头脑中有关疾病的内容图式,产生如包含 hospital, scientist, patient, disease 等的图式结构;如果读者拥有更丰富的医学图式,那么对 Parkinson(帕金森症)可能会有一些认知,则激活有如 shake, paralysis 这样的更明确的图式。而以上所有图式会在读者阅读文章内容时(以第一自然段为例)促进与文章新信息产生关联,帮助理解。

Can a Sleep Disorder Predict Parkinson?

  Calming the tremors of Parkinson disease remains a challenge for both patients and doctors alike, but new research suggests that future therapies for the condition may emerge from an unlikely place: people's sleep habits.

  读者也许对 tremor 这个词感到陌生,但看到前后的 calm 和 Parkinson 时,会通过内容图式的帮助,预测出 tremor 的意义,即描述帕金森症的一种症状,推断出类似"抖动"或"颤抖"的意思。

  在自上而下处理这篇阅读理解时,读者还可以依靠修辞图式的帮助来判断文章的体裁,譬如读者在继续阅读上篇文章内容时，会发现每段的开头和结尾有符合他们已有的说明文图式结构，从而判断出此篇文章的体裁是说明文。

Scientists at Sacre Coeur Hospital at the University of Montreal report in the journal *Neurology* that Parkinson can be predicted relatively accurately up to 12 years before the first muscle tremors appear...

REM sleep disorder itself can be treated with medications, but those drugs still won't slow the decline in nerve function that's responsible for Parkinson. ... "But once we have those agents, as far as I'm concerned, every patient with REM sleep disorder should be taking it."

在自上而下处理阅读信息时，读者已有的内容图式越丰富就越能帮助读者掌握新材料的背景知识；新材料与已有图式产生关联可以最大限度地处理与储存新材料的知识信息。读者的修辞图式、修辞手段图式（如明、暗喻图式）等，也可以促进读者提高阅读理解水平。

而自下而上处理阅读信息时，读者头脑中的语言图式被激活（比如句子和段落理解中的单词图式），此时在阅读中若遇到某语言知识的理解障碍时，读者会依照语言图式的引导加以处理。例如："Do you see any green in my eyes？""green"在读者的语言图式中表示"绿色"和"无经验的、未成熟的"，如果将"绿色"关联至句子理解，那么这个句子的意思会是"你从我的眼睛里看到绿色吗？"这种句意会破坏读者对上下文的正确理解。那么，有经验的读者会寻找"green"的另一图式产生正确的理解，它应该是"你以为我是好欺骗的吗？"

不难看出，图式对读者正确有效地处理阅读理解篇章具有一定的重要意义，它影响着阅读速度的快慢、阅读能力的提高等一系列问题。读者应该在平时积累各种图式结构，在阅读中积极激活这些图示，与新知识产生关联，从而促进其阅读理解水平的提高。

四、全国大学英语四、六级考试新题型简介

自2013年12月考次起，全国大学英语四、六级考试委员会对四、六级考试的试卷结构、测试内容与题型进行了局部调整。调整后的四级和六级的试卷构成相同，由写作、听力理解、阅读理解和翻译四个部分组成，满分仍为710分。新的大学英语四、六级的试卷结构、测试内容、测试题型、分值比例和考试时间如表1所示：

表1 四、六级考试结构、测试内容与题型、分值比例和考试时间表

试卷结构	测试内容		测试题型	分值比例	考试时间
写作	写作		短文写作	15%	30分钟
听力理解	听力对话	短对话	多项选择	8%	30分钟
		长对话	多项选择	7%	
	听力理解	短文	多项选择	10%	
		听写	单词、词组听写	10%	
阅读理解	词汇理解		选词填空	5%	40分钟
	长篇阅读		信息匹配	10%	
	仔细阅读		多项选择	20%	
翻译	汉译英		段落翻译	15%	30分钟
总计				100%	130分钟

(一) 大学英语四、六级考试内容与题型介绍

与调整前的考试题型相比,新的四、六级考试题型出现了单词及词组听写、信息匹配和段落翻译这样的新内容,取消了句子听写、快速阅读、完形填空等的题型设置。为了使广大考生对调整后的考试有一个全面的认识,现将试卷的测试内容与题型介绍如下。

1. 写作

写作部分测试学生用英语进行书面表达的能力,所占分值比例为15%,考试时间30分钟。写作测试选用考生所熟悉的题材,要求考生根据所提供的信息及提示(如:提纲、情景、图片或图表等)写出一篇短文,四级120～180词,六级150～200词。

2. 听力理解

听力理解部分测试学生获取口头信息的能力。录音材料用标准的英式或美式英语朗读,语速四级约每分钟130词,六级约每分钟150词。听力部分分值比例为35%,其中对话占15%,短文占20%。

对话部分包括短对话和长对话,采用多项选择题的形式进行考核。短对话有8段,每段提一个问题;长对话有2段,每段提3～4个问题;对话部分共15题。每段对话均朗读一遍,每个问题后留有13～15秒的答题时间。

短文部分包括短文理解及单词和词组听写。短文理解有3篇,采用多项选择题的形式进行考核。四级每篇长度为220～250词,六级为240～270词。每篇短文朗读一遍,提3～4个问题,每个问题后留有13～15秒的答题时间,共10题。单词及词组听写采用1篇短文,四级的长度为220～250词,六级为240～270词。要求考生在听懂短文的基础上用所听到的原文填写空缺的单词或词组,共10题。短文播放三遍。

3. 阅读理解

阅读理解部分包括1篇长篇阅读和3篇仔细阅读,测试学生在不同层面上的阅读理解能力,包括理解篇章或段落的主旨大意和重要细节、综合分析、推测判断以及根据上下文推测词义等能力。该部分所占分值比例为35%,其中长篇阅读占10%,仔细阅读占25%。考试时间40分钟。

长篇阅读代替了原来的快速阅读,但篇章长度和难度保持不变。总长度四级约1000词,六级约1200词。阅读速度四级约每分钟100词,六级约每分钟120词。篇章后附有10个句子,每句一题。每句所含的信息出自篇章的某一段落,要求考生找出与每句所含信息相匹配的段落。有的段落可能对应两题,有的段落可能不对应任何一题。

仔细阅读部分要求考生阅读3篇短文。2篇为多项选择题型的短文理解测试,每篇长度四级为300～350词,六级为400～450词;1篇为选词填空,篇章长度四级为200～250词,六级为250～300词。短文理解每篇后有若干个问题,要求考生根据对文章的理解,从每题的四个选项中选择最佳答案。选词填空要求考生阅读一篇删去若干词汇的短文,然后从所给的选项中选择正确的词汇填空,使短文复原。

4. 翻译

翻译部分测试学生把汉语所承载的信息用英语表达出来的能力,原来的单句汉译英调整为段落汉译英。翻译内容涉及中国的历史、文化、经济、社会发展等。四级长度为140～160个汉字;六级长度为180～200个汉字。

(二) 大学英语四、六级考试分数解释

考试中心对考试的分数解释是:大学英语四、六级考试是标准相关—常模参照的标准化考试。标准相关体现在:(1)试卷各部分的设计和命题参照大学英语的教学要求规定的技能和标准;(2)写作和翻译部分的阅卷依据评分标准。常模参照体现在考后各部分的原始分转换成报道分时,分别参照各部分的常模。因此,考试既是标准相关又具有常模参照的性质。

大学英语四、六级考试不设及格线。经过等值处理后的原始总分参照总分常模转换成常模正态分,均值为500,标准差为70,报道总分在220分至710分之间。在将原始分转换成报道分时,各部分采用不同的分数量表,从而使各部分报道分的简单相加之和等于报道总分。

采用常模参照旨在保证考试分数解释的稳定性。考生的任何一次四、六级考试成绩均可在四级或六级常模中找到其百分位位置,即考生成绩在相应级别的常模群体中所处的相对位置。考试委员会网站上(http://www.cet.edu.cn)已公布了总分和各部分的百分位对照表,以供考试成绩使用者了解考生的相对能力水平。

(三) 成绩报道

成绩报道分为总分和单项分。单项分包括:(1)听力;(2)阅读;(3)翻译和写作。每次考试后,考试委员会向总分在220分及以上的考生发放成绩报告单,报告其总分和各部分的单项分。考试委员会同时向参加考试的各个院校提供该校考生的成绩(总分和各部分单项分)和有关该校的各种统计数据。

(四) 评分标准

大学英语四、六级考试卷中的作文与翻译评分标准如下:

1. 作文评分标准

作文满分为15分,成绩分为六个档次,分别为:13~15分、10~12分、7~9分、4~6分、1~3分和0分。各档次的评分标准见表2:

表2 作文评分标准表

档次	评分标准
13~15分	切题。表达思想清楚,文字通顺、连贯,基本上无语言错误,仅有个别小错。
10~12分	切题。表达思想清楚,文字较连贯,但有少量语言错误。
7~9分	基本切题。有些地方表达思想不够清楚,文字勉强连贯;语言错误相当多,其中有一些是严重错误。
4~6分	基本切题。表达思想不清楚,连贯性差。有较多的严重语言错误。
1~3分	条理不清,思路紊乱,语言支离破碎或大部分句子均有错误,且多数为严重错误。
0分	未作答,或只有几个孤立的词,或作文与主题毫不相关。

2. 翻译评分标准

翻译满分为15分,成绩分为六个档次:13~15分、10~12分、7~9分、4~6分、1~3分和0分。各档次的评分标准见表3:

表3 翻译评分标准表

档次	评分标准
13~15分	译文准确表达了原文的意思。用词贴切,行文流畅,基本上无语言错误,仅有个别小错。
10~12分	译文基本上表达了原文的意思。文字通顺、连贯,无重大语言错误。
7~9分	译文勉强表达了原文的意思。用词欠准确,语言错误相当多,其中有些是严重语言错误。
4~6分	译文仅表达了一小部分原文的意思。用词不准确,有相当多的严重语言错误。
1~3分	译文支离破碎。除个别词语或句子,绝大部分文字没有表达原文意思。
0分	未作答,或只有几个孤立的词,或译文与原文毫不相关。

通过上述的介绍,考生可以基本掌握大学英语四、六级考试新的结构设置、测试内容与题型等信息。总体来说,四、六级考试的整体难度较前有所调整:单词(词组)听写较之前的长句听写降低了难度;长篇阅读的信息匹配题题型新、难度大;汉译英翻译难度提升最大,这就要求考生应具备较好的语法和语言运用能力。此外,由于撤销了完形填空和快速阅读的选择题,以往考生凭借技巧来猜测答案的投机行为也会受到极大的遏制。调整后的大学英

语四、六级考试给广大考生带来了新的挑战,如何正确面对考试的调整和有效提高考试的成绩自然而然地成了考生亟待解决的问题。然而,万变不离其宗,要想在考试中取得好成绩,最快的捷径仍在于持之以恒的练习。通过多听、多说、多读、多写,不断加强和提高词汇及语法的运用能力,考生终会水到渠成,取得良好成绩。

(五)长篇阅读之段落信息匹配题

自2013年12月起,四、六级考试阅读理解中的长篇阅读替代了原来的快速阅读,但篇章长度和难度保持不变,即四级总长度约1000词,六级约1200词。阅读速度四级每分钟约100词,六级每分钟约120词。篇章后附有10个句子,每句一题。每句所含的信息出自篇章的某一段落,要求考生找出与每句所含信息相匹配的段落。有的段落可能对应两题,有的段落可能不对应任何一题。四级考试需要看十个左右的段落,然后匹配十个信息点;六级考试需要看十五个段落,匹配十个信息点,难度无疑增加了不少。

段落信息匹配题是国外语言考试如托福、雅思中的一种常考题型,该题型主要考查学生的信息匹配能力。信息题干不是对原文的完全照搬,比如有时可能是同义句的改写等。

下面以2013年12月全国大学英语四、六级考试考次的样题为例,介绍3种段落信息匹配题的解题方法。

段落信息匹配样题:

Section B

Directions: In this section, you are going to read a passage with ten statements attached to it. Each statement contains information given in one of the paragraphs. Identify the paragraph from which the information is derived. You may choose a paragraph more than once. Each paragraph is marked with a letter. Answer the questions by marking the corresponding letter on Answer Sheet 2.

Universities Branch Out

A) As never before in their long history, universities have become instruments of national competition as well as instruments of peace. They are the place of the scientific discoveries that move economies forward, and the primary means of educating the talent required to obtain and maintain competitive advantage. But at the same time, the opening of national borders to the flow of goods, services, information and especially people has made universities a powerful force for global integration, mutual understanding and geopolitical stability.

B) In response to the same forces that have driven the world economy, universities have become more self-consciously global: seeking students from around the world who represent the entire range of cultures and values, sending their own students abroad to prepare them for global careers, offering courses of study that address the challenges of an interconnected world and collaborative (合作的) research programs to advance science for the benefit of all humanity.

C) Of the forces shaping higher education none is more sweeping than the movement across borders. Over the past three decades the number of students leaving home each year to study abroad has grown at an annual rate of 3.9 percent, from 800,000 in 1975 to 2.5 million in 2004. Most travel from one developed nation to another, but the flow from developing to developed countries is growing rapidly. The reverse flow, from developed to developing countries, is on the rise, too. Today foreign students earn 30 percent of the doctoral degrees awarded in the United States and 38 percent of those in the United Kingdom. And the number crossing borders for undergraduate study is growing as well, to 8 percent of the undergraduates at America's best institutions and 10 percent of all undergraduates in the U.K. In the United States, 20 percent of the newly hired professors in science and engineering are foreign-born, and in China many newly hired faculty members at the top research universities received their graduate education abroad.

D) Universities are also encouraging students to spend some of their undergraduate years in another country. In Europe, more than 140,000 students participate in the Erasmus program each year, taking courses for credit in one of 2,200 participating institutions across the continent. And in the United States, institutions are helping place students in summer internships (实习) abroad to prepare them for global careers. Yale and Harvard have led the way, offering every undergraduate at least one international study or internship opportunity—and providing the financial resources to make it possible.

E) Globalization is also reshaping the way research is done. One new trend involves sourcing portions of a research program to another country. Yale professor and Howard Hughes Medical Institute investigator Tian Xu directs a research center focused on the genetics of human disease at Shanghai's Fudan University, in collaboration with faculty colleagues from both schools. The Shanghai center has 95 employees and graduate students working in a 4,300-square-meter laboratory facility. Yale faculty, postdoctors and graduate students visit regularly and attend videoconference seminars with scientists from both campuses. The arrangement benefits both countries; Xu's Yale lab is more productive, thanks to the lower costs of conducting research in China, and Chinese graduate students, postdoctors and faculty get on-the-job training from a world-class scientist and his U.S. team.

F) As a result of its strength in science, the United States has consistently led the world in the commercialization of major new technologies, from the mainframe computer and the integrated circuit of the 1960s to the Internet infrastructure (基础设施) and applications software of the 1990s. The link between university-based science and industrial application is often indirect but sometimes highly visible: Silicon Valley was intentionally created by Stanford University, and Route 128 outside Boston has long housed companies spun off from MIT and Harvard. Around the world, governments have encouraged copying of this model, perhaps most successfully in Cambridge, England, where Microsoft and scores of other leading software and biotechnology companies have set up shop around the university.

G) For all its success, the United States remains deeply hesitant about sustaining the research-university model. Most politicians recognize the link between investment in science and national economic strength, but support for research funding has been unsteady. The budget of the National Institutes of Health doubled between 1998 and 2003, but has risen more slowly than inflation since then. Support for the physical sciences and engineering barely kept pace with inflation during that same period. The attempt to make up lost ground is welcome, but the nation would be better served by steady, predictable increases in science funding at the rate of long-term GDP growth, which is on the order of inflation plus 3 percent per year.

H) American politicians have great difficulty recognizing that admitting more foreign students can greatly promote the national interest by increasing international understanding. Adjusted for inflation, public funding for international exchanges and foreign-language study is well below the levels of 40 years ago. In the wake of September 11, changes in the visa process caused a dramatic decline in the number of foreign students seeking admission to U.S. universities, and a corresponding surge in enrollments in Australia, Singapore and the U.K. Objections from American university and business leaders led to improvements in the process and a reversal of the decline, but the United States is still seen by many as unwelcoming to international students.

I) Most Americans recognize that universities contribute to the nation's well-being through their scientific research, but many fear that foreign students threaten American competitiveness by taking their knowledge and skills back home. They fail to grasp that welcoming foreign students to the United States has two important positive effects: first, the very best of them stay in the States and—like immigrants throughout history—strengthen the nation; and second, foreign students who study in the United States become ambassadors for many of its most cherished (珍视) values when they return home. Or at least they understand them better. In America as elsewhere, few instruments of foreign policy are as effective in promoting peace and stability as welcoming international university students.

注意：此部分试题请在答题卡2上作答。

46. American universities prepare their undergraduates for global careers by giving them chances for international study or internship.
47. Since the mid-1970s, the enrollment of overseas students has increased at an annual rate of 3.9 percent.
48. The enrollment of international students will have a positive impact on America rather than threaten its competitiveness.
49. The way research is carried out in universities has changed as a result of globalization.
50. Of the newly hired professors in science and engineering in the United States, twenty percent come from foreign countries.
51. The number of foreign students applying to U.S. universities decreased sharply after September 11 due to changes in the visa process.
52. The U.S. federal funding for research has been unsteady for years.
53. Around the world, governments encourage the model of linking university-based science and industrial application.

54. Present-day universities have become a powerful force for global integration.
55. When foreign students leave America, they will bring American values back to their home countries.

(六) 长篇阅读之段落信息匹配题的解题方法与能力训练

1. 明确考点要求

信息匹配题可称为信息包含题,即 Which paragraph contains this information。该题型的考点不是要求考生去找到问题的答案所在,而是寻找在哪一段中出现考点的信息。传统的阅读练习往往会让考生的思维形成定式,即认为文中一定有答案点,要找到答案点必须对一些话语进行反复推敲等。改革后的长篇阅读之设题形式不仅仅涉及某一具体细节,更是要求考生能把握文章的整体等;再者,信息匹配题的信息题干也并非完全照搬原文中的句子。

2. 预览题干,明确关键词

题干中的关键词可以用来定位文中信息。考生需依靠所划的关键词迅速找到信息所在的段落,从而得到答案。以四级样卷的Q47为例,"Since the mid-1970s, the enrollment of overseas students has increased at an annual rate of 3.9 percent."考生可将"mid-1970s","rate of 3.9 percent"当做定位的关键词,然后带着它快速地浏览文章便会发现它出现在段落C中,"Over the past three decades the number of students leaving home each year to study abroad has grown at an annual rate of 3.9 percent, from 800,000 in 1975 to 2.5 million in 2004."这种定位关键词的方式属于细节信息的定位。又如四级样卷的Q53,"Around the world, governments encourage the model of linking university-based science and industrial application."考生可能选择"university-based science"为关键词,它是有连字符的合成词。有经验的考生会对文中信息进行寻找、归纳,发现段落F中出现"is often indirect but sometimes highly visible",从"highly visible"可归纳出"encourage"的趋势,从而确定答案为段落F。这种定位关键词的方式属于细节归纳的定位。再以四级样卷的Q54为例,"Present-day universities have become a powerful force for global integration."考生会比较自然地把"global integration"当做定位的关键词,然后带着它快速地浏览文章,很快会发现它出现在段落A的最后一句中,"But at the same time, the opening of national borders to the flow of goods, services, information and especially people has made universities a powerful force for global integration, mutual understanding and geopolitical stability."这种定位关键词属于隐含信息的定位。

为此,划定关键词是考生答题的关键环节;快速、准确地找寻到关键词是提高信息匹配能力的有效途径。下面列出2013年12月全国大学英语四、六级考试的样题中段落信息匹配题的关键词以供学习参考。

表4 四级样卷段落信息匹配样题的关键词

题号	答案	关键词	定位方式	关键词特点
46	D	internship	细节归纳	斜体、括号
47	C	mid-1970s, 3.9 percent	细节信息	数字
48	I	competitiveness, positive	细节归纳	冒号
49	E	research, globalization	细节信息	段落首句
50	C	20 percent	细节信息	数字
51	H	after September 11	细节信息	数字、特殊事件
52	G	funding, unsteady	细节信息	转折
53	F	university-based	细节归纳	特殊词汇、连字符
54	A	global integration	隐含信息	首段句尾
55	I	values	隐含信息	最高级most

表5 六级样卷段落信息匹配样题的关键词

题号	答案	关键词	定位方式	关键词特点
46	F	employers, older workers	细节信息	段落中心句
47	K	recent study	细节信息	研究内容
48	D	reforms	细节信息	转折
49	A	report, sustainability	细节信息	首段尾句
50	M	shortage, war	细节信息	举例
51	I	one-child	细节归纳	转折
52	B	books, conflicts (warfare)	细节归纳	书籍
53	J	innovative, risks	细节信息	比较than
54	E	the best solution, pension	细节信息	最高级most
55	H	immigration, rich countries	隐含信息	尾句

3. 速读文章段首尾句,牢记关键词、信号词等

速读文章中的每一段落,特别是段首句、段尾句和段落内的关键词汇和信号词汇。读者从段首或段尾句可以迅速了解本段主要内容,从关键词汇掌握段内重点信息的范围。与此

同时,要熟知一些信号词汇的用法,考生从以上信息词汇中能梳理大量信息的逻辑关系,把握行文脉络。现将常用的词汇罗列如下:表因果转折类的词汇but, however, since, because, thus, hence 等;表递进关系的词汇 not only, but also, furthermore, additionally, moreover 等;表让步关系的词汇 although, though 等;表序数的词汇 first, second, at last 等;事实罗列的词汇 for example, for instance, such as 等。特殊词汇包括精确数据、非文章高频词的大写或专有名词、斜体或援引内容等。如 51 题 The number of foreign students applying to U.S. universities decreased sharply after September 11 due to changes in the visa process. September 11 是一个非高频专有大写,直接定位至 H 段即成功。

4. 扩大词汇量,提高同义替换能力

在备考四、六级的学习过程中,考生应注意积累词汇,不断扩大词汇量,特别是词汇或短语的英文解释。因速读中经常会遇到无法匹配的段落与题目,此时可以使用同义替换的做题原则。以六级样卷的 Q54 为例,"The best solution to the pension crisis is to postpone the retirement age." 考生通常会把 "postpone the retirement age" 作为定位的关键词,然后还是带着它去浏览文章。在段落 E 中会看到这样一句话 "By far the most effective method to restrain pension spending is to give people the opportunity to work longer, because it increases tax revenues and reduces spending on pensions at the same time." 之中的 "to give people the opportunity to work longer" 与选择的关键词表述的正是同一个意思,此时使用同义替换可以答题。

同义替换的使用对于考生来说是一项挑战,它不是一蹴而就的,而是一个需要积累和锻炼的过程。英语学习者平时应积极积累词汇,注意同义词、近义词和短语的表达方式,通过大量阅读以提高快速阅读的能力,从而顺利地通过大学英语四、六级考试这一关。

5. 关注篇章标题

关注阅读篇章的主标题或副标题。考生看过文章标题,如样题中题目 Universities Branch Out 之后,可以马上了解文章所围绕的主题是美国大学的扩张,产生相关的联想,激发起内在的有关美国大学的信息图式,在短时间内帮助其掌握文章主旨大意。而副标题是主标题的补充,对主标题所概括的核心内容进一步解释,考生也不应忽视。

长篇阅读之信息匹配题的设题形式不算新鲜,雅思考试从一诞生就包含这一题型,考研英语也是备选题型之一。四、六级考生对改革后的信息匹配题应建立积极解题的心态,从阅读篇章的标题入手,速读段落首、尾句,准确判断文章关键词汇、信息词汇或特殊词汇,结合题干内容逆向式在各首尾句、关键词、信息词之间寻找定位信息,并适当运用同义替换技巧完成题干与段落的信息匹配任务,如此,考生一定会取得良好的成绩。

阅读新题型练习题

Passage One

Why Integrity Matters

A. The key to integrity is consistency — not only setting high personal standards for oneself (honesty, responsibility, respect for others, fairness) but also living up to those standards each day. One who has integrity is bound by and follows moral and ethical standards even when making life's hard choices, choices which may be clouded by stress, pressure to succeed, or temptation.

B. What happens if we lie, cheat, steal, or violate other ethical standards? We feel disappointed in ourselves and ashamed. But a lapse of integrity also affects our relationships with others. Trust is essential in any important relationship, whether personal or professional. Who can trust someone who is dishonest or unfair? Thus, integrity must be one of our most important goals.

C. We are each responsible for our own decisions, even if the decision-making process has been undermined by stress or peer pressure. The real test of character is whether we can learn from our mistake, by understanding why we acted as we did, and then exploring ways to avoid similar problems in the future.

D. Making ethical decisions is a critical part of avoiding future problems. We must learn to recognize risks, because if we can't see the risks we're taking, we can't make responsible choices. To identify risks, we need to know the rules and be aware of the facts. For example, one who doesn't know the rules about plagiarism may accidentally use words or ideas without giving proper credit, or one who fails to keep careful research notes may unintentionally fail to quote and cite sources as required. But the fact that such a violation is "unintentional" does not excuse the misconduct. Ignorance is not a defense.

E. Most people who get in trouble do know the rules and facts, but manage to fool themselves about the risks they're taking by using excuses: "Everyone else does it," "I'm not hurting anyone," or "I really need this grade." Excuses can get very elaborate: "I know I'm looking at another's exam, even though I'm supposed to keep my eyes on my own paper, but that's not cheating because I'm just checking my answers, not copying." We must be honest about our actions, and avoid excuses. If we fool ourselves into believing we're not doing anything wrong, we can't see the real choice we're making — and that leads to bad decisions.

F. To avoid fooling yourself, watch out for excuses and try this test: Ask how you would feel if your actions were public, and anyone could be watching over your shoulder. Would you feel proud or ashamed of your actions? If you'd rather hide your actions, that's a good indication that you're taking a risk and rationalizing it to yourself.

G. To decide whether a risk is worth taking, you must examine the consequences, in the future as well as right now, negative as well as positive, and to others as well as to yourself. Those who take risks they later regret usually focus on immediate benefits ("what's in it for me"), and simply haven't considered what might go wrong. The consequences of getting caught are serious, and may include a "0" on a test or assignment; an "F" in the class; suspension or dismissal from school; transcript notation; and a tarnished reputation. In fact, when you break a rule or law, you lose control over your life, and give others the power to impose punishment: you have no control over what that punishment might be. This is an extremely precarious and vulnerable position. There may be some matters of life and death, or highest principle, which might justify such a risk, but there aren't many things that fall in this category.

H. Those who don't get caught pay an even higher price. A cheater doesn't learn from the test, depriving him/herself of an education. Cheating undermines confidence and independence:

the cheater is a fraud, and knows that without dishonesty, he/she would have failed. Cheating destroys self-esteem and integrity, leaving the cheater ashamed, guilty, and afraid of getting caught. Worst of all, a cheater who doesn't get caught the first time usually cheats again, not only because he/she is farther behind, but also because it seems "easier." This slippery slope of eroding ethics and bigger risks leads only to disaster. Eventually, the cheater gets caught, and the later he/she gets caught, the worse the consequences. Students have been dismissed from school because they didn't get this simple message: Honesty is the ONLY policy that works.

I. Cheaters often feel invisible, as if their actions "don't count" and don't really hurt anyone. But individual choices have a profound cumulative effect. Cheating can spread like a disease, and a cheater can encourage others just by being seen from across the room. Recent statistics suggest 30% or more of college students cheat. If a class is graded on a curve, cheating hurts others' grades. Even if there is no curve, cheating "poisons" the classroom, and others may feel pressured to join in. ("If I don't cheat, I can't compete with those who do.") Cheating also has a destructive impact on teachers. The real reward of good teaching is seeing students learn, but a cheater says, "I'm not interested in what you're trying to teach; all I care about is stealing a grade, regardless of the effect on others." The end result is a blatant and destructive attack on the quality of your education. Finally, cheating can hurt the reputation of the University, and harm those who worked hard for their degree.

J. If cheating becomes the norm, then we are in big trouble. We must rely on the honesty and good faith of others every day. If not, we couldn't put money in the bank, buy food, clothing, or medicine from others, drive across a bridge, get on a plane, go to the dentist—the list is endless. There are many examples of the vast harm that is caused when individuals forget or ignore the effect their dishonesty can have. The savings and loan scandal, the stock market and junk bond swindles, and, of course, Watergate, have undermined the faith of many Americans in the integrity of political and economic leaders and society as a whole. Such incidents take a tremendous toll on our nation's economy and our individual well-being. For example, but for the savings and loan debacle, there might be funds available to reduce the national debt and pay for education.

K. In sum, we all have a common stake in our school, our community, and our society. Our actions do matter. It is essential that we act with integrity in order to build the kind of world in which we want to live.

1. Although some people are familiar with the rules and facts, they still try to find certain excuses to fool themselves about the risks they are taking.
2. Many Americans lost faith in the integrity of their political leaders as a result of Watergate scandal.
3. Violation of a rule is misconduct even if it is claimed to be unintentional.
4. Integrity is the basis of mutual trust in personal and professional relationships.

5. We learn to identify the risks we are going to take to ensure we make responsible choices.
6. Those who take risks they regret later on value immediate benefits most.
7. Cheaters at exam don't care about their education, all they care about is how to steal a grade.
8. A person of integrity not only sets high moral and ethical standards but also sticks to them in their daily life.
9. Students who cheat will be dismissed from school because they simply don't know that honesty is the best policy.
10. A cheater is very likely to be caught finally and the severity of the consequences depends on how soon he gets caught.

Key: 1. E 2. J 3 D 4. B 5. D 6. G 7. I 8. A 9. H 10. H

Passage Two

Into the Unknown

The world has never seen population ageing before. Can it cope?

A. Until the early 1990s nobody much thought about whole populations getting older. The UN had the foresight to convene a "world assembly on ageing" back in 1982, but that came and went. By 1994 the World Bank had noticed that something big was happening. In a report entitled "Averting the Old Age Crisis," it argued that pension arrangements in most countries were unsustainable.

B. For the next ten years a succession of books, mainly by Americans, sounded the alarm. They had titles like Young vs Old, Gray Dawn and The Coming Generational Storm, and their message was blunt: health-care systems were heading for the rocks, pensioners were taking young people to the cleaners, and soon there would be intergenerational warfare.

C. Since then the debate has become less emotional, not least because a lot more is known about the subject. Books, conferences and research papers have multiplied. International organizations such as the OECD and the EU issue regular reports. Population ageing is on every agenda, from G8 economic conferences to NATO summits. The World Economic Forum plans to consider the future of pensions and health care at its prestigious Davos conference early next year. The media, including this newspaper, are giving the subject extensive coverage.

D. Whether all that attention has translated into sufficient action is another question. Governments in rich countries now accept that their pension and health-care promises will soon become unaffordable, and many of them have embarked on reforms, but so far only timidly. That is not surprising: politicians with an eye on the next election will hardly rush to introduce unpopular measures that may not bear fruit for years, perhaps decades.

E. The outline of the changes needed is clear. To avoid *fiscal* (财政) meltdown, public pensions and health-care provision will have to be reined back severely and taxes may have to go up. By far the most effective method to restrain pension spending is to give people the opportunity to work longer, because it increases tax revenues and reduces spending on pensions at the same time. It may even keep them alive longer. John Rother, the AARP's head of policy and strategy, points to studies showing that other things being equal, people who remain at work have lower death rates than their retired peers.

F. Younger people today mostly accept that they will have to work for longer and that their pensions will be less generous. Employers still need to be persuaded that older workers are worth holding on to. That may be because they have had plenty of younger ones to choose from, partly thanks to the post-war baby-boom and partly because over the past few decades many more women have entered the labour force, increasing employers' choice. But the reservoir of women able and willing to take up paid work is running low, and the baby-boomers are going grey.

G. In many countries immigrants have been filling such gaps in the labor force as have already emerged (and remember that the real shortage is still around ten years off). Immigration in the developed world is the highest it has ever been, and it is making a useful difference. In still-fertile America it currently accounts for about 40% of total population growth, and in fast-ageing western Europe for about 90%.

H. On the face of it, it seems the perfect solution. Many developing countries have lots of young people in need of jobs; many rich countries need helping hands that will boost tax revenues and keep up economic growth. But over the next few decades labor forces in rich countries are set to shrink so much that inflows of immigrants would have to increase enormously to compensate: to at least twice their current size in western Europe's most youthful countries, and three times in the older ones. Japan would need a large multiple of the few immigrants it has at present. Public opinion polls show that people in most rich countries already think that immigration is too high. Further big increases would be politically unfeasible.

I. To tackle the problem of ageing populations at its root, "old" countries would have to *rejuvenate* (使年轻) themselves by having more of their own children. A number of them have tried, some more successfully than others. But it is not a simple matter of offering financial incentives or providing more child care. Modern urban life in rich countries is not well adapted to large families. Women find it hard to combine family and career. They often compromise by having just one child.

J. And if fertility in ageing countries does not pick up? It will not be the end of the world, at least not for quite a while yet, but the world will slowly become a different place. Older societies may be less innovative and more strongly disinclined to take risks than younger ones. By 2025 at the latest, about half the voters in America and most of those in western European countries will be over 50—and older people turn out to vote in much greater number than younger ones. Academic studies have found no evidence so far that older voters have used their power at the ballot box to push for policies that specifically benefit them, though if in future there are many more of them they might start doing so.

K. Nor is there any sign of the intergenerational warfare predicted in the 1990s. After all, older people themselves mostly have families. In a recent study of parents and grown-up children in 11 European countries, Karsten Hank of Mannheim University found that 85% of them lived within 25km of each other and the majority of them were in touch at least once a week.

L. Even so, the shift in the centre of gravity to older age groups is bound to have a profound effect on societies, not just economically and politically but in all sorts of other ways too. Richard Jackson and Neil Howe of America's CSIS, in a thoughtful book called The Graying of the Great Powers, argue that, among other things, the ageing of the developed countries will have a number of serious security implications.

M. For example, the shortage of young adults is likely to make countries more reluctant to commit the few they have to military service. In the decades to 2050, America will find itself playing an ever-increasing role in the developed world's defence effort. Because America's population will still be growing when that of most other developed countries is shrinking, America will be the only developed country that still matters *geopolitically* (地缘政治上).

N. There is little that can be done to stop population ageing, so the world will have to live with it. But some of the consequences can be alleviated. Many experts now believe that given the right policies, the effects, though grave, need not be catastrophic. Most countries have recognized the need to do something and are beginning to act.

O. But even then there is no guarantee that their efforts will work. What is happening now is historically unprecedented. Ronald Lee, director of the Centre on the Economics and Demography of Ageing at the University of California, Berkeley, puts it briefly and clearly: "We don't really know what population ageing will be like, because nobody has done it yet."

1. Employers should realize it is important to keep older workers in the workforce.
2. A recent study found that most old people in some European countries had regular weekly contact with their adult children.
3. Few governments in rich countries have launched bold reforms to tackle the problem of population aging.
4. In a report published some 20 years ago, the sustainability of old-age pension systems in most countries was called into doubt.
5. Countries that have a shortage of young adults will be less willing to send them to war.
6. One-child families are more common in aging societies due to the stress of urban life and the difficulties of balance between family and career.
7. A series of books, mostly authored by Americans, warned of conflicts between the older and younger generations.
8. Compared with younger ones, older societies tend to less innovative and take fewer risks.
9. The best solution to the pension crisis is to postpone the retirement age.
10. Immigration as a means to boost the shrinking labor force may meet resistance in some rich countries.

Key: 1. F 2. K 3. D 4. A 5. M 6. I 7. B 8. J 9. E 10. H

Passage Three

Rising Drug Costs in Canada

A. Canada's premiers (the leaders of provincial governments), if they have any breath left after complaining about Ottawa at their late July annual meeting, might spare a moment to do something, together, to reduce health-care costs.

B. They're all groaning about soaring health budgets, the fastest-growing component of which are pharmaceutical costs. According to the Canadian Institute for Health Information, prescription drug costs have risen since 1997 at twice the rate of overall health-care spending. Part of the increase comes from drugs being used to replace other kinds of treatments. Part of it arises from new drugs costing more than older kinds. Part of it is higher prices.

C. What to do? Both the Romanow commission and the Kirby committee on health care — to say nothing of reports from other experts — recommended the creation of a national drug agency. Instead of each province having its own list of approved drugs, bureaucracy, procedures and limited bargaining power, all would pool resources, work with Ottawa, and create a national institution.

D. What does "national" mean? Roy Romanow and Senator Michael Kirby recommended a federal-provincial body much like the recently created National Health Council.

E. But "national" doesn't have to mean that. "National" could mean interprovincial — provinces combining efforts to create one body.

F. Either way, one benefit of a "national" organization would be to negotiate better prices, if possible, with drug manufacturers. Instead of having one province — or a series of hospitals within a province — negotiate a price for a given drug on the provincial list, the national agency would negotiate on behalf of all provinces.

G. Rather than, say, Quebec, negotiating on behalf of seven million people, the national agency would negotiate on behalf 31 million people. Basic economics suggests the greater the potential consumers, the higher the likelihood of a better price.

H. Of course the pharmaceutical companies will scream. They like divided buyers; they can lobby better that way. They can use the threat of removing jobs from one province to another. They can hope that, if one province includes a drug on its list, the pressure will cause others to include it on theirs. They wouldn't like a national agency, but self-interest would lead them to deal with it.

I. A small step has been taken in the direction of a national agency with the creation of the Canadian Coordinating Office for Health Technology Assessment, funded by Ottawa and the provinces. Under it, a Common Drug Review recommends to provincial lists which new drugs should be included. Predictably, and regrettably, Quebec refused to join.

J. A few premiers are suspicious of any federal-provincial deal-making. They (particularly Quebec and Alberta) just want Ottawa to fork over additional billions with few, if any, strings attached. That's one reason why the idea of a national list hasn't gone anywhere while drug costs keep rising fast.

K. So, if the provinces want to run the health-care show, they should prove they can run it, starting with an interprovincial health list that would end duplication, save administrative costs, prevent one province from being played off against another, and bargain for better drug prices.

L. Premiers love to quote Mr. Romanow's report selectively, especially the parts about more federal money. Perhaps they should read what he had to say about drugs: "A national drug agency would provide governments more influence on pharmaceutical companies in order to constrain the ever-increasing cost of drugs."

M. Or they could read Mr. Kirby's report: "the substantial buying power of such an agency would strengthen the public prescription-drug insurance plans to negotiate the lowest possible purchase prices from drug companies."

N. So when the premiers gather in Niagara Falls to assemble their usual complaint list, they should also get cracking about something in their jurisdiction that would help their budgets and patients.

1. The pharmaceutical corporations would be reluctant to accept a national medical system in that they prefer divided consumers of drugs.
2. The national list of drugs hasn't been very successful partly because of the resistance of some provinces such as Quebec who wants Ottawa to cover the expense.
3. Since the late 1990s, the costs of medicines which should be prescribed have grown faster the speed of overall health-care spending.
4. The provinces would cooperate with the central government to put resources together and set up a nationwide system of drugs instead of a local one in each province.
5. There is much good chance that more buyers mean the more reasonable prices of drugs, as the simple knowledge of economics shows.
6. The cost of new drugs is higher than that of old ones, which makes the cost of prescription drugs higher.
7. In one report, it is said that lower prices of drugs may result from the high purchasing power of a national agency.
8. One possible advantage which a nationwide system may bring about is to talk with drug manufacturers about the prices of medicines.
9. Despite their complaints, the provinces should try to do something to lower the spending of health care.
10. Premiers are only interested in part of the report of Mr. Romanow.

Key: 1. H 2. J 3. B 4. C 5. G 6. B 7. M 8. F 9. A 10. L

Passage Four

Creative Book Report Ideas

A. Are you at a loss for creative book report ideas for your students? If yes, then this article will help you make reading and reviewing books more creative for your class. In an age of PSPs, Xbox, anime and gaming arcades, reading has lost its foothold in the list of hobbies that children tend to cite. Most of the reading that kids do today comes in the form of compulsory books that they need to read for school and maybe that is the reason they find reading to be an insurmountable and boring task. If you want to inculcate the love for languages and literary masterpieces in your students and want them to devour books everyone should read, then a good way of going about the same would be to get them to start working on creative book report ideas. While working on creative ideas for book reports, your students will have to understand the book in a way that allows them to come up with new ways to present to the class, the essence of the book.

B. As a teacher while egging your students to activate their creative gray cells, you will have to help them out with basic ideas that they can work on. Depending on the age bracket that your students belong to, the creative book report ideas will vary. This is so, not just because of the varying attention spans that children of various age groups posses but also because of the amount of work that kids can put into the report. While a middle school student will be comfortable handling a handy cam, a student from elementary school will be more fascinated if he is working with paints and puppets. So do you want to know how to write a book report creatively? In this article, we will list out for you, a couple of good creative book report ideas for elementary students and for middle school students.

C. A book report sandwich is a good creative idea for book reports. As a teacher you can get drawings of a sandwich on sheets of paper that are of the color of the ingredients of your sandwich, for example, a cream sheet of paper to resemble mayonnaise, red to represent tomato and likewise. Obviously, each ingredient should be cut in a way that when assembled together, it looks like a sandwich. Now, give each of your students one of these book sandwiches to create their book report. It can start with the name of the book and the author's name on the top slice of the sandwich. The second ingredient can have the summary of the book on it. Each subsequent ingredient can have a description of the main characters, the setting of the book, the plot, and then his or her views about the book. Once they are done with their book reports, they can staple the book sandwich together and then, you can create a class bulletin board with all the book report sandwiches on display.

D. One of the good techniques to retell a story, it is also one of the favorite creative book report ideas among students. The job that the student will have is to read the book and then pick a few objects at his/her home which will allow him/her to retell the story in a way that makes it interesting for his/her audience. Every time he/she picks out an object from the bag to report the book he/she has read, there has to be a valid connection between the book and the object, which the student can first ask the audience to guess and then go ahead and explain it. This idea is spin-off on the normal show and tells and allows for an interactive book report session.

E. This is one of the creative ideas for book reports in which, as the teacher, you will have to divide your class into groups and give them one book each. The students can then read the book and get together and write a play and act it out for the class. To give a deeper insight into the book, one of the students can play the role of the author and as a group, the students can try and recreate the thought process of the author. The student playing the role of the author can then interrupt the play at important junctures and talk about the reasons for these twists in the play and how he/she came up with these plot lines.

F. As a young adult, your student's fascination may go beyond the immediate concerns of the book. He/she may want to understand the circumstances in which the book was written, the times then, the events happening in the world and get the author's perspective about the book. Encourage your students to mink on those lines. Divide the class into pairs and give each pair one book to read. Let them then do the roles of the author and a journalist. You can have an interview session in front of the class, enabling them to dissect the book and get a peek into the author's world.

G. In a technology-obsessed world, it may be a very tiny minority of your class that does not get excited with the Drospect of shooting a film. One of the best creative book report ideas for middle school, you will need to divide the class into groups and give them at least two months to adapt the book that they have been assigned, into a film. The movie should have a well-adapted screenplay and all other prerequisites, like a lighting engineer, sound engineer, costume designer, etc. At the end of the given time, the film can be screened in front of the class and then discussed.

H. If you are on the lookout for good individual creative book report ideas, then this one could be for you. Assign every student a book and then ask them to start maintaining a diary, from the author's point of view. Ask them to come up with imaginary incidents from the author's life and use historical events to explain why the author wrote the book in a certain manner. Alternately, you can also ask your students to give a surrogate ending to the story.

I. These are just a few of the options that you could use to inspire your students to come up with creative book report ideas. As kids we tend to be more imaginative and creative. Encourage your students to think out of the box and appreciate them for their efforts. This will help you have a class that is not only lively and inquisitive by nature but also a class that will cultivate a love for words.

1. Teachers can create a class bulletin board to display all the book report sandwiches after their students finish their reports.
2. Adopting the method of knowing your author, teachers can encourage students to think beyond the immediate concerns of the book.
3. Asking me students to write from their own point of view is suitable for teachers who are on the lookout for good individual creative book report ideas.

4. Retelling a story is one of the favorite creative book report ideas among students and it tells and allows for an interactive book report session.
5. Nowadays, most of books children read are those they need to read for school.
6. Teachers tend to be more imaginative and creative as kids.
7. While working on creative ideas for book reports, students will have to understand the book.
8. The creative book report ideas vary according to ages because children in different age groups have different attention span.
9. If teachers ask their students to shoot a film about a book, they should give them no fewer than two months.
10. Teachers have to divide their class into groups and give them one book each is a good creative book report ideas.

Key: 1. C 2. F 3. H 4. D 5. A 6. I 7. A 8. B 9. G 10. E

Passage Five

Protect Your Privacy When Job-hunting Online

A. Identity theft and identity fraud are terms used to refer to all types of crime in which someone wrongfully obtains and uses another person's personal data in some way that involves fraud or deception, typically for economic gain.

B. The numbers associated with identity theft are beginning to add up fast these days. A recent General Accounting Office report estimates that as many as 750,000 Americans are victims of identity theft every year. And that number may be low, as many people choose not to report the crime even if they know they have been victimized.

C. Identity theft is "an absolute epidemic," states Robert Ellis Smith, a respected author and advocate of privacy. "It's certainly picked up in the last four or five years. It's worldwide. It affects everybody, and there's very little you can do to prevent it and, worst of all, you can't detect it until it's probably too late."

D. Unlike your fingerprints, which are unique to you and cannot be given to someone else for their use, you personal data, especially your social security number, your bank account or credit card number, your telephone calling card number, and other valuable identifying data, can be used, if they fall into the wrong hands, to personally profit at your expense. In the United States and Canada, for example, many people have reported that unauthorized persons have taken funds out of their bank or financial accounts, or, in the worst cases, taken over their identities altogether, running up vast debts and committing crimes while using the victims' names. In many cases, a victim's losses may included not only out-of-pocket financial losses, but substantial additional financial costs associated with trying to restore his reputation in the community and correcting erroneous information for which the criminal is responsible.

E. According to the FBI, identity theft is the number one fraud committed on the Internet. So how do job seekers protect themselves while continuing to circulate their resumes online?

The key to a successful online job search is learning to manage the risks. Here are some tips for staying safe while conducting a job search on the Internet.

F. Check for a privacy policy. If you are considering posting your resume online, make sure the job search site your are considering has a privacy policy, like CareerBuilder.com. The policy should spell out how your information will be used, stored and whether or not it will be shared. You may want to think twice about posting your resume on a site that automatically shares your information with others. You could be opening yourself up to unwanted calls from *solicitors* (推销员). When reviewing the site's privacy policy, you'll be able to delete your resume just as easily as you posted it. You won't necessarily want your resume to remain out there on the Internet once you land a job. Remember, the longer your resume remains posted on a job board, the more exposure, both positive and not-so-positive, it will receive.

G. Take advantage of site features. Lawful job search sites offer levels of privacy protection. Before posting your resume, carefully consider your job search objective and the level of risk you are willing to assume. CareerBuilder.com, for example, offers three levels of privacy from which job seekers can choose. The first is standard posting. This option gives job seekers who post their resumes the most visibility to the broadest employer audience possible. The second is *anonymous* (匿名的) posting. This allows job seekers the same visibility as those in the standard posting category without any of their contact information being displayed. Job seekers who wish to remain anonymous but want to share some other information may choose which pieces of contact information to display. The third is private posting. This option allows a job seeker to post a resume without having it searched by employers. Private posting allows job seekers to quickly and easily apply for jobs that appear on CareerBuilder.com without retyping their information.

H. Safeguard your identity. Career experts say that one of the ways job seekers can stay safe while using the Internet to search out jobs is to conceal their identities. Replace your name on your resume with a *generic* (泛指的) identifier, such as "Intranet Developer Candidate," or "Experienced Marketing Representative." You should also consider eliminating the name and location of your current employer. Depending on your title, it may not be all that difficult to determine who you are once the name of your company is provided. Use a general description of the company such as "Major auto manufacturer," or "International packaged goods supplier." If your job title is unique, consider using the generic equivalent instead of the exact title assigned by your employer.

I. Establish and email address for your search. Another way to protect your privacy while seeking employment online is to open up an email account specifically for your online job search. This will safeguard your existing email box in the event someone you don't know gets hold of your email address and shares it with others. Using an email address specifically for you job search also eliminates the possibility that you will receive unwelcome emails in your primary mailbox. When naming your new email address, be sure that it doesn't contain references to your name or other information that will give away your identity. The best solution is an email address that is relevant to the job you are seeking such as salesmgr2004@provider.com.

J. Protect your reference. If your resume contains a section with the names and contact information of your references, take it out. There's no sense in safeguarding your information while sharing private contact information of your references.

K. Keep *confidential* (机密的) information confidential. Do not, under any circumstances, share your social security, driver's license, and bank account numbers or other personal information, such as race or eye color. Honest employers do not need this information with an initial application. Don't provide this even if they say they need it in order to conduct a background check. This is one of the oldest tricks in the book — don't fall for it.

1. Those who post their resumes online for a long time will run an increased risk of becoming victims of identity theft.
2. Robert Ellis Smith says that identity theft is spreading around the world and hard to detect beforehand.
3. Victims of identity theft may suffer additional financial losses in order to restore their reputation and correct wrong information.
4. In the US, 750,000 people are estimated to become victims of identity theft each year.
5. It is a safer way to find a job online when you use an email account specifically.
6. One is supposed to learn how to manage the risks if he or she is going to seek jobs online safely.
7. Standard posting allows fullest potential audience to browse through the resumes posted online.
8. Honest employers will not ask their initial job applicants to reveal their social security account, driver's license or bank account numbers.
9. Make sure that your email address will not be named in a way that could let out your personal information.
10. Job seekers are advised to describe the company they are serving right now in a general way instead of giving an exact name.

Key: 1. F   2. C   3. D   4. B   5. I   6. E   7. G   8. K   9. I   10. H

参考目录：

1. 李永芳. 快速阅读障碍与技巧[J]. 安徽大学学报(哲学社会科学版), 1994(03).
2. 尹德谟. 新编实用英语快速阅读教程[M]. 上海:上海外语教育出版社, 2004.
3. 张维友. 图式知识与阅读理解[J]. 外语界, 1995(02).
4. 张法科,王顺玲. 图式理论在EFL阅读教学中的应用研究——以《综合教程》教学为例[J]. 外语界, 2010(02).
5. 张同乐等. 实用英语技能训练教程[M]. 北京:北京大学出版社, 2010.
6. 端木庆一. 英文阅读图示、空缺与图示建构[J]. 河南师范大学学报(哲学社会科学版), 2004 (02).
7. "NSA Building Quantum Supercomputer". VOA News. Jan, 2014 < http://www.voanews.com/content/nsa-building-a-quantum-supercomputer/1822963.html>.
8. "Diagnosing Disease with the Touch of a Button". Newsweek. Dec, 2013 <http://www.newsweek.com/diagnosing-diseases-touch-button-224058>.

阅读练习参考目录：

1. Cloud, John. "Talk Therapy for Kids' Pain: Better than Pills?". TIME. Jan, 2010 <http://www.time.com/time/health/article/0,8599,1882901,00.html>.
2. Fitzpatrick, Laura. "Job Forecast for College Seniors: Grimmer Than Ever". TIME. Jan, 2010 <http://www.time.com/time/business/article/0,8599,1882979,00.html>.
3. "Wal-mart Closes Ohio Lab; 650 Out of Work". Wall Street Journal. March, 2009 <http://online.wsj.com/article/BT-CO-20090327-711420.html>.
4. Kahn, Michael. "Very hot tea may cause throat cancer: study". LONDON (Reuters). Jan, 2010 <http://www.reuters.com/article/idUSTRE52Q01620090327>.
5. Solomon, Howard. "Worldwide cellphone sales to drop". IT World Canada. Jan, 2010 <http://www.itworldcanada.com/blogs/nw-watch/2009/03/26/worldwide-cellphone-sales-to-drop/49988/>.
6. Lu, Carmen. "Yale professors join NASA investigation". Yale Daily News. Jan, 2010 <http://www.yaledailynews.com/news/scitech-news/2009/03/27/yale-professors-join-nasa-investigation/>.
7. Kelly, Martin. "Geronimo and Fort Pickens". About.com: American History. Jan,2010 <http://americanhistory.about.com/od/nativeamericans/a/geronimo.htm>.
8. "Earth hour dims lights around globe". ShanghaiDaily.com. Jan,2010 <http://www.shanghaidaily.com/sp/article/2009/200903/20090329/article_395831.htm>.
9. (意)马基雅维利. 君主论[M]. 北京:外语教学与研究出版社, 2010.
10. (美)潘恩. 常识[M]. 张源译, 南京:译林出版社, 2012.
11. (英)密尔. 论自由[M]. 顾肃译, 南京:译林出版社, 2012.
12. "TP01-24全套阅读文本". Docin.com. Jan, 2014. <http://www.docin.com/p-408148752.html?qq-pf-to=pcqq.c2c>.

听力技能与训练

作为一项重要的外语技能,听力在听、说、读、写、译五种外语技能中占有重要的地位。本篇内容将以大学英语四、六级英语听力为基础,分项讲解听力技巧及注意事项,并配以丰富的听力练习以帮助读者提高听力理解能力。

一、语音

良好的语音识别能力是听懂英语材料的前提条件。在平时的练习中要注意英语正确的发音规则,熟悉较为典型的语音现象,只有这样才能听懂相关内容。

1. 音标

英语音标由48个音素构成,其中包括20个元音和28个辅音。学好音标是听懂英文材料的基础。

英语国际音标表(48个)

元音(20个)

长元音	/ɑː/	/ɔː/	/ɜː/	/iː/	/uː/			
短元音	/ʌ/	/ɒ/	/ə/	/ɪ/	/ʊ/	/e/	/æ/	
双元音	/eɪ/	/aɪ/	/ɔɪ/	/ɪə/	/eə/	/ʊə/	/əʊ/	/aʊ/

辅音(28个)

清辅音	/p/	/t/	/k/	/f/	/θ/	/s/
浊辅音	/b/	/d/	/g/	/v/	/ð/	/z/
清辅音	/ʃ/	/h/	/ts/	/tʃ/	/tr/	
浊辅音	/ʒ/	/r/	/dz/	/dʒ/	/dr/	
鼻音	/m/	/n/	/ŋ/			
半元音	/j/	/w/				
边音	/l/					

在听音过程中不易区分的元音为 /iː/和/i/,/e/和/æ/。

/iː/是长元音,如 bee, tea, heat 等,但是在快速朗读的时候往往会弱读成短音/i/的音。

/i/是短元音,如 big, it, hit 等。

/e/和/æ/都是短元音,如 bed/bad pen/pan get/gap smell/smash。 注意:在发/e/音时的嘴型要小于发/æ/音时的嘴型。

2. 重音

每个英语单词都有一个重音。在双音节和多音节词中,有一个音节读得较其他音节重,这个音节就称作重读音节,其余的音节读得较轻,为非重读音节。重音不同,词义和词性也不同。如果把重音读在错误的音节上,这个单词就可能会发生歧义,或很难听懂。例如:

desert /ˈdzət/ *n.* 沙漠　　　　　　desert /dɪˈzɜːt/ *v.* 抛弃

record /ˈrekɔːd/ n. 唱片　　　　　record /rɪˈkɔːd/ v. 录音
content /ˈkɒntent/ n. 内容　　　　content /kənˈtent/ v. 使满足

一般说来，双音节词的重音在第一个音节上，多音节词的重音在倒数第三个音节上。例如：

English　　　　paper　　　　level　　　　fellow
cinema　　　　ability　　　　university　　　elephant

在连贯的句子中，有的词需要重读，有的词要弱读。重读的词通常是名词、形容词、数词、副词和实意动词等。需弱读的词通常是冠词、介词、连词、人称代词等。例如：

They will ˈgraduate in ˈone ˈyear.

但是，有时也会出现为了突出某个词的意思而改变重音。例如：

I didn't know ˈ**he** was coming.

he 作为人称代词本不该重读，但此句中的重音改变是有言外之意的："我不知道他（而不是别人）要来。"句重音的改变是说话人表达意思的一种手段，也是听话人理解其话外音的重要依据。

3. 连读

在语速比较快时，同一意群中，如果前一个词结尾是辅音，后一个词的开头是元音，在语流中常发生连着发音的现象。另外，某些辅音与辅音、元音与元音，也可以连起来读。例如：

not at all 连读后读成 /ˈnɔtəˈtɔl/。

look out of 连读后读成 /ˈlʊkaʊtəf/。

在 Do open the door, please 中，do open 连读后读成 /ˈdʊwəʊpen/。

4. 同化

两个相邻的音相互影响，发生了变化，如果同化发生在两个词之间，那么这两个词之间有着平滑的过渡，主要有以下三种方式：

辅音[d]与[j]相邻时，被同化为[dʒ]：Would you...?
辅音[t]与[j]相邻时，被同化为[tʃ]：Can't you...?
辅音[s]与[j]相邻时，被同化为[ʃ]：Miss you.

5. 失爆

也称为不完全爆破。当两个爆破音相邻，发前面一个爆破音时不送气，只做出发此音的口型，听起来好像吞掉了这个音。例如：

big cake
dad told me
huge change
good-bye

6. 语调

英语是语调语言，一般分为升调和降调。说同一句话时用不同的语调会表达出不同的意思。英语中陈述句、特殊疑问句、祈使句和感叹句通常用降调。一般疑问句、婉转祈使句以及表达不确定或疑问的陈述句用升调。说话人有时会用语调表达自己的态度或口气。同样的句子，所用语调不同，表达的意思就会不同。要注意的一点是，在反意疑问句中，如果疑问部分用降调，表示说话人认为自己所说的正确，只是希望听者证实。如果疑问部分用升调，则表示说话人对于所说的心存疑问，希望听者给出自己的看法或意见。例如：

He is a bus driver, isn't he? ↘

说话人用降调,说明自己确信他是个公交车驾驶员。

He is a bus driver, isn't he? ↗

说话人用升调,说明自己不确定他是否是个公交车驾驶员,想听取他人意见。

7. 英音与美音的差别

目前我国大多数英语教学的发音以英音为主,但美式英语近年来借助其强大的经济和文化势力逐渐风行起来。一些英语考试中的听力部分就出现了英音和美音交替现象。这给许多只熟悉英式英语发音的听者带来了麻烦。因此要注意并熟悉美音与英音的不同,并在练习中注意区分。这里把两种发音的主要区别举例说明。例如:英音中的元音 /ɑ:/在美音中通常读作/æ/;/eɪ/通常读作/e/;而/ɒ/和/ɔ:/则读作/ʌ/。这里举几个单词为例:

英音	美音
bath /bɑ:θ/	bath /bæθ/
half /hɑ:f/	half /hæf/
chance /tʃɑ:ns/	chance /tʃæns/
plant /plɑ:nt/	plant /plænt/
cake /keɪk/	cake /kek/
gate /geɪt/	gate /get/
say /seɪ/	say /se/
got /gɒt/	got /gʌt/
job /dʒɒb/	job /dʒʌb/

另外 /r/音也要注意。英音中只有当字母r位于元音之前时,才发 /r/音,而当字母r位于元音之后时,是不发 /r/音的。但是美音只要有r出现总是要发音的。例如:

英音	美音
red /red/	red /red/
ear /ɪə/	ear /ɪər/
course /kɔ:s/	course /kɔ:rs/

在练习听力的时候要反复朗读或跟读、模仿,让自己熟悉其正确的发音,才能达到良好的效果。

以下列出的是英音与美音发音不同的一些常见词:

英音		美音
adult	/ˈædʌlt/	/əˈdʌlt/
cassette	/kɑːˈset/	/kəˈset/
cupboard	/ˈkʌbəd/	/ˈkʌbərd/
either	/ˈaɪðə/	/ˈiːðə/
garage	/ˈgærɑːʒ/	/gəˈrɑːʒ/
laboratory	/ləˈbɒrətəri/	/ˈlæbərətɔːri/
neither	/ˈnaɪðə/	/ˈniːðə/
record	/ˈrekɔːd/	/ˈrekərd/
secretary	/ˈsekrətri/	/ˈsekrəteri/

英语和汉语一样,说话人通过不同的语调和重音的变化表达不同的意思。重读的每一处都具有提示作用。因而在考试中,考生要注意说话人的语音语调及不同的单词或句子的重音,从中推测出人物的心理活动、观点和态度。

二、听力习惯及文化背景

许多人没有养成良好的听力习惯,在平时的练习中,他们或趴在桌子上,或闭着眼睛以减少干扰。实际上,听是语言沟通的重要手段,在大多数情况下,听和说都是在正常状态下进行的,所以在日常的练习中要注意做到正常、正规、正确。正常是指正常姿态;正规是指用正规的方法做笔记帮助答题;正确是指有正确的做题方法。听材料时不要趴着或闭着眼,手中的笔要随时准备做笔记,重点记录人名、地名、数字、时间等容易忘记或不易区分的词;在听之前要把所给的选项浏览一遍,预测将要听到内容,做到心中有数。如果参加考试,在考前要充分休息,保证充沛的精力;考试的过程中要保持平稳的心态,既要沉着冷静又要反应灵敏,同时把握好节奏,即听前审题+预测,听时记录+思考,听后判断+下题预测。

在平时的学习中要注意积累有关英语国家的文化背景知识,了解了这些国家的历史、地理、风土人情及政治体制等知识对于理解所听内容是有很大帮助的。

三、听力主要内容及技巧

2013年12月进行的大学英语四、六级考试中听力题型虽然有所变化,但不变的依然是对考生的英语听力理解、单词拼写等能力的考查。它往往考的不是考生是否听见,而是考考生是否听懂。把命题中的对话和段落原封不动地照搬到答案里,等着考生把它挑出来的题型,在如今的四、六级听力考试中几乎没有了。绝大多数的题目是要求考生把听到的原文进行变换和归纳,然后对应到选项中。这些能力是靠平时多听、多练、多积累而一步步地培养起来的。下面就英语四、六级听力考试中较为常见的题目类型进行讲解和分析。

1. 对话

在常听的对话中通常分为短对话和长对话。短对话所涉及的内容通常涉及日常生活、学习或工作等方面,句子结构及用词都相对较为简单。长对话的内容信息量比较大,句子比较长,结构较为复杂,注重语篇层次上的理解。长短对话后所提问的问题通常分为明示问题和暗示问题两大类。明示问题直接可以从对话中得出,比如明确提及的时间、地点、人物等;而暗示问题则要通过分析判断才能得到正确的回答。听者通常要根据所听对话对于事件发生的时间、地点、人物的描述以及说话人所用的语调和口气来推测说话人的真实意图和想法。

短对话

短对话所涉及的内容以及问题主要涉及的主题可大致分为:时间数字、地点方向、身份关系、态度观点、原因结果、推理判断和细节辨认题等。听者要注意听懂双方对话中话语的隐含意义。在大学英语四、六级听力的考试中,听者可以根据自己在听的时候的理解以及听之前的预测迅速地在题目的选项上做一些自己明白的记号,比如在认为有可能成为答案的选项或者根本没有可能成为答案的选项后面分别做不同的记号,这样当听到问题的时候就可以很确定地选择答案。

时间数字

这一类题目不仅需要听者听清所说的时间或数字,问题的答案往往需要简单的计算才

能得出。例如:

M: I'll have these shoes. Please tell me how much I owe you.

W: They are $40 a pair and three pairs make a total of $120. But today we offer a 10% discount.

Q: How much does the man have to pay?

[A] $120. [B] $90.
[C] $108. [D] $40.

在听的时候如果注意记笔记,然后听清问题,再进行简单运算,就不难得出正确的答案[C]。

听数字时注意区分13—19和30—90的发音,例如14(fourteen)和40(forty),这些数字的发音比较容易混淆,区分的办法是通过把握此类词的重音:fourteen /fɔːˈiːn/, forty /fɔːti/。

地点方向

这类题目一是要听清指方向时用的副词或介词,理清它们之间的关系;二是要注意以所用的词来判断所在场所。例如:

W: George, look at the long waiting line. I'm glad you've made a reservation.

M: More and more people enjoy eating out now. Besides, this place is especially popular with the oversea students.

Q: Where did the conversation most probably take place?

[A] At a theatre. [B] At a booking office.
[C] At a railway. [D] At a restaurant.

从本题中用到 eating out 就可轻松判断[D]为正确答案。

身份关系

在这类对话中,说话人的关系不同,所用的词、句子及语气都有所不同。职业不同,所用场景词汇也不同,这些都是听音时做出正确判断的关键。例如:

W: John, what are you doing on your computer? Don't you remember your promise?

M: This is not a game. It's only a crossword puzzle that helps increase my vocabulary.

Q: What is the probable relationship between the speakers?

[A] Colleagues. [B] Employer and employee.
[C] Husband and wife. [D] Mother and son.

本题说的是孩子与父母间的 promise 的问题,女士所用的语气明显有一种至上而下的感觉,所以答案应为最后一个。

态度观点

这类题目有些时候说话人的观点、看法会直接说出来,但多数情况下,需要听者从说话人的语气、语调及所用词汇通过推理来判断,也就是要听"话外音"。例如:

M: What was it like growing up in New York's Bronx District, was it safe?

W: To me it was. It was all I knew. My mom was sending me to the shop and I'd go and buy when I was 8 years old.

Q: What do we learn from the conversation?

[A] The woman did not feel any danger growing up in the Bronx.

[B] The man thinks it was quite safe living in the Bronx district.

[C] The woman started working at an early age to support her family.

[D] The man doesn't think it safe to send an 8-year-old to buy things.

从女士所说的 To me it was 可以推断出答案是[A]。而接下来女士所说的信息可侧面支持她的看法。

原因结果

此类题目一般由第二位说话者说出原因,因此要注意听第二个人所说的内容。通常是先说出赞同的态度,然后再用转折词说出直接原因。例如:

M: My computer doesn't work properly. I wonder if I can use yours for a while.

W: You certainly could if I had one, but I gave mine to my daughter last month.

Q: What is said about the woman's computer?

[A] She has no computer at the moment.

[B] She has only one computer.

[C] She will lend the man her computer.

[D] Her computer has broken down.

女士先说了一个虚拟句 You certainly could if I had one. 然后又用 but 进一步补充了原因。答案为[A]。

推理判断

这类题目的特点是说话人所用方式比较含蓄委婉,听者要仔细揣摩说者的"话外音"。例如:

M: What was it like working with those young stars?

W: It was a great group. I always got mad that people said that we didn't get along just because we are girls. There was never a fight. We had a great time.

Q: What does the woman mean?

[A] The girls got on well with each other.

[B] It's understandable that girls don't get along.

[C] She was angry with the other young stars.

[D] The girls lacked the courage to fight.

其实从女士的第一句话就能推断出正确答案为[A]。但由于女士说的比较长,干扰信息比较多,所以可能会错选。

细节辨认题

此类题目既考查听力能力,又考查短期记忆力,所以比较难。关键要及时做好笔记,把每个选项所提供的时间、地点、人物、爱好、动作等对应起来,做出正确判断。例如:

M: I can't find the key to my car. I need it to go for a drive.

W: I'll look for it later. Right now I need your help fixing the shelf before I paint it.

Q: What will they do first?

[A] Write the letter.   [B] Fix the shelf.

[C] Paint the shelf.   [D] Look for the pen.

问题是问先做什么。对话中提到一些不同的事情,但女士所说的 before 是本题的关键,它给出了事情的先后顺序。答案是[B]。

听力技能与训练

长对话

长对话所涉及的主题与短对话的主题相似,常与学校生活、休闲娱乐有关,如:讨论学习、生活和娱乐等等。长对话是短对话和短文的结合,需要听者具有综合听力素质,既要注意细节,又要把握好整体。做这部分试题的时候,要注意以下几点:听音前,尽量把有关的试题选项浏览一遍,根据选项猜测可能出现的问题及提问方式。听音时,抓住与选项及所猜测问题有关的关键词,速记有关内容或者在选项后面做记号。听清问题,修正猜测问题,做出正确选择。另外在长对话中,由于问题不止一个,为了防止听了后面,忘了前面,因此在听的过程中,参照各题的选项,做一些简要的笔记,特别是听到数字、时间、年龄、地点等问题时,适当的笔记对正确的答题尤为重要。

因此,加强短文和短对话的练习,掌握好两部分的听力技巧,应对长对话也就比较容易了。例如:

W: Oh! I'm fed up with my job!

M: Hey! There's a perfect job for you in the paper today. You might be interested.

W: Oh? What is it? What do they want?

M: Wait a minute...Ah, here it is. The European Space Agency. It's recruiting translators.

W: The European Space Agency?

M: Well, that's what it says. They need an English translator to work from French or German.

W: So they need a degree in French or German, I suppose. Well, I've got that. What's more? I have plenty of experience. What else are they asking for?

M: Just that. A university degree, and 3 or 4 years of experience as a translator in a professional environment. They also say, the person should have a lively and inquiring mind, effective communication skills, and the ability to work individually, or as a part of the team.

W: Well, if I stay on my present job much longer, I won't have any mind or skills left. By the way, what about salary? I just hope it isn't lower than what I get now.

M: It's said to be negotiable. It depends on the applicant's education and experience. In addition to basic salary, there's a list of extra benefits. Have a look yourself.

W: Um...travel and social security plus relocation expenses are paid. Hey, this isn't bad. I really want the job.

Questions:

1. Why is the woman trying to find a new job?

   [A] She is thirsty for promotion.

   [B] She wants a much higher salary.

   [C] She is tired of her present work.

   [D] She wants to save travel expenses.

2. What position is being advertised in the paper?

   [A] Translator.

   [B] Travel agent.

   [C] Language instructor.

   [D] Environmental engineer.

3. What are the key factors that determine the salary of the new position?

   [A] Lively personality and inquiring mind.

   [B] Communication skills and team spirit.

   [C] Devotion and work efficiency.

   [D] Education and experience.

这段长对话中划线部分的内容就是3道题目的答案。细心的听者如果能在听的过程中做一些笔记，答案是不难判断出的，而且也会发现题目的顺序和文章的叙述顺序是一致的。所以，答案分别是[C]，[A]，[D]。

2. 短文

短文的信息量大、内容广、题材多样，选材多涉及学校生活、家庭社会、娱乐文化、音乐艺术、历史地理以及科普知识等方面，难度相对较大。需要听者既具备一定的文化背景知识，又要有较快的反应力和较强的记忆力。因此，听者不但要提高英语听力水平，平时还应该多注意收集这些方面的材料，掌握一些不必太专业的简单词汇和常识，在考试中就能起到提示主题的作用。在平时的练习中，要注意做到一下几点：

（1）预测问题内容

预测将要听到的内容是听力理解的基本技巧，主要取决于听者对关键词的捕捉，对背景知识的掌握以及对语言环境的熟悉程度。预测时要依靠所给出的选择项内容，以及所听的词和短语迅速准确地推断短文内容和问题类型。

（2）听大意抓要点

听短文时不必要求听懂全部内容，而是主要通过听懂文章的开头及结尾部分，再抓住文章中的一些关键词和短语来了解文章大意。

（3）做记录记细节

要养成边听边记的好习惯，尤其听到数字、时间、地名及人名时一定要随手记下，否则可能会忘记。但不要看见有和自己记下的内容相同的选项就选上，而是要先听清楚问题，在综合考虑之后再做出判断。

（4）学会同义替换

在短文所给题目中可能会用不同的词或短语替换短文中出现的词和短语，所以在平时的练习中，要多掌握具有相同或相近意思的词和词组，以及各种常用句式的表达法。

3. 复合式听写

复合式听写考题没有太强的专业性，取材仍然围绕日常生活、科技发展、历史起源、人物回顾、文化娱乐等展开文段。但在大学英语四、六级考试中，考查的不仅是听者对语言的理解能力，还对听者的词汇、拼写、语法等语言知识的运用能力进行全面的考查，同时还要求听音者具有一定的快速书写能力，这对培养听者的语言实际运用能力有很大的好处。在听写开始之前预读内容，重点阅读文章的开头和结尾的几句可以帮助听者把握文章主旨。如果时间允许，听者还可观察一下空格前后的语法信息，从而帮助单词听写、判断词性、单复数以及时态、语态等内容。

听力技能与训练

2013年新大学英语四、六级听力的重大变化是复合式听写由以前的听写8个单词3个句子变为10个单词或词组。复合式听写部分短文播放三遍。听力理解的总时间从35分钟缩短到30分钟,听写三遍的播放速度保持一致,播放中不停顿,要求考生注意把握好时间。

总而言之,英语听力技能的提高实际上就是综合技能的提高。它不仅涉及听者所掌握的语音、词汇、语法、句法水平,也涉及听者听音时的心理状态、所积累的文化背景知识的水平等因素。同时也与是否经常听读英语,有无英语听音环境密切相关。所以平时要注意创造英语环境,多听、多读、多练,努力提高自己的英语综合水平,只有这样,英语听力水平才能随之水涨船高。

听力练习
短对话

Directions: *There are 80 short conversations in this section. Listen to each conversation once and choose the best answer from the four choices marked A, B, C, and D.*

1. A) Place another order. B) Call to check on it.
   C) Wait patiently. D) Go and find the furniture.
2. A) She doesn't need the job. B) She hasn't got a job yet.
   C) She has got a good job. D) She is going to start work soon.
3. A) She got home before 9 o'clock. B) She had a bad cold.
   C) She had a car accident. D) She was delayed.
4. A) She hasn't gone camping for several weeks.
   B) She likes to take long camping trips.
   C) She prefers not to go camping on weekends.
   D) She often spends a lot of time planning her camping trips.
5. A) A writer.   B) A teacher.   C) A reporter.   D) A student.
6. A) She has not heard of Prof. Johnson.
   B) She has not heard of Prof. Johnson's brother.
   C) She is a good friend of Prof. Johnson's brother.
   D) She does not know Prof. Johnson's brother.
7. A) Coming back for a later show. B) Waiting in a queue.
   C) Coming back in five minutes. D) Not going to the movie today.
8. A) He has got a heart attack. B) He has unharmed.
   C) He was badly hurt. D) He has fully recovered from the shock.
9. A) The man went to Australia during Christmas.
   B) The man visited Australia during the summer vacation.
   C) The man didn't have a good time because of the different weather.
   D) The man remained home while his parents went to see his uncle.
10. A) To attend a party at a classmate's home.
    B) To do homework with her classmate.
    C) To attend an evening class.
    D) To have supper out with her classmate.

11. A) Look for a more expensive hotel. B) Try to find a quiet place.
    C) Go to another hotel by bus. D) Take a walk around the city.
12. A) They're talking about nice children.
    B) The man has a house for sale.
    C) The woman lives in a nice house.
    D) The man has three children.
13. A) In a hotel B) At a dinner table.
    C) In the street. D) At the man's house.
14. A) Relatives. B) Roommates. C) Colleagues. D) Neighbors.
15. A) 5:00. B) 5:15. C) 5:30. D) 5:45.
16. A) He wants to have more sleep. B) Women need more sleep than men.
    C) His wife doesn't sleep well. D) He doesn't need as much sleep as his wife.
17. A) A student. B) A reporter. C) A visitor. D) A lecturer.
18. A) To the school. B) To a friend's house.
    C) To the post office. D) Home.
19. A) He is afraid he won't be chosen for the trip.
    B) The boss has not decided where to go.
    C) Such a trip is necessary for the company.
    D) It's not certain whether the trip will take place.
20. A) It was boring. B) It was entertaining.
    C) It was touching. D) It was encouraging.
21. A) The man wants to attend tomorrow's show.
    B) There aren't any tickets left for tonight's show.
    C) There aren't any tickets left for tomorrow's show.
    D) The man doesn't want to attend tomorrow's show.
22. A) Detective stories. B) Stories about jail escapes.
    C) Love stories. D) Stories about royal families.
23. A) It was a long lecture, but easy to understand.
    B) It was not as easy as she had thought.
    C) It was as difficult as she had expected.
    D) It was interesting and easy to follow.
24. A) To put him through to the director.
    B) To have a talk with the director about his work.
    C) To arrange an appointment for him with the director.
    D) To go and see if the director can meet him right now.
25. A) Margaret wanted to return some magazines to the woman.
    B) Margaret wanted to lend some magazines to the woman.
    C) Margaret wanted to borrow some magazines from the woman.
    D) Margaret wanted to get some magazines back from the woman.

26. A) He doesn't care much about it.
    B) He enjoys it very much.
    C) He doesn't mind ever though it's tedious.
    D) He hates working overtime.
27. A) The woman doesn't think it exciting to travel by air.
    B) They'll stay at home during the holidays.
    C) They are offered some plane tickets for their holidays.
    D) They'll be flying somewhere for their vacation.
28. A) Something went wrong with the bus.
    B) She took somebody to hospital.
    C) Something prevented her from catching the bus.
    D) She came on foot instead of taking a bus.
29. A) Do her homework.   B) Clean the backyard.
    C) Wash clothes.   D) Enjoy the beautiful day.
30. A) The man is looking for a place to live in.
    B) The man has a house for rent.
    C) The woman is a secretary.
    D) The two speakers are old friends.
31. A) They are twins.   B) They are classmates.
    C) They are friends.   D) They are colleagues.
32. A) The man is planning a trip to Austin.
    B) The man has not been to Austin before.
    C) The man doesn't like Austin.
    D) The man has been to Austin before.
33. A) The size of the room.   B) Long working hours.
    C) The hot weather.   D) The fan in the room.
34. A) The man has changed his destination.
    B) The man is returning his ticket.
    C) The man is flying to New York tomorrow morning.
    D) The man can't manage to go to New York as planned.
35. A) It is difficult to identify.   B) It has been misplaced.
    C) It is missing.   D) It has been borrowed by someone.
36. A) Looking for a timetable.   B) Buying some furniture.
    C) Reserving a table.   D) Window shopping.
37. A) Cold and windy.   B) Snow will be replaced by strong winds.
    C) It will get better.   D) Rainy and cold.
38. A) It is no longer available.
    B) It has been reprinted four times.
    C) The store doesn't have it now, but will have it soon.
    D) The information in the book is out of date.

39. A) Henry doesn't like the color.
    B) Someone else painted the house.
    C) There was no ladder in the house.
    D) Henry painted the house himself.
40. A) In a cotton field.   B) At a railway station.
    C) On a farm.   D) On a train.
41. A) She is not interested in the article.
    B) She has given the man much trouble.
    C) She would like to have a copy of the article.
    D) She doesn't want to take the trouble to read the article.
42. A) He saw the big tower he visited on TV.
    B) He has visited the TV tower twice.
    C) He has visited the TV tower once.
    D) He will visit the TV tower in June.
43. A) The woman has trouble getting along with the professor.
    B) The woman regrets having taken up much of the professor's time.
    C) The woman knows the professor has been busy.
    D) The woman knows the professor has run into trouble.
44. A) He doesn't enjoy business trips as much as he used to.
    B) He doesn't think he is capable of doing the job.
    C) He thinks the pay is too low to support his family.
    D) He wants to spend more time with his family.
45. A) The man thought the essay was easy.
    B) They both had a hard time writing the essay.
    C) The woman thought the essay was easy.
    D) Neither of them has finished the assignment yet.
46. A) In the park.   B) Between two buildings.
    C) In his apartment.   D) Under a huge tree.
47. A) It's awfully dull.   B) It's really exciting.
    C) It's very exhausting.   D) It's quite challenging.
48. A) A movie.   B) A lecture.   C) A play.   D) A speech.
49. A) The weather is mild compared to the past years.
    B) They are having the coldest winter ever.
    C) The weather will soon get warmer.
    D) The weather may get even colder.
50. A) A mystery story.
    B) The hiring of a shop assistant.
    C) The search for a reliable witness.
    D) An unsolved case of robbery.

51. A) A math teacher and his colleague.　　B) A teacher and his student.
    C) A student and his classmate.　　D) A librarian and a student.
52. A) Tony could not continue the experiment.
    B) Tony finished the experiment last night.
    C) Tony thought the experiment was well done.
    D) Tony had expected the experiment to be easier.
53. A) She can't put up with the noise.
    B) She wants to save money to buy a piano.
    C) The present apartment is too expensive.
    D) She has found a job in a neighboring area.
54. A) He is not very enthusiastic about his English lessons.
    B) He has made great progress in his English.
    C) He is a student of the music department.
    D) He is not very interested in English songs.
55. A) At home.　　B) In a restaurant.　　C) In a car.　　D) On the street.
56. A) His injury kept him at home.
    B) He didn't think it necessary.
    C) He was too weak to see the doctor.
    D) He failed to make an appointment.
57. A) 5:15.　　B) 5:10.　　C) 4:30.　　D) 5:00.
58. A) The man needs help.　　B) The man is complaining.
    C) The man likes his job.　　D) The man is talking with his boss.
59. A) Wear a new dress.　　B) Make a silk dress.
    C) Attend a party.　　D) Go shopping.
60. A) He played his part quite well.　　B) He was not dramatic enough.
    C) He performed better than the secretary.　　D) He exaggerated his part.
61. A) The man saw Mark on the street two months ago.
    B) The woman had forgotten Mark's phone number.
    C) The woman made a phone call to Mark yesterday.
    D) Mark and the woman had not been in touch for some time.
62. A) The man is late for the trip because he is busy.
    B) The woman is glad to meet Mr. Brown in person.
    C) The man is meeting the woman on behalf of Mr. Brown.
    D) The woman feels sorry that Mr. Brown is unable to come.
63. A) At 10:30.　　B) At 10:25.　　C) At 10:40.　　D) At 10:45.
64. A) The man no longer smokes.
    B) The man is under pressure from his wife.
    C) The man usually follows his wife's advice.
    D) The man refuses to listen to his doctor's advice.

65. A) Move to a big city.　　　　　　　B) Become a teacher.
　　C) Go back to school.　　　　　　　D) Work in New York.
66. A) Quit delivering flowers.　　　　　B) Work at a restaurant.
　　C) Bring her flowers every day.　　　D) Leave his job to work for her.
67. A) She can find the right person to help the man.
　　B) She can help the man out.
　　C) She's also in need of a textbook.
　　D) She picked up the book from the bus floor.
68. A) The man was confused about the date of the appointment.
　　B) The man wants to change the date of the appointment.
　　C) The man is glad he's got in touch with the doctor.
　　D) The man can't come for the appointment at 4:15.
69. A) The two speakers are at a loss what to do.
　　B) The man is worded about his future.
　　C) The two speakers are seniors at college.
　　D) The woman regrets spending her time idly.
70. A) She has learned a lot from the novel.
　　B) She also found the plot difficult to follow.
　　C) She usually has difficulty remembering names.
　　D) She can recall the names of most characters in the novel.
71. A) Skating.　　　　　　　　　　　　B) Swimming.
　　C) Boating and swimming.　　　　　D) Boating and skating.
72. A) Put her report on his desk.
　　B) Read some papers he recommended.
　　C) Improve some parts of her paper.
　　D) Mail her report to the publisher.
73. A) She takes it as a kind of exercise.
　　B) She wants to save money.
　　C) She loves doing anything that is new.
　　D) Her office isn't very far.
74. A) A shop assistant.　　　　　　　　B) A telephone operator.
　　C) A waitress.　　　　　　　　　　　D) A clerk.
75. A) A railway porter.　　　　　　　　B) A bus conductor.
　　C) A taxi driver.　　　　　　　　　　D) A postal clerk.
76. A) Most people killed in traffic accidents are heavy drinkers.
　　B) She does not agree with the man.
　　C) Drunk drivers are not guilty.
　　D) People should pay more attention to the danger of drunk driving.
77. A) $1.40.　　　　B) $4.30.　　　　C) $6.40.　　　　D) $8.60.

78. A) Collect papers for the man.
    B) Do the typing once again.
    C) Check the paper for typing errors.
    D) Read the whole newspaper.
79. A) The woman does not want to go to the movies.
    B) The man is too tired to go to the movies.
    C) The woman wants to go to the movies.
    D) The man wants to go out for dinner.
80. A) By bus.   B) By bike.   C) By taxi.   D) On foot.

短对话原文

1. M: I haven't received the furniture I ordered yet. Maybe I should call to check on it.
   W: Don't worry. It takes at least a week to arrive.
   Q: What does the woman think the man should do?

2. M: Congratulations! I understand you've got a job. When will you start to work?
   W: You must be thinking of someone else. I'm still waiting to hear the good news.
   Q: What does the woman mean?

3. W: If it hadn't been snowing so hard, I might have been home by 9 o'clock.
   M: It's too bad you didn't make it. Jane was here and she wanted to see you.
   Q: What happened to the woman?

4. M: Janet is quite interested in camping, isn't she?
   W: Yes, she often goes for weeks at a time.
   Q: What does the woman say about Janet?

5. W: Good evening, Professor David. My name is Susan Gray. I'm with the local newspaper. Do you mind if I ask you a few questions?
   M: Not at all. Go ahead, please?
   Q: What does Susan Gray do?

6. M: Do you know Professor Johnson's brother?
   W: I've never met him, but I've heard that he is as well-known as Johnson herself.
   Q: What do we learn from the woman's reply?

7. W: The movie starts in 5 minutes and there's bound to be a long line.
   M: Why don't we come back for the next show? I'm sure it would be less crowded.
   Q: What is the man suggesting?

8. W: Were you hurt in the accident?
   M: I was shocked at the time, but wasn't hurt at all. My bike was totally damaged though.
   Q: What do we know about the man?

9. W: Where were you on Christmas, David? I called you several times and nobody was home.
   M: My parents and I traveled to Australia to visit my uncle. It was quite an experience to spend Christmas in summer.
   Q: What do we learn from this conversation?

10. M: It's seven o'clock already. Mary should be home by now.
    W: Oh. I forgot to tell you that she called this afternoon and told me that she was going to a party at her classmate's house and wouldn't be home until 10.
    Q: What did Mary say she was going to do?

11. M: I don't think we can find a better hotel around here at this time.
    W: Let's walk a little further to see if there is another one. I just can't bear the traffic noise here.
    Q: What will the speakers most probably do?

12. W: Hi! I'm calling about the three-bedroom house you advertised in yesterday's paper. It sounds really nice.
    M: It is — especially if you have children.
    Q: What do we learn from the conversation?

13. W: Dear, I feel hungry now. How about you?
    M: So do I. Let me call Room Service. Hello, Room Service? Please send a menu to 320 right away.
    Q: Where are the two speakers?

14. M: I've just brought your ladder back. Thanks for lending it to me. Where shall I leave it?
    W: Just lean it against the wall there. Use the ladder again any time.
    Q: What's the probable relationship between these two speakers?

15. M: What's the time for departure?
    W: 5:30. That only leaves us 15 minutes to go through the customs and check our baggage.
    Q: At what time did the conversation take place?

16. W: Look here, darling. The paper says people tend to feel unwell if they sleep less than six hours a day.
    M: That may be true for you, but it certainly isn't true for me.
    Q: What can we conclude from the man's reply?

17. M: Are there any more questions on this lecture? Yes, Mary.
    W: Dr. Baker, do you think an independent candidate could become president?
    Q: What most probably is Mary?

18. M: Can you stay for dinner?
    W: I'd love to, but I have to go and send some registered mail before picking up the children from school.
    Q: Where will the woman go first?

19. W: How many people has the boss chosen for the business trip to France?
    M: Well, as far as I know, whether there'll be such a trip is yet to be decided.
    Q: What does the man mean?

20. W: The speech the blind girl gave this evening was extremely moving.
    M: I think everyone felt the same.
    Q: How did the man feel about the girl's speech?

21. M: I would like two tickets for the 9 o'clock show this evening.
    W: I'm sorry, Sir. They are sold out. But we have a few left for tomorrow.
    Q: What do we learn from this conversation?

22. W: I'd love to see a different type of movie for a change. I'm tired of movies about romantic stories.
    M: I agree. Let's go and see a new movie at the Royal Theatre. I hear it's a real story of two prison breakers.
    Q: What kind of movie does the woman find boring?

23. M: What do you think of Professor Brown's lecture?
    W: The topic was interesting, but the lecture was much more difficult to follow than I had expected.
    Q: What does the woman say about the lecture?

24. M: I'd like to have a talk with your director sometime this week. Could you arrange it for me?
    W: He's rather busy these days. But I'll see what I can do.
    Q: What's the man asking the woman to do?

25. M: Why did Margaret call yesterday?
    W: She wanted to pick up some magazines she lent me.
    Q: What do we learn from the conversation?

26. W: You seem to have a lot of work to do at your office. You're always staying late and working overtime.
    M: That's true. But it's no bother to me. The work is interesting. I don't mind extra hours at all.
    Q: How does the man feel about his job?

27. M: Well, the holiday will soon be here.
    W: Yes, isn't it exciting by this time next week, we'll be on the plane?
    Q: What do we learn from the conversation?

28. M: What happened to you? You are so late.
    W: The bus I took broke down in front of the hospital and I had to walk from there.
    Q: Why was the woman so late?

29. M: It's such a beautiful day. Why not sit out in the back yard for a while and enjoy it?
    W: I'd love to. But there's a lot of laundry to do.
    Q: What will the woman probably do?

30. M: I believe you have a room to let.
    W: That's so. Yes, won't you come in?
    Q: What can we learn from the conversation?

31. W: I often mistake Jim for Bob. Can you tell them apart?
    M: No, they look so much alike that they even confused their mother sometimes when they were young.
    Q: What is the most probable relationship between Jim and Bob?

32. W: I'm thinking of going to Austin for a visit. Do you think it's worth seeing?
    M: Well, I wish I had been there.
    Q: What do we learn from the conversation?

33. M: It's so hot today. I simply can't work. I wish there were a fan in this room.
    W: So do I. I'll fall asleep if I stay here any longer.
    Q: What are they complaining about?

34. M: Excuse me, I have a ticket for the 6 o'clock flight to New York. But I'm afraid I can't make it. Is there a seat available for tomorrow morning?
    W: Let me see. I'm sorry. All the morning flights have been booked up. The earliest we can get for you is the two o'clock flight in the afternoon.
    Q: What does the conversation tell us?

35. W: Jack, I can't find Volume Ten. Could you check for me who borrowed it?
    M: Here it is, on the upper shelf, next to Volume Two.
    Q: Why can't the woman find the book?

36. M: Have you a table for four?
    W: Certainly, Sir. A corner table or would you rather be near the window?
    Q: What is the man doing?

37. W: It's been very cold in the past two days.
    M: We haven't seen the worst of it yet. More snow is forecast next week accompanied by strong winds.
    Q: What will the weather be like?

38. W: I'd like to buy a copy of Professor Franklin's book on sea shells.
    M: I'm sorry. Ms. That book has been out of print for some time now.
    Q: What does the man say about the book?

39. M: Did Henry paint the whole house himself?
    W: He had it painted, because he doesn't like climbing ladders.
    Q: What do we learn from the conversation?

40. W: Look at that big field of cotton. And there's a farm with some beautiful houses.
    M: You really get to know the country when you go by train, don't you?
    Q: Where did the conversation most probably take place?

41. M: Would you like a copy of Professor Smith's article?
    W: Thanks, if it's not too much trouble.
    Q: What does the woman imply?

42. W: Did you visit the Television Tower when you had your vacation in Shanghai last summer?
    M: I couldn't make it last June. But I finally visited it two months later. I plan to visit it again sometime next year.
    Q: What do we learn about the man?

43. M: Prof. Kennedy has been very busy this semester. As far as I know, he works until midnight every day.
    W: I wouldn't have troubled him so much if I had known he was so busy.
    Q: What do we learn from the conversation?

44. W: If I were you, I would have accepted the job.
    M: I turned down the offer because it would mean frequent business trips away from my family.
    Q: Why didn't the man accept the job?

45. M: How are you getting on with your essay, Mary? I'm having a real hard time with mine.
    W: After two sleepless nights, I'm finally through with it.
    Q: What do we learn from this conversation?

46. W: Where did you say you found this bag?
    M: It was lying under a big tree between the park and the apartment building.
    Q: Where did the man find the bag?

47. M: Wouldn't you get bored with the same routine year teaching the same things to children?
    W: I don't think it would be as boring as working in an office. Teaching is most stimulating.
    Q: What does the woman imply about office work?

48. M: I was terribly embarrassed when some of the audience got up and left in the middle of the performance.
    W: Well, some people just can't seem to appreciate real-life drama.
    Q: What are they talking about?

49. W: Oh, it's so cold. We haven't had such a severe winter for so long, have we?
    M: Yes, the forecast says it's going to get worse before it warms up.
    Q: What do we learn from the conversation?

50. M: You were seen hanging about the store on the night when it was robbed, weren't you?
    W: Me? You must have made a mistake. I was at home that night.
    Q: What are they talking about?

51. W: I heard you got a full mark in math exams. Congratulations!
    M: Thanks! I'm sure you also did a good job.
    Q: What's the probable relationship between the two speakers?

52. W: Hi, Tony. How did your experiment go yesterday?
    M: Well, it wasn't as easy as I had thought. I have to continue doing it tonight.
    Q: What do we learn from the conversation?

53. M: I hear you are moving into a new apartment soon?
    W: Yes, but it is more expensive. My present neighbor plays piano all night long.
    Q: Why is the woman moving?

54. W: Mr. Jones, your student, Bill, shows great enthusiasm for music instruments.
    M: I only wish he showed half as much for his English lessons.
    Q: What do we learn from the conversation about Bill?

55. W: Oh, dear! I'm starving, I can't walk any farther.

    M: Let's go to the restaurant across the street and get something to eat.

    Q: Where are the two people?

56. W: Why didn't you make an appointment to see the doctor last week when you first twisted your ankle?

    M: The injury didn't seem serious then. I decided to go today, because my foot still hurt when I put my weight on it.

    Q: Why didn't the man see the doctor earlier?

57. M: I wonder if Suzy will be here by 5 o'clock.

    W: Her husband said she left home at 4:30. She should be here at 5:10, and 5:15 at the latest.

    Q: What time did Suzy leave home?

58. W: When will you be through with your work, John?

    M: Who knows? My boss usually finds something for me to do at the last minute.

    Q: What do we learn from the conversation?

59. W: I don't know what I'm going to wear to the party. All of my clothes look so old and I can't afford something new.

    M: Why don't you wear your black silk dress?

    Q: What is the woman going to do?

60. M: How did you like yesterday's play?

    W: Generally speaking, it was quite good. The part of secretary was played wonderfully, but I think the man who played the boss was too dramatic to be realistic.

    Q: How does the woman feel about the man's acting in the play?

61. M: I ran into our friend Mark yesterday on the street, and he said he hadn't heard from you in two months.

    W: Yes, I know. But I've been too busy to phone him.

    Q: What can be inferred from the conversation?

62. M: Mr. Brown asked me to tell you that he's sorry he can't come to meet you in person. He's really too busy to make the trip.

    W: That's okay. I'm glad you've come in his place.

    Q: What do we learn from the conversation?

63. M: So, when are the other guys going to get here? The train is leaving in 10 minutes. We can't wait here forever!

    W: It's 10:30 already? They are supposed to be here by now! I told everybody to meet here by 10:15.

    Q: When is the train leaving?

64. W: So you've finally listened to your wife's advice and given up smoking?

    M: It was my doctor's advice. I'm suffering from high blood pressure.

    Q: What do we learn from the conversation?

65. W: Frank, I thought you were working in New York.
    M: I was, but I've moved back. I just couldn't get used to living in a big city, so here I am back in school taking courses for a teacher's certificate.
    Q: What is Frank planning to do?

66. M: Washing dishes at the restaurant every day is really boring.
    W: Why don't you quit and deliver flowers for me?
    Q: What does the woman advise the man to do?

67. M: Can I borrow your math textbook? I lost mine on the bus.
    W: You've asked the right person. I happen to have an extra copy.
    Q: What does the woman mean?

68. W: Hello, this is Dr. Gray's office. We're calling to remind you of your 4:15 appointment for your annual checkup tomorrow.
    M: Oh, thanks. It's a good thing you called. I thought it was 4:15 today.
    Q: What do we learn from the conversation?

69. W: I just can't believe this is our last year. College is going by fast.
    M: Yeah. We'll have to face the real world soon. So, have you figured out what you're going to do after you graduate?
    Q: What do we learn from the conversation?

70. M: I had a hard time getting through this novel.
    W: I share your feeling. Who can remember the names of 35 different characters?
    Q: What does the woman imply?

71. M: Boating and skating are my favorite sports.
    W: I like swimming but not boating or skating.
    Q: Which sport does the woman like?

72. W: Have you finished reading my research report? I put it on your desk last week.
    M: Yes, but you have to revise some parts of it, I'm afraid, if you want to get it published.
    Q: What does the man suggest that the woman should do?

73. M: Hi, Susan. I hear that you walk all the way to the office these days.
    W: Yes. I have found great pleasure in walking. That's the type of exercise I enjoy very much.
    Q: Why does the woman walk all the way to the office?

74. M: How about the food I ordered? I've been waiting for twenty minutes already.
    W: I'm very sorry, sir. I'll be back with your order in a minute.
    Q: What's the woman's job?

75. W: Excuse me, sir. I'm going to send this parcel to London. What's the postage for it?
    M: Let me see. It's one pound and fifty.
    Q: Who is the woman most probably speaking to?

76. M: I think it's high time we turned our attention to the danger of drunk driving now.
    W: I can't agree with you more. You see, countless innocent people are killed by drunk drivers each year.
    Q: What does the woman mean?

77. W: Here's a ten-dollar bill. Give me two tickets for tonight's show, please.

   M: Sure. Two tickets and here's a dollar forty cents change.

   Q: How much does one ticket cost?

78. M: Are you sure you've corrected all the typing errors in this paper?

   W: Perhaps I'd better read it through again.

   Q: What's the woman going to do?

79. M: Mary, would you like to go to the movies with me after dinner?

   W: Well, I'll go if you really want me to, but I'm rather tired.

   Q: What can we conclude from this conversation?

80. M: If I were you, I'd ride a bike to work. Taking a crowded bus during rush hours is really terrible.

   W: Thank you for your advice, but my bike has got a flat tyre.

   Q: How would the woman most probably get to work?

短对话答案

1. C) Wait patiently.
2. B) She hasn't got a job yet.
3. D) She was delayed.
4. B) She likes to take long camping trips.
5. C) A reporter.
6. D) She does not know Prof. Johnson's brother.
7. A) Coming back for a later show.
8. B) He has unharmed.
9. A) The man went to Australia during Christmas.
10. A) To attend a party at a classmate's home.
11. C) Go to another hotel by bus.
12. B) The man has a house for sale.
13. A) In a hotel.
14. D) Neighbours.
15. B) 5:15.
16. D) he doesn't need as much sleep as his wife.
17. A) A student.
18. C) To the post office.
19. D) It's not certain whether the trip will take place.
20. C) It was touching.
21. B) There aren't any tickets left for tonight's show.
22. C) Love stories.
23. B) It was not as easy as she had thought.
24. C) To arrange an appointment for him with the director.
25. D) Margaret wanted to get some magazines back from the woman.

26. B) He enjoys it very much.
27. D) They'll be flying somewhere for their vacation.
28. A) Something went wrong with the bus.
29. C) Wash clothes.
30. A) The man is looking for a place to live in.
31. A) They are twins.
32. B) The man has not been to Austin before.
33. C) The hot weather.
34. D) The man can't manage to go to New York as planned.
35. B) It has been misplaced.
36. C) Reserving a table.
37. A) Cold and windy.
38. A) It is no longer available.
39. B) Someone else painted the house.
40. D) On a train.
41. C) She would like to have a copy of the article.
42. C) He has visited the TV tower once.
43. B) The woman regrets having taken up much of the professor's time.
44. D) He wants to spend more time with his family.
45. B) They both had a hard time writing the essay.
46. D) Under a huge tree.
47. A) It's awfully dull.
48. C) A play.
49. D) The weather may get even colder.
50. D) An unsolved case of robbery.
51. C) A student and his classmate.
52. D) Tony had expected the experiment to be easier.
53. A) She can't put up with the noise.
54. A) He is not very enthusiastic about his English lessons.
55. D) On the street.
56. B) He didn't think it necessary.
57. C) 4:30.
58. B) The man is complaining.
59. C) Attend a party.
60. D) He exaggerated his part.
61. D) Mark and the woman had not been in touch for some time.
62. C) The man is meeting the woman on behalf of Mr. Brown.
63. C) At 10:40.
64. A) The man no longer smokes.
65. B) Become a teacher.

66. D) Leave his job to work for her.
67. B) She can help the man out.
68. A) The man was confused about the date of the appointment.
69. C) The two speakers are seniors at college.
70. B) She also found the plot difficult to follow.
71. B) Swimming.
72. C) Improve some parts of her paper.
73. A) She takes it as a kind of exercise.
74. C) A waitress.
75. D) A postal clerk.
76. D) People should pay more attention to the danger of drunk driving.
77. B) $4.30.
78. C) Check the paper for typing errors.
79. A) The woman does not want to go to the movies.
80. A) By bus.

长对话

Directions: *There are ten long conversations in this section. Listen to each conversation twice and choose the best answers from the four choices marked A, B, C and D.*

Questions 1 to 4 are based on the conversation you have just heard.

1. A) A notice by the electricity board.
   B) Ads promoting electric appliances.
   C) The description of a thief in disguise.
   D) A new policy on pensioners' welfare.
2. A) Speaking with a proper accent.
   B) Wearing an official uniform.
   C) Making friends with them.
   D) Showing them his ID.
3. A) To be on the alert when being followed.
   B) Not to leave senior citizens alone at home.
   C) Not to let anyone in without an appointment.
   D) To watch out for those from the electricity board.
4. A) She was robbed near the parking lot.
   B) All her money in the bank disappeared.
   C) The pension she had just drawn was stolen.
   D) She was knocked down in the post office.

Questions 5 to 7 are based on the conversation you have just heard.

5. A) Marketing consultancy.
   B) Professional accountancy.
   C) Luxury hotel management.
   D) Business conference organization.
6. A) Having a good knowledge of its customs.
   B) Knowing some key people in tourism.
   C) Having been to the country before.
   D) Being able to speak Japanese.
7. A) It will bring her potential into full play.
   B) It will involve lots of train travel.
   C) It will enable her to improve her Chinese.
   D) It will give her more chances to visit Japan.

Questions 8 to 11 are based on the conversation you have just heard.

8. A) He prefers the smaller evening classes.
   B) He has signed up for a day course.
   C) He has to work during the day.
   D) He finds the evening course cheaper.
9. A) Learn a computer language.
   B) Learn data processing.
   C) Buy some computer software.
   D) Buy a few course books.
10. A) Thursday evening, from 7:00 to 9:45.
    B) From September 1 to New Year's eve.
    C) Every Monday, lasting for 12 weeks.
    D) Three hours a week, 45 hours in total.
11. A) What to bring for registration.
    B) Where to attend the class.
    C) How he can get to Frost Hall.
    D) Whether he can use a check.

Questions 12 to 14 are based on the conversation you have just heard.

12. A training coach.
    B) A trading adviser.
    C) A professional manager.
    D) A financial trader.
13. A) He can save on living expenses.
    B) He considers cooking creative.

C) He can enjoy healthier food.

   D) He thinks take-away is tasteless.

14. A) It is something inevitable.

   B) It is frustrating sometimes.

   C) It takes patience to manage.

   D) It can be a good thing.

Questions 15 to 18 are based on the conversation you have just heard.

15. A) The hotel clerk had put his reservation under another name.

   B) The hotel clerk insisted that he didn't make any reservation.

   C) The hotel clerk tried to take advantage of his inexperience.

   D) The hotel clerk couldn't find his reservation for that night.

16. A) A grand wedding was being held in the hotel.

   B) There was a conference going on in the city.

   C) The hotel was undergoing major repairs.

   D) It was a busy season for holiday-makers.

17. A) It was free of charge on weekends.

   B) It had a 15% discount on weekdays.

   C) It was offered to frequent guests only.

   D) It was 10% cheaper than in other hotels.

18. A) Demand compensation from the hotel.

   B) Ask for an additional discount.

   C) Complain to the hotel manager.

   D) Find a cheaper room in another hotel.

Questions 19 to 21 are based on the conversation you have just heard.

19. A) To make a business report to the woman.

   B) To be interviewed for a job in the woman's company.

   C) To resign from his position in the woman's company.

   D) To exchange stock market information with the woman.

20. A) He is head of a small treading company.

   B) He works in an international insurance company.

   C) He leads s team of brokers in a big company.

   D) He is a public relations officer in a small company.

21. A) The woman thinks Mr. Saunders is asking for more than they can offer.

   B) Mr. Saunders will share one third of the woman's responsibilities.

   C) Mr. Saunders believes that he deserves more paid vacations.

   D) The woman seems to be satisfied with Mr. Saunders' past experience.

Questions 22 to 25 are based on the conversation you have just heard.

22. A) She's worried about the seminar.
    B) The man keeps interrupting her.
    C) She finds it too hard.
    D) She lacks interest in it.
23. A) The lecturers are boring.
    B) The course is poorly designed.
    C) She prefers Philosophy to English.
    D) She enjoys literature more.
24. A) Karen's friend.
    B) Karen's parents.
    C) Karen's lecturers.
    D) Karen's herself.
25. A) Changing her major.
    B) Spending less of her parents' money.
    C) Getting transferred to the English Department.
    D) Leaving the university.

Questions 26 to 28 are based on the conversation you have just heard.

26. A) An employee in the city council at Birmingham.
    B) Assistant Director of the Admissions Office.
    C) Head of the Overseas Students Office.
    D) Secretary of Birmingham Medical School.
27. A) Nearly fifty percent are foreigners.
    B) About fifteen percent are from Africa.
    C) A large majority are from Latin America.
    D) A small number are from the Far East.
28. A) She will have more contact with students.
    B) It will bring her capability into fuller play.
    C) She will be more involved in policy-making.
    D) It will be less demanding than her present job.

Questions 29 to 32 are based on the conversation you have just heard.

29. A) Journalist of a local newspaper.
    B) Director of evening radio programs.
    C) Producer of television commercials.
    D) Hostess of the weekly "Business World."
30. A) He ran three restaurants with his wife's help.
    B) He and his wife did everything by themselves.

C) He worked both as a cook and a waiter.

D) He hired a cook and two local waitresses.

31. A) He hardly needs to do any advertising nowadays.

B) He advertises a lot on radio and in newspapers.

C) He spends huge sums on TV commercials every year.

D) He hires children to distribute ads in shopping centers.

32. A) The restaurant location.

B) The restaurant atmosphere.

C) The food variety.

D) The food price.

Questions 33 to 35 are based on the conversation you have just heard.

33. A) She was a bank manager.

B) She was a victim of the robbery.

C) She was a defence lawyer.

D) She was a witness to the crime.

34. A) A tall man with dark hair and a moustache.

B) A youth with a distinguishing mark on his face.

C) A thirty-year-old guy wearing a light sweater.

D) A medium-sized young man carrying a gun.

35. A) Identify the suspect from pictures.

B) Go upstairs to sign some document.

C) Have her photo taken for their files.

D) Verify the record of what she had said.

长对话原文

Long conversation 1:

W: Gosh! Have you seen this, Richard?

M: See what?

W: In the paper. It says, there is a man going around pretending he's from the electricity board. He's been calling at people's homes, saying he is coming to check that all their appliances are safe. Then he gets around them to make him a cup of tea, and while they are out of the room he steals their money, handbag whatever and makes off with it.

M: But you know, Jane, it's partly their own fault; you should never let anyone like that in unless you're expecting them.

W: It's all very well to say that. But someone comes to the door, and says electricity or gas and you automatically think they are OK, especially if they flash a card to you.

M: Does this man have an ID then?

W: Yes, that's just it. It seems he used to work for the electricity board at one time according to the paper. The police are warning people especially pensioners not to admit anyone unless they have an appointment. It's a bit sad. One old lady told them she'd just been to the post-office to draw her pension when he called. She said he must have followed her home. He stole the whole lot.

M: But what does he look like? Surely they must have a description.

W: Oh, yes they have. Let's see, in his thirties, tall, bushy dark hair, slight northern accent, sounds a bit like you actually.

Questions 1 to 4 are based on the conversation you have just heard.

1. What does the woman want the man to read in the newspaper?
2. How did the man mentioned in the newspaper try to win further trust from the victims?
3. What is the warning from the police?
4. What does the woman speaker tell us about the old lady?

Long conversation 2

M: Miss Jones, could you tell me more about your first job with hotel marketing concept?

W: Yes, certainly. I was a marketing consultant responsible for marketing 10 UK hotels. They were all luxury hotels in a leisure sector all of a very high standard.

M: Which markets were you responsible for?

W: For Europe and Japan.

M: I see from your resume that you speak Japanese. Have you ever been to Japan?

W: Yes, I have. I spent months in Japan 2006. I met all the key people in the tourist industry, the big tour operators and the tourist organizations. As I speak Japanese I had a very big advantage.

M: Yes, of course. Have you had any contact with Japan in your present job?

W: Yes, I've had a lot. Cruises have become very popular with the Japanese both for holidays and for business conferences. In fact, the market for all types of luxury holidays for the Japanese has increased a lot recently.

M: Really, I'm interested to hear more about that, but first tell me have you ever traveled on the luxury train, the Orient Express, for example?

W: No, I haven't. But I've traveled on the Glacial Express through Switzerland and I traveled across China by train about 8 years ago. I love train travel. That's why I'm very interested in this job.

Questions 5 to 7 are based on the conversation you have just heard.

5. What did the woman do in her first job?
6. What gave the woman an advantage during her business trip in Japan?
7. Why is the woman applying for the new job?

Long conversation 3:

W: Hello, Parkson College. May I help you?

M: Yes. I'm looking for information on courses in computer programming. I would need it for the fall semester.

W: Do you want a day or evening course?

M: Well, it would have to be an evening course since I work during the day.

W: Aha. Have you taken any courses in data processing?

M: No.

W: Oh! Well, data processing is a course you have to take before you can take computer programming.

M: Oh, I see. Well, when is it given? I hope it is not on Thursdays.

W: Well, there's a class that meets on Monday evenings at 7.

M: Just once a week?

W: Yes. But that's almost 3 hours from 7 to 9:45.

M: Oh! Well, that's alright. I could manage that. How many weeks does the course last?

W: Mm, let me see. 12 weeks. You start the first week in September, and finish, oh, just before Christmas. December 21st.

M: And how much is the course?

W: That's 300 dollars including the necessary computer time.

M: Ah-hum. Okay, Eh, where do I go to register?

W: Registration is on the second and third of September between 6 and 9 in Frost Hall.

M: Is that the round building behind the parking lot?

W: Yes, that's the one.

M: Oh, I know how to get there. Is there anything that I should bring with me?

W: No, just your checkbook.

M: Well, thank you very much.

W: You're very welcome. Bye!

M: Bye!

Questions 8 to 11 are based on the conversation you have just heard.

8. Why does the man choose to take an evening course?
9. What does the man have to do before taking the course of computer programming?
10. What do we learn about the schedule of the evening course?
11. What does the man want to know at the end of the conversation?

Long conversation 4:

W: So, why exactly does your job have a reputation for being stressful?

M: Stress is generally driven by the feeling of being out of control of a situation and the feeling of a situation controlling you. Trading in financial markets combines both.

W: How do you relax in the evening?

M: I very rarely do anything work-related so it's easy to escape the markets. I generally go to the gym or go for a run, especially if I've had a bad day. I always cook a meal rather than have a take-away. To do something my brain would regard as creative.

W: Do you think what you do for relaxation is an effective way to beat stress?

M: I don't think there is a specific rule about how to beat stress. I generally find out what I do is effective for me.

W: Would you consider changing your job because of the high stress factor?

M: I have considered leaving my job due to stress-related factors. However, I do think that an element of stress is a good thing, and if used the right way, it can actually be a positive thing.

W: What do you enjoy about the stressful aspects of your job?

M: Having said all that, I do actually enjoy an element of uncertainty. I enjoy a mental challenge. Trading generates a wide range of emotions second by second. How you deal with and manage those emotions dictates short, medium and long term trading performance and success.

Questions 12 to 14 are based on the conversation you have just heard.

12: What is the man's job?

13: Why does the man prefer to cook a meal rather than have a take-away?

14: What does the man say about an element of stress in his job?

Long conversation 5:

M: Hello, I have a reservation for tonight.

W: Your name, please.

M: Nelson, Charles Nelson.

W: Ok, Mr. Nelson. That's a room for five and...

M: But excuse me, you mean a room for five pounds? I didn't know the special was so good.

W: No, no, no ··· according to our records, a room for 5 guests was booked under your name.

M: No, no··· hold on. You must have two guests under the name.

W: Ok, let me check this again. Oh, here we are.

M: Yeah?

W: Charles Nelson, a room for one for the 19th...

M: Wait, wait. It's for tonight, not tomorrow night.

W: Em..., I don't think we have any rooms for tonight. There's a conference going on in town and...er, let's see...yeah, no rooms.

M: Oh, come on! You must have something, anything!

W: Well, let...let me check my computer here...Ah!

M: What?

W: There has been a cancellation for this evening. A honeymoon suite is now available.

M: Great, I'll take it.

W: But, I'll have to charge you 150 pounds for the night.

M: What? I should have a discount for the inconvenience!

W: Well, the best I can give you is a 10% discount plus a ticket for a free continental at breakfast.

M: Hey, isn't the breakfast free anyway?

W: Well, only on weekends.

M: I want to talk to the manager.

W: Wait, wait, wait...Mr. Nelson, I think I can give you an additional 15% discount...

Questions 15 to 18 are based on the conversation you've just heard.

15. What's the man's problem?

16. Why did the hotel clerk say they didn't have any rooms for that night?

17. What did the clerk say about the breakfast in the hotel?

18. What did the man imply he would do at the end of the conversation?

Long conversation 6:

W: Please have a seat, Mr. Thunders. I received your resume last week, and was very impressed.

M: Thank you!

W: We are a small financial company trading mostly stocks and bonds. May I ask you why you are interested in working for us?

M: Your company has an impressive reputation and I always want to work for a smaller company.

W: That's good to hear. Would you mind telling me a little bit about your present job?

M: I'm currently working in a large international company in charge of a team of 8 brokers. We buy and sell stocks for major clients worldwide.

W: Why do you think you are the right candidate for this position?

M: As a head broker, I have a lot of experience in the stock market, I deal with the clients on the daily bases, and I enjoy working with people.

W: Well, you might just be the person we've been looking for. Do you have any questions?

M: Uh-hum, if I were hired, how many accounts would I be handling?

W: You will be working with two other head brokers, in another words, you will be handling about a third of our clients.

M: And who would I report to?

W: Directly to me.

M: I see. What kind of benefits package do you offer?

W: Two weeks of paid vacation in your first year employment. You are also been entitled to medical and dental insurance, but this is something you should discuss with our Personnel Department. Do you have any other questions?

M: No, not at the moment.

W: Well, I have to discuss your application with my colleagues and we'll get back to you early next week.

M: OK, thanks, it's been nice meeting you!

W: Nice meeting you too! And thanks for coming in today.

Questions 19 to 21 are based on the conversation you have just heard.

19. What's the purpose of Mr. Thunders' visit?
20. What is Mr. Thunders' current job?
21. What can we conclude from the conversation?

Long conversation 7:

M: Hey, Karen, you are not really reading it, are you?

W: Pardon?

M: The book! You haven't turned the page in the last ten minutes.

W: No, Jim, I suppose I haven't. I need to get through although, but I keep drifting away.

M: So it doesn't really hold your interest?

W: No, not really. I wouldn't bother with it, to be honest, but I have to read it for a seminar. I'm at the university.

M: It's a labor of labor then rather than a labor of love.

W: I should say, I don't like Dickens at all really, the author, indeed, I am starting to like the whole course less and less.

M: It's not just the book, it's the course as well?

W: Yeah, in a way, although the course itself isn't really that bad, a lot of it is pretty good, in fact, and the lecturers are fine. It's me, I suppose. You see, I wanted to do philosophy rather than English, but my parents took me out of it.

M: So the course is OK as such. It's just that hadn't been left to you. You would have chosen a different one.

W: Oh, they had my best interest at heart, of course, my parents. They always do, don't they? They believe that my job prospects would be pretty limited with the degree of philosophy. Plus they give me a really generous allowance, but I am beginning to feel that I'm wasting my time and their money. They would be so disappointed though if I told them I was quitting.

Questions 22 to 25 are based on the conversation you have just heard.

22. Why can't Karen concentrate on the book?
23. Why is Karen starting to like the course less and less?
24. Who thinks philosophy graduates have limited job opportunities?
25. What is Karen thinking of doing?

Long conversation 8:

M: Sarah, you work in the admissions office, don't you?

W: Yes, I'm...I've been here ten years as an assistant director.

M: Really? What does that involve?

W: Well, I'm in charge of all the admissions of postgraduate students in the university.

M: Only postgraduates?

W: Yes, postgraduates only. I have nothing at all to do with undergraduates.

M: Do you find that you get particular...sort of...different national groups? I mean, do you get large numbers from Latin America or...

W: Yes. Well, of all the students enrolled last year, neary half were from overseas. They were from African countries, the Far East, the Middle East, and Latin America.

M: Em. But have you been doing just that for the last 10 years, or, have you done other things?

W: Well, I've been doing the same job. Er, before that, I was secretary of the medical school at Birmingham; and further back, I worked in the local government.

M: Oh, I see.

W: So I've done different types of things.

M: Yes, indeed. How do you imagine your job might develop in the future? Can you imagine shifting into a different kind of responsibility or doing something...

W: Oh, yeah, from October 1, I'll be doing an entirely different job. There's going to be more committee work. I mean, more policy work, and less dealing with students, unfortunately...I'll miss my contact with students.

Questions 26 to 28 are based on the conversation you've just heard:

26. What is the woman's present position?
27. What do we learn about the postgraduates enrolled last year in the woman's university?
28. What will the woman's new job be like?

Long conversation 9:

W: Good evening and welcome to this week's Business World, a programs for and about business people. Tonight we have Mr. Angelino who came to the United States six years ago, and is now an established businessman with three restaurants in town. Tell us, Mr. Angelino, how did you get started?

M: Well, I started off with a small diner. I did all the cooking myself and my wife waited on tables. It was really too much work for two people. My cooking's great. And word got around town about the food. Within a year, I had to hire another cook and four waitresses. When that restaurant became very busy, I decided to expand my business. Now with three places, my main concern is keeping the business successful and running smoothly.

W: Do you advertise?

M: Oh yes. I don't have any TV commercials, because they are too expensive. But I advertise a lot on radio and in local newspapers. My children used to distribute ads in nearby shopping centers, but we don't need to do that anymore.

W: Why do you believe you've been so successful?

M: Um, I always serve the freshest possible food and I make the atmosphere as comfortable and as pleasant as I can, so that my customers will want to come back.

W: So you always aim to please the customers?

M: Absolutely! Without them I would have no business at all.

W: Thank you, Mr. Angelino. I think your advice will be helpful to those just staring out in business.

Questions 29 to 32 are based on the conversation you've just heard:

29. What is the woman's occupation?
30. What do we learn about Mr. Angelino's business at its beginning?
31. What does Mr. Angelino say about advertising his business?
32. What does the man say contribute to the success of his business?

Long conversation 10:

M: Mrs. Dawson, thanks very much for coming down to the station. I just like to go over some of the things that you told police officer Parmer at the bank.

W: All right.

M: Well, could you describe the man who robbed the bank for this report that we're filling out here? Now, anything at all that you can remember would be extremely helpful to us.

W: Well, just, I can only remember basically what I said before.

M: That's all right.

W: The man was tall, six foot, and he had dark hair, and he had moustache.

M: Very good. All right, did he have any other distinguishing marks?

W: Um, no, none that I can remember.

M: Do you remember how old he was by any chance?

W: Well, I guess around 30, maybe younger, give or take a few years.

M: Mm, all right. Do you remember anything about what he was wearing?

W: Yes, yes, he had on a dark sweater, a solid color.

M: OK. Um, anything else that strikes you at the moment?

W: I remember he was wearing a light shirt under the sweater. Yes, yes.

M: All right. Mrs. Dawson, I really appreciate what you've been through today. I'm just going to ask you to look at some photographs before you leave if you don't mind. It won't take very long. Can you do that for me?

W: Oh, of course.

M: Would you like to step this way with me, please?

W: OK, sure.

M: Thank you.

Questions 33 to 35 are based on the conversation you have just heard.

33. What do we learn about the woman?
34. What did the suspect look like?
35. What did the man finally ask the woman to do?

长对话答案

1. C) The description of a thief in disguise.
2. D) Showing them his ID.
3. C) Not to let anyone in without an appointment.
4. C) The pension she had just drawn was stolen.
5. A) Marketing consultancy.
6. D) Being able to speak Japanese.
7. B) It will involve lots of train travel.
8. C) He has to work during the day.
9. B) Learn data processing.
10. C) Every Monday, lasting for 12 weeks.
11. A) What to bring for registration.
12. D) A financial trader.
13. B) He considers cooking creative.
14. D) It can be a good thing.
15. A) The hotel clerk had put his reservation under another name.
16. B) There was a conference going on in the city.
17. A) It was free of charge on weekends.
18. C) Complain to the hotel manager.
19. B) To be interviewed for a job in the woman's company.
20. C) He leads s team of brokers in a big company.
21. D) The woman seems to be satisfied with Mr.Saunders' past experience.
22. D) She lacks interest in it.
23. C) She prefers Philosophy to English.
24. B) Karen's parents.
25. A) Changing her major.
26. B) Assistant Director of the Admissions Office.
27. A) Nearly fifty percent are foreigners.
28. C) She will be more involved in policy-making.
29. D) Hostess of the weekly "Business World."
30. B) He and his wife did everything by themselves.
31. B) He advertises a lot on radio and in newspapers.
32. B) The restaurant atmosphere.
33. D) She was a witness to the crime.
34. A) A tall man with dark hair and a moustache.
35. A) Identify the suspect from pictures.

听力技能与训练

复合式听力

Directions: There are ten passages in this section. Listen to each passage three times and fill in the blanks according to what you hear.

Passage 1

Very few people can get a college degree before 11, but Michael was an exception. He started high school when he was 5, finishing in just nine months. He became the (1) _____ youngest college graduate when he was 10 years and 4 months old, earning an (2) _____ degree. Now at 11 Michael's working on a master's degree in (3) _____ intelligence. But Michael's (4) _____ hasn't always come easy. (5) _____ his intelligence, he still lacks important life (6) _____. In one class, he had to struggle to understand (7) _____ novels, because, he says, "I'm 11. I've never been in love before." Another challenge was his size. In high school physical education was difficult, because all of the (8) _____ was too big for the then five-year-old student. He likes computers so much that in (9) _____ he's studying how to make them think like people. He wants to make robots do all the heavy tasks. Michael is smart, but he is like (10) _____ kid.

Passage 2

If you are a young college student, most of your concerns about your health and happiness in life are probably (1) _____ on the present. Basically, you want to feel good physically, mentally, and (2) _____ now. You probably don't spend much time worrying about the (3) _____ future, such as whether you will develop heart disease, or (4) _____, how you will take care of yourself in your (5) _____ years, or how long you are going to live. Such thoughts may have (6) _____ your mind once in a while however, if you are in your thirties, forties, fifties, or older, such health related thoughts are likely to become (7) _____ important to you. (8) _____ your age, you can make a number of important changes in your current lifestyle that will help you feel better physically and mentally. Recently researchers have found that, even in late adulthood, exercise, strength training with weights, and better food can help elderly individuals significantly improve their health and add happiness to their life. We know much more about (9) _____ health today than our parents and grandparents did in the past, giving us the opportunity to avoid some of health problems that have troubled them. And these new knowledge can (10) _____ our children to help them become healthier than our generation.

Passage 3

In police work, you can never (1) _____ the next crime or problem. No working day is (2) _____ to any other, so there is no "typical" day for a police officer. Some days are relatively slow, and the job is boring; other days are so busy that there is no time to eat. I think I can describe police work in one word: (3) _____. Sometimes it is dangerous. One day, for example, I was working (4) _____; that is, I was on the job, but I was wearing normal clothes, not my police uniform. I was trying to catch some robbers who were (5) _____ money from people as they walked down the street. Suddenly, seven bad men (6) _____ at me, one of them had a knife. We got into a fight. Another policeman arrived, and together, we (7) _____ three of them; but the other four (8) _____. Another day, I helped a woman who was going to have a baby. She was trying to get to the hospital, but there was a bad (9) _____. I put her in my police car to get there faster. I thought she was going to have the baby right there in my car. But (10) _____, the baby waited to arrive until we got to the hospital.

Passage 4

Last summer Tom and his friends George and Bill wanted to take a vacation, but they did not have much money. They decided that a short (1) _____ expedition was the only trip they could (2) _____. Since each of them was (3) _____ climbing, the vacation would be a lot of fun. Tom made all the plans. He decided that they should (4) _____ the expenses for food and gas equally and that each one should bring some (5) _____ clothes because the weather at high (6) _____ is usually cold. The boys were not in a hurry, so they climbed (7) _____ the first day. The weather was pleasant, and they enjoyed the fresh air as they (8) _____ a narrow path.

Tom expected the weather to stay nice, but late in the afternoon there was a storm. The boys rushed toward a cave and decided to camp there that night. When the sun rose the next morning, they (9) _____. As the boys went higher, the climbing became more dangerous, and by late that afternoon the trip (10) _____ endless. When they finally reached the top of the mountain, they saw a beautiful sight. The colors of the sunset were yellow, red, and gold. The boys relaxed and enjoyed the view.

Passage 5

In the past, American families tended to be quite large. Parents raising five or more children were common. Over the years the size of the family has (1) _____. One reason for this is an increase in the cost of living. (2) _____, children attend schools for more years than they used to, making them financially (3) _____ on their families longer. Moreover, children nowadays are better dressed and have more money to spend on (4) _____. The parents usually take the responsibility for all the expenses.

Meanwhile, families are (5) _____ than they used to be. More and more American mothers work away from home. The break-up of the family occurs when the parents divorce. A lot of children in the U.S. live part of their young lives with only one parent. Broken families usually (6) _____ problems for children and parents alike. Children blame them when their parents separate. They grow up feeling (7) _____ as they are moved back and forth between parents.

Usually one parent takes the (8) _____ for raising the children. These single parents must (9) _____ the children's emotional and psychological needs while also supporting them financially. This is very (10) _____ and leaves very little time for the parent's own personal interests. Single parents often marry other single parents. In this type of family, unrelated children are forced to develop brother or sister relationship.

Passage 6

The Library of Congress is America's national library. It has millions of books and other objects. It has newspapers and popular publications, (1) _____ letters of historical interest. It also has maps, photographs, art (2) _____, movies, sound recordings, and musical (3) _____. All together, it has more than 100 million objects. The Library of Congress is open to the public Monday through Saturday (4) _____ public holidays. Anyone may go there and read anything in the collection. But no one is (5) _____ to take books out of the building. The Library of Congress was established in 1800. It started with 11 boxes of books in one room of the Capitol Building. By 1814, the collection had increased to about 3,000 books. They were all destroyed that year, when the Capitol was (6) _____ during America's war with Britain. To help rebuild the library, Congress bought the books of President Thomas Jefferson. Mr. Jefferson's collection included 7,000 books in seven languages. In 1897, the library (7) _____ its own building across the street from the Capitol. Today, three buildings hold the library's collection. The library provides books and materials to the U.S. Congress and also lends books to other American libraries, government (8) _____, and foreign libraries. It buys some of its books and gets others as gifts. It also gets materials through its (9) _____ office. Anyone who wants copyright (10) _____ for a publication in the U.S. must send two copies to the library. This means the Library of Congress receives almost everything that is published in the United States.

Passage 7

A new study reports the common drug aspirin greatly reduces life (1) _____ problems after an operation to replace (2) _____ blood vessels to the heart. More than 800,000 people around the world have this heart surgery each year. The doctors who (3) _____ the study say giving aspirin to patients soon after the operation could save thousands of lives. People usually take aspirin to control pain and reduce high body (4) _____. Doctors also advise some people to take aspirin to help (5) _____ heart attacks. About 10-15 percent of these heart operations (6) _____ death or damage to the heart or other organs. The new study shows that even a small amount of aspirin reduced such threats. The doctors said the chance of death for patients who took aspirin would fall by 67%. They (7) _____ this was true if the aspirin was given within 48 hours of the operation. The doctors believe aspirin helps (8) _____ patients because it can prevent blood from (9) _____ and blood vessels from being blocked. However, the doctors warned that people who have stomach bleeding or other bad (10) _____ from aspirin should not take it after heart surgery.

Passage 8

One winter day in 1891, a class of training school in Massachusetts, U. S. A, went into the gym for their daily exercises. Since the football (1) _____ had ended, most of the young men felt they were in for a boring time. But their teacher, Jones Nasmith had other ideas. He had been (2) _____ a long time on the new game that would have the (3) _____ of American football. Nasmith showed the men a basket he had hung at the each end of the gym, and explained that they were going to use a round European football. At first everybody tried to throw the ball into the basket (4) _____ where he was standing. "Pass! Pass!" Nasmith kept shouting, (5) _____ his whistle to stop the excited players. Slowly, they began to understand what was wanted of them. The problem with the new game, which was soon called "basketball," was getting the ball (6) _____ the basket. They used ordinary food baskets with (7) _____, and the ball, of course, stayed inside. At first, someone had to climb up every time a basket was (8) _____. It was several years before someone (9) _____ the idea of removing the bottom of the basket and letting the ball (10) _____. There have been many changes in the rules since then, and basketball has become one of the world's most popular sports.

Passage 9

More and more of the world's (1) _____ are living in towns or cities. The speed at which cities are growing in the less developed countries is alarming. Between 1920 and 1960, big cities in developed countries increased two and a half times (2) _____, but in other parts of the world the growth was eight times their size. The (3) _____ size of growth is bad enough, but there are now also very (4) _____ signs of trouble in the (5) _____ of percentages of people living in towns and percentages of people working in industry. During the 19th century, cities grew as a result of the growth of industry. In Europe, the (6) _____ of people living in cities was always smaller than that of the work force working in factories. Now, however, the (7) _____ is almost always true in the newly industrialized world. The percentage of people living in cities is much higher than the percentage working in industry. Without a (8) _____ of people working in industry, these cities cannot pay for their growth. There is not enough money to build adequate houses for the people that live there, (9) _____ the new arrivals. There has been little opportunity to build water supplies or other facilities. So the figures for the growth of towns and cities (10) _____ proportional growth of unemployment and underemployment, a growth in the number of hopeless and despairing parents and starving children.

Passage 10

When couples (1) _____, they usually plan to have children. Sometimes, however, a couple can not have a child of their own. In this case, they may decide to adopt a child. In fact, (2) _____ is very common today. There are about 60 thousand adoptions each year in the United States alone. Some people (3) _____ adopt infants, others adopt older children, some couples adopt children from their own countries, others adopt children from foreign countries. (4) _____, they all adopt children for the same reason — they care about children and want to give their adopted child a happy life.

Most adopted children know that they are adopted. Psychologists and (5) _____ experts generally think this is a good idea. However, many adopted children or adoptees have very little information about their (6) _____ parents. As a matter of fact, it is often very difficult for adoptees to find out about their birth parents because the birth records of most adoptees are usually (7) _____. This information is secret so no one can see it.

Naturally, adopted children have different feelings about their birth parents. Many adoptees want to (8) _____ them, but others do not. The decision to search for birth parents is a difficult one to make. Most adoptees have (9) _____ feelings about finding their biological parents. (10) _____ adoptees do not know about their natural parents, they do know that their adopted parents want them, love them and will care for them.

复合式听力原文

Passage 1

Very few people can get a college degree before 11, but Michael was an exception. He started high school when he was 5, finishing in just nine months. He became the world's youngest college graduate when he was 10 years and 4 months old, earning an architecture degree. Now at 11 Michael's working on a master's degree in artificial intelligence. But Michael's success hasn't always come easy. Despite his intelligence, he still lacks important life experiences. In one class, he had to struggle to understand romantic novels, because, he says, "I'm 11. I've never been in love before." Another challenge was his size. In high school physical education was difficult, because all of the equipment was too big for the then five-year-old student. He likes computers so much that in graduate school he's studying how to make them think like people. He wants to make robots do all the heavy tasks. Michael is smart, but he is like every other kid.

Passage 2

If you are a young college student, most of your concerns about your health and happiness in life are probably focused on the present. Basically, you want to feel good physically, mentally, and emotionally now. You probably don't spend much time worrying about the distant future, such as whether you will develop heart disease, or cancer, how you will take care of yourself in your retirement years, or how long you are going to live. Such thoughts may have crossed your mind once in a while however, if you are in your thirties, forties, fifties, or older, such health related thoughts are likely to become increasingly important to you. Regardless of your age, you can make a number of important changes in your current lifestyle that will help you feel better physically and mentally. Recently researchers have found that, even in late adulthood, exercise, strength training with weights, and better food can help elderly individuals significantly improve their health and add happiness to their life. We know much more about preventive health today than our parents and grandparents did in the past, giving us the opportunity to avoid some of health problems that have troubled them. And these new knowledge can be transmitted to our children to help them become healthier than our generation.

Passage 3

In police work, you can never predict the next crime or problem. No working day is identical to any other, so there is no "typical" day for a police officer. Some days are relatively slow, and the job is boring; other days are so busy that there is no time to eat. I think I can describe police work in one word: variety. Sometimes it is dangerous. One day, for example, I was working undercover; that is, I was on the job, but I was wearing normal clothes, not my police uniform. I was trying to catch some robbers who were stealing money from people as they walked down the street. Suddenly, seven bad men jumped out at me, one of them had a knife. We got into a fight. Another policeman arrived, and together, we arrested three of them; but the other four ran away. Another day, I helped a woman who was going to have a baby. She was trying to get to the hospital, but there was a bad traffic jam. I put her in my police car to get there faster. I thought she was going to have the baby right there in my car. But fortunately, the baby waited to arrive until we got to the hospital.

Passage 4

Last summer Tom and his friends George and Bill wanted to take a vacation, but they did not have much money. They decided that a short mountain climbing expedition was the only trip they could afford. Since each of them was accustomed to climbing, the vacation would be a lot of fun. Tom made all the plans. He decided that they should share the expenses for food and gas equally and that each one should bring some extra clothes because the weather at high altitudes is usually cold. The boys were not in a hurry, so they climbed casually the first day. The weather was pleasant, and they enjoyed the fresh air as they climbed up a narrow path.

Tom expected the weather to stay nice, but late in the afternoon there was a storm. The boys rushed toward a cave and decided to camp there that night. When the sun rose the next morning, they continued climbing. As the boys went higher, the climbing became more dangerous, and by late that afternoon the trip appeared endless. When they finally reached the top of the mountain, they saw a beautiful sight. The colors of the sunset were yellow, red, and gold. The boys relaxed and enjoyed the view.

Passage 5

In the past, American families tended to be quite large. Parents raising five or more children were common. Over the years the size of the family has decreased. One reason for this is an increase in the cost of living. On the average, children attend schools for more years than they used to, making them financially dependent on their families longer. Moreover, children nowadays are better dressed and have more money to spend on entertainment. The parents usually take the responsibility for all the expenses.

Meanwhile, families are less close than they used to be. More and more American mothers work away from home. The break-up of the family occurs when the parents divorce. A lot of children in the U.S. live part of their young lives with only one parent. Broken families usually result in problems for children and parents alike. Children blame them when their parents separate. They grow up feeling unsettled as they are moved back and forth between parents.

Usually one parent takes the responsibility for raising the children. These single parents must care for the children's emotional and psychological needs while also supporting them financially. This is very demanding and leaves very little time for the parent's own personal interests. Single parents often marry other single parents. In this type of family, unrelated children are forced to develop brother or sister relationship.

Passage 6

The Library of Congress is America's national library. It has millions of books and other objects. It has newspapers and popular publications, as well as letters of historical interest. It also has maps, photographs, art prints, movies, sound recordings, and musical instruments. All together, it has more than 100 million objects. The Library of Congress is open to the public Monday through Saturday except for public holidays. Anyone may go there and read anything in the collection. But no one is permitted to take books out of the building. The Library of Congress was established in 1800. It started with 11 boxes of books in one room of the Capitol Building. By 1814, the collection had increased to about 3,000 books. They were all destroyed that year, when the Capitol was burned down during America's war with Britain. To help rebuild the library, Congress bought the books of President Thomas Jefferson. Mr. Jefferson's collection included 7,000 books in seven languages. In 1897, the library moved into its own building across the street from the Capitol. Today, three buildings hold the library's collection. The library provides books and materials to the U.S. Congress and also lends books to other American libraries, government agencies, and foreign libraries. It buys some of its books and gets others as gifts. It also gets materials through its copyright office. Anyone who wants copyright protection for a publication in the U.S. must send two copies to the library. This means the Library of Congress receives almost everything that is published in the United States.

Passage 7

A new study reports the common drug aspirin greatly reduces life threatening problems after an operation to replace blocked blood vessels to the heart. More than 800,000 people around the world have this heart surgery each year. The doctors who carried out the study say giving aspirin to patients soon after the operation could save thousands of lives. People usually take aspirin to control pain and reduce high body temperature. Doctors also advise some people to take aspirin to help prevent heart attacks. About 10-15 percent of these heart operations end in death or damage to the heart or other organs. The new study shows that even a small amount of aspirin reduced such threats. The doctors said the chance of death for patients who took aspirin would fall by 67%. They claimed this was true if the aspirin was given within 48 hours of the operation. The doctors believe aspirin helps heart surgery patients because it can prevent blood from thickening and blood vessels from being blocked. However, the doctors warned that people who have stomach bleeding or other bad reactions from aspirin should not take it after heart surgery.

Passage 8

One winter day in 1891, a class of training school in Massachusetts, U. S. A, went into the gym for their daily exercises. Since the football season had ended, most of the young men felt they were in for a boring time. But their teacher, Jones Nasmith had other ideas. He had been working for a long time on the new game that would have the excitement of American football. Nasmith showed the men a basket he had hung at the each end of the gym, and explained that they were going to use a round European football. At first everybody tried to throw the ball into the basket no matter where he was standing. "Pass! Pass!" Nasmith kept shouting, blowing his whistle to stop the excited players. Slowly, they began to understand what was wanted of them. The problem with the new game, which was soon called "basketball," was getting the ball out of the basket. They used ordinary food baskets with bottoms, and the ball, of course, stayed inside. At first, someone had to climb up every time a basket was scored. It was several years before someone came up with the idea of removing the bottom of the basket and letting the ball fall through. There have been many changes in the rules since then, and basketball has become one of the world's most popular sports.

Passage 9

More and more of the world's population are living in towns or cities. The speed at which cities are growing in the less developed countries is alarming. Between 1920 and 1960, big cities in developed countries increased two and a half times in size, but in other parts of the world, the growth was eight times their size. The sheer size of growth is bad enough, but there are now also very disturbing signs of trouble in the comparison of percentages of people living in towns and percentages of people working in industry. During the 19th century, cities grew as a result of the growth of industry. In Europe, the proportion of people living in cities was always smaller than that of the workforce working in factories. Now, however, the reverse is almost always true in the newly industrialized world. The percentage of people living in cities is much higher than the percentage working in industry. Without a base of people working in industry, these cities cannot pay for their growth. There is not enough money to build adequate houses for the people that live there, let alone the new arrivals. There has been little opportunity to build water supplies or other facilities. So the figures for the growth of towns and cities represent proportional growth of unemployment and underemployment, a growing in the number of hopeless and despairing parents and starving children.

Passage 10

When couples get married, they usually plan to have children. Sometimes, however, a couple can not have a child of their own. In this case, they may decide to adopt a child. In fact, adoption is very common today. There are about 60,000 adoptions each year in the United States alone. Some people prefer to adopt infants. Others adopt older children. Some couples adopt children from their own countries. Others adopt children from foreign countries. In any case, they all adopt children for the same reason. They care about children and want to give their adopted child a happy life.

Most adopted children know that they are adopted. Psychologists and childcare experts generally think this is a good idea. However, many adopted children or adoptees have very little information about their biological parents. As a matter of fact, it is often very difficult for adoptees to find out about their birth parents because the birth records of most adoptees are usually sealed. This information is secret, so no one can see it.

Naturally, adopted children have different feelings about their birth parents. Many adoptees want to search for them, but others do not. The decision to search for birth parents is a difficult one to make. Most adoptees have mixed feelings about finding their biological parents. Even though adoptees do not know about their natural parents, they do know that their adoptive parents want them, love them and will care for them.

复合式听力答案

Passage 1
1. world's
2. architecture
3. artificial
4. success
5. Despite
6. experiences
7. romantic
8. equipment
9. graduate school
10. every other

Passage 2
1. focused
2. emotionally
3. distant
4. cancer
5. retirement
6. crossed
7. increasingly
8. regardless of
9. preventive
10. be transmitted to

Passage 3

1. predict
2. identical
3. variety
4. undercover
5. stealing
6. jumped out
7. arrested
8. ran away
9. traffic jam
10. fortunately

Passage 4

1. mountain climbing
2. afford
3. accustomed to
4. share
5. extra
6. altitudes
7. casually
8. climbed up
9. continued climbing
10. appeared

Passage 5

1. decreased
2. On the average
3. dependent
4. entertainment
5. less close
6. result in
7. unsettled
8. responsibility
9. care for
10. demanding

Passage 6

1. as well as
2. prints
3. instruments

4. except for
5. permitted
6. burned down
7. moved into
8. agencies
9. copyright
10. protection

Passage 7
1. threatening
2. blocked
3. carried out
4. temperature
5. prevent
6. end in
7. claimed
8. heart surgery
9. thickening
10. reactions

Passage 8
1. season
2. working for
3. excitement
4. no matter
5. blowing
6. out of
7. bottoms
8. scored
9. came up with
10. fall through

Passage 9
1. population
2. in size
3. sheer
4. disturbing
5. comparison
6. proportion
7. reverse

8. base
9. let alone
10. represent

Passage 10
1. get married
2. adoption
3. prefer to
4. In any case
5. child-care
6. biological
7. sealed
8. search for
9. mixed
10. Even though

短篇文章

Directions: *There are 15 passages in this section. Listen to each passage three times and answer the following questions according to what you hear.*

Passage 1

Questions 1 to 3 are based on the passage you have just heard.

1. A) He fell into the river but couldn't swim.
   B) He fell into the river together with his bike.
   C) He had his foot caught between two posts in the river.
   D) He dived into the river but couldn't reach the surface.
2. A) He jumped into the river immediately.
   B) He took off his coat and jumped into the water.
   C) He dashed down the bridge to save the boy.
   D) He shouted out for help.
3. A) He asked what the young man's name was.
   B) He asked the young man to take him home.
   C) He gave his name and then ran away.
   D) He thanked the young man and then ran away.

Passage 2

Questions 4 to 6 are based on the passage you have just heard.

4. A) Alcohol helps develop people's intelligence.
   B) Heavy drinking is not necessarily harmful to one's health.
   C) Controlled drinking helps people keep their wits as they are.
   D) Drinking, even moderately, man harms one's health.

5. A) Worried.
   B) Pleased.
   C) Surprised.
   D) Unconcerned.
6. A) At a conference.
   B) In a newspaper.
   C) On television.
   D) In a journal.

Passage 3
Questions 7 to 10 are based on the passage you have just heard.
7. A) To seek adventure there.
   B) To be with her mother on Christmas.
   C) To see the animals and plants there.
   D) To join her father on Christmas.
8. A) She was seriously injured.
   B) She survived the accident.
   C) She lost consciousness.
   D) She fell into a stream.
9. A) To avoid hostile Indians.
   B) To avoid the rain.
   C) To avoid the strong sunlight.
   D) To avoid wild animals.
10. A) They gave Julia food to eat.
    B) They drove Julia to a hospital.
    C) They invited Julia to their hut.
    D) They took Julia to a village by boat.

Passage 4
Questions 11 to 13 are based on the passage you have just heard.
11. A) He wanted to find a place to read his papers.
    B) He wanted to kill time before boarding the plane.
    C) He felt thirsty and wanted some coffee.
    D) He went there to meet his friends.
12. A) Toys for children.
    B) Important documents.
    C) Food and coffee.
    D) Clothes and scientific papers.
13. A) The woman took his case on purpose.
    B) All his papers had been stolen.

C) He had taken the woman's case.

D) The woman played a joke on him.

Passage 5

Questions 14 to 16 are based on the passage you have just heard.

14. A) The liberation movement of British women.

B) Rapid economic development in Britain.

C) Changing attitudes to family life.

D) Reasons for changes in family life in Britain.

15. A) Because millions of men died in the war.

B) Because women had proved their worth.

C) Because women were more skillful than men.

D) Because factories preferred to employ women.

16. A) The concept to "the family" as a social unit.

B) The attitudes to birth control.

C) The attitudes to religion.

D) The ideas of authority and tradition.

Passage 6

Questions 17 to 20 are based on the passage you have just heard.

17. A) Those who are themselves spoiled and self-centered.

B) Those who expected to have several children but could only have one.

C) Those who like to give expensive jewels to their children.

D) Those who give birth to their only children when they are below 30.

18. A) Because their parents want them to share the family burden.

B) Because their parents are too strict with them in their education.

C) Because they have nobody to play with.

D) Because their parents want them to grow up as fast as possible.

19. A) Two types of only children.

B) Parents' responsibilities.

C) The necessity of family planning.

D) The relationship between parents and children.

20. A) They have no sisters or brothers.

B) They are overprotected by their parents.

C) Their parents expect too much of them.

D) Their parents often punish them for minor faults.

Passage 7
Questions 21 to 23 are based on the passage you have just heard.

21. A) They invited him to a party.
    B) They asked him to make a speech.
    C) They gave a special dinner for him.
    D) They invited his wife to attend the dinner.

22. A) He was embarrassed.
    B) He felt greatly encouraged.
    C) He felt sad.
    D) He was deeply touched.

23. A) Sam's wife did not think that the company was fair to Sam.
    B) Sam's wife was satisfied with the gold watch.
    C) Sam did not like the gold watch.
    D) The company had some financial problems.

Passage 8
Questions 24 to 26 are based on the passage you have just heard.

24. A) The number of students they take in is limited.
    B) They receive little or no support from public taxes.
    C) They are only open to children from rich families.
    D) They have to pay more taxes.

25. A) Private schools admit more students.
    B) Private schools charge less than religious schools.
    C) Private schools run a variety of programs.
    D) Private schools allow students to enjoy more freedom.

26. A) The churches.
    B) The program designers.
    C) The local authorities.
    D) The state government.

Passage 9
Questions 27 to 30 are based on the passage you have just heard.

27. A) She was found stealing in a bookstore.
    B) She caught someone in the act of stealing.
    C) She admitted having stolen something.
    D) She said she was wrongly accused of stealing.

28. A) A book.
    B) $3,000.
    C) A handbag.
    D) A Christmas card.

29. A) She was questioned by the police.

   B) She was shut in a small room for 20 minutes.

   C) She was insulted by the shopper around her.

   D) She was body-searched by the store manager.

30. A) They refused to apologize for having followed her through the town.

   B) They regretted having wrongly accused her of stealing.

   C) They still suspected that she was a thief.

   D) They agreed to pay her $3,000 damages.

Passage 10

Questions 31 to 34 are based on the passage you have just heard.

31. A) They want to change the way English is taught.

   B) They learn English to find well paid jobs.

   C) They want to have an up to date knowledge of English.

   D) They know clearly what they want to learn.

32. A) Professionals.

   B) College students.

   C) Beginners.

   D) Intermediate learners.

33. A) Courses for doctors.

   B) Courses for businessmen.

   C) Courses for reporters.

   D) Courses for lawyers.

34. A) Three groups of learners.

   B) The importance of business English.

   C) English for Specific Purposes.

   D) Features of English for different purposes.

Passage 11

Questions 35 to 37 are based on the passage you have just heard.

35. A) To show off their wealth.

   B) To feel good.

   C) To regain their memory.

   D) To be different from others.

36. A) To help solve their psychological problems.

   B) To play games with them.

   C) To send them to the hospital.

   D) To make them aware of its harmfulness.

37. A) They need care and affection.

   B) They are fond of round-the-world trips.

    C) They are mostly from broken families.

    D) They are likely to commit crimes.

Passage 12

Questions 38 to 40 are based on the passage you have just heard.

38. A) Because it was too heavy.

    B) Because it did not bend easily.

    C) Because it did not shoot far.

    D) Because its string was short.

39. A) It went out of use 300 years ago.

    B) It was invented after the short bow.

    C) It was discovered before fire and the wheel.

    D) It's still in use today.

40. A) They are accurate and easy to pull.

    B) Their shooting range is 40 yards.

    C) They are usually used indoors.

    D) They took 100 years to develop.

Passage 13

Questions 41 to 43 are based on the passage you have just heard.

41. A) Because the bird couldn't repeat his master's name.

    B) Because the bird screamed all day long.

    C) Because the bird uttered the wrong word.

    D) Because the bird failed to say the name of the town.

42. A) The cruel master.

    B) The man in the kitchen.

    C) The pet bird.

    D) The fourth chicken.

43. A) The bird had finally understood his threat.

    B) The bird managed to escape from the chicken house.

    C) The bird had learned to scream back at him.

    D) The bird was living peacefully with the chickens.

Passage 14

Questions 44 to 46 are based on the passage you have just heard.

44. A) They are kept in open prisons.

    B) They are allowed out of the prison grounds.

    C) They are ordered to do cooking and cleaning.

    D) They are a small portion of the prison population.

45. A) Some of their prisoners are allowed to study or work outside prisons.
    B) Most of their prisoners are expected to work.
    C) Their prisoners are often sent to special centers for skill training.
    D) Their prisoners are allowed freedom to visit their families.
46. A) They are encouraged to do maintenance for the training centre.
    B) Most of them get paid for their work.
    C) They have to cook their own meals.
    D) They can choose to do community work.

Passage 15

Questions 47 to 50 are based on the passage you have just heard.

47. A) Because they have a driving license.
    B) Because they have received special training.
    C) Because the traffic conditions in London are good.
    D) Because the traffic system of the city is not very complex.
48. A) Two to four months.
    B) About three weeks.
    C) At least half a year.
    D) Two years or more.
49. A) Government officers are hard to please.
    B) The learner has to go through several tough tests.
    C) The learner usually fails several times before he passes it.
    D) The driving test usually lasts two months.
50. A) They don't want their present bosses to know what they're doing.
    B) They want to earn money from both jobs.
    C) They cannot earn money as taxi drivers yet.
    D) They look forward to further promotion.

短篇文章听力原文

Passage 1

　　A young man who refused to give his name dived into the river yesterday morning to save a twelve-year-old boy. The boy ran away after he was rescued. He had been swimming in the river and had caught his foot between two concrete posts under the bridge. He shouted out for help, at the time a young man was riding across the bridge on his bicycle. He quickly got down and dived into the river. He then freed the boy's foot and helped him to the river bank where a small crowd had collected. The boy thanked his rescuer sincerely, then ran off down the road. He was last seen climbing over a gate before disappearing over the top of the hill. The young man who was about 20 years of age said, "I don't blame the boy for not giving his name. Why should he? If he wants to swim in the river, that's his business. And if I wanted to help him, that's mine. You can not have my name either." He then ran back to the bridge, got on his bicycle and rode away.

Questions 1 to 3 are based on the passage you have just heard.

1. What happened to the 12-year-old boy?
2. What did the young man do when he saw the boy in danger?
3. What did the little boy do after he was rescued?

Passage 2

Researchers have discovered a link between drinking and thinking. A moderate amount of alcohol may help us keep our mental abilities as we age. Brain scans show alcohol abuse kills brain cells. But little is known about the effects of life-long drinking. So moderate drinkers may want to toast new findings from researchers at Duke and Indiana Universities. Dr. Joe Christian of Indiana Universities says men who have one or two drinks each day retain slightly stronger comprehension skills than the non-drinker or the heavy drinker. The doctor and his colleagues gave mental tests to nearly 4000 male twins between the ages of 66 and 76. The moderate drinkers had slightly better reasoning ability than their brothers who drink more or less. Other studies have found that alcohol in moderation can help the heart. But alcohol abuse can cause bone loss and other health problems. This study was presented at an alcoholism meeting in San Antonio.

Questions 4 to 6 are based on the passage you have heard.

4. What has recent research found about drinking?
5. How would moderate drinkers feel about the new research findings?
6. Where was the result of the study first made public?

Passage 3

On Christmas Eve 1971, Julia Smith was taking a flight in Peru with her mother to join her father, a Professor, who was an expert on the jungle and plants and animals living there. Unfortunately, the plane crashed in a storm. The passengers all died except Julia who only had a few cuts. She was determined to survive. She had no map, only a bag of sweets and her torn clothes. She found a stream and followed it, trying to keep in the shade as much as possible, because she had no hat. For ten days, she walked along the river, eating fruits from the trees. At night she slept near the river bank, on the ground which was wet from the rain. She often felt weak, but she refused to give up. On the 10th day, she arrived at a small hut. The three Indian hunters who visited the hut every two weeks rescued her and took her by boat to a small village from where she was flown to a hospital. She was safe at last.

Questions 7 to 10 are based on the passage you have just heard.

7. Why was Julia taking a flight in Peru?
8. What happened to Julia after the plane crash?
9. Why did Julia try to stay in the shade when she walked along the river?
10. What did the three Indian hunters do?

Passage 4

    I had to go to Amsterdam last week for a conference. I arrived at the airport in plenty of time and checked in, but I only had one small case so I decided to take it on the plane as hand luggage. As the flight was not due to board for 45 minutes, I went to a cafe, sat down, and ordered a cup of coffee.

    While I was sitting there drinking my coffee and reading the paper, I was vaguely aware of a woman and her child coming to sit at the next table. I did not pay much attention to them, though, and when my flight was called I reached for my case and left.

    An hour later, the plane was in the air and I decided to look at the conference program to see what I wanted to attend. Imagine my horror when I opened the case and found that it was full of picture books and children's toys — and imagine what the woman must have thought about a case full of men's clothes and scientific papers!

Questions 11 to 13 are based on the passage you have just heard.

    11. Why did the speaker go to a cafe?
    12. What was in the speaker's case?
    13. What did the speaker find out on board the plane?

Passage 5

    There are many reasons why family life in Britain has changed so much in the last fifty years. The liberation of women in the early part of the twentieth century and the social and economic effects of World War II had a great impact on traditional family life. Women became essential to industry and the professions. During the war they had worked in factories and proved their worth, now, with the loss of millions of men, their services were indispensable to the nation.

    More recently, great advances in scientific knowledge, and particularly in medicine, have had enormous social consequences. Children are better cared for and are far healthier. Infant death rate is low. Above all, parents can now plan the size of their family if they wish through more effective means of birth control.

    Different attitudes to religion, authority and tradition generally have also greatly contributed to changes in family life. But these developments have affected all aspects of society. It is particularly interesting to note that the concept of "the family" as a social unit has survived all these challenges.

Questions 14 to 16 are based on the passage you have just heard.

    14. What is this passage mainly about?
    15. Why did British women become indispensable to industry after World War II?
    16. What remained unchanged in spite of all the challenges in family life?

Passage 6

    The key question for any only child is this: why were you an only child? It's a key question for at least two reasons. If your parents had wanted several children but could have you only, they are most likely to pour into you all the energy and attention that had been intended for several children. I call this the "special jewel" phenomenon. Only children who are special jewels often arrive when their parents are older — usually in their thirties. These special jewels can become very spoiled and self-centered.

On the other hand, you may be an only child because your parents planned for only one and stuck to their plan. Your parents may give you a very strict and well-structured education to make you "a little adult". Many only children grow up feeling unhappy because they always had to be such "little adults".

Questions 17 to 20 are based on the passage you have just heard.

17. Who are likely to treat their only children as "special jewels"?
18. Why do some only children become "little adults"?
19. What does the passage mainly discuss?
20. Why do some only children feel unhappy?

Passage 7

Sam had worked 30 years for the same company and now he had to retire. As a sign of gratitude, the company held a dinner in his honor. "Sam," announced his boss, "It is my great honor to present this gift to you on behalf of the company." Sam walked down to the front of the table and accepted the gift with pride. It was a gold watch and on it was written "To faithful Sam for 30 years of service." Sam wept. "I am at a loss for words." At home, Sam's wife looked at the gold watch critically. "For this you worked 30 years? A cheap gold-plated watch?" "It's the thought, dear." answered Sam. "The important thing is that I am not working any more." His wife held the gold watch to her ear and said: "Neither is your watch."

Questions 21 to 23 are based on the passage you have just heard.

21. What did the company do to honor Sam?
22. How did Sam feel when he saw what was written on the watch?
23. What can we infer from the story?

Passage 8

Religious and private schools receive little or no support from public taxes in the United States. As a result, they are more expensive to attend. The religious schools in America are usually run by churches. Therefore they tend to be less expensive than private schools. When there is free education available to all children in the United States, why do people spend money on private schools? Americans offer a great variety of reasons for doing so. Some parents send their children to private schools because the classes there are usually smaller. In their opinion the public schools in their area are not of high enough quality to meet their needs. Private schools in the United States range widely in size and quality, and they offer all kinds of programs to meet the needs of certain students.

Questions 24 to 26 are based on the passage you have just heard.

24. Why is it usually expensive to attend religious and private schools?

25. What is one of the reasons for people to send their children to private schools?

26. Who usually runs religious schools in the United States?

Passage 9

An elderly woman yesterday made a legal claim against a department store because it had wrongly accused her of stealing a Christmas card. Ms. Doss White, 72 years old, is claiming $3000 damages from the store for wrongful arrest and false imprisonment. Ms. White visited the store while doing Christmas shopping, but did not buy anything. She was followed through the town by a store manager. He had been told that a customer saw her take a card and put it in her shopping bag. He stopped her at a bookstore as she was reading a book. Ms. White said. "This man, a total stranger, suddenly grasped my bag and asked if he could look in it." She was taken back to the store and shut in a small room in full view of shoppers for 20 minutes until the police arrived. At the police station she was body-searched and nothing was found. Her lawyer said the department store sent an insincere apology and they insisted that she may have been stealing. The hearing continues today.

Questions 27 to 30 are based on the passage you have just heard.

27. What does the story tell us about the old woman?

28. What was said to have been stolen?

29. What happened to Ms. White after she was taken back to the store?

30. What was now the attitude of the department store in this legal case?

Passage 10

There are three groups of English learners: beginners, intermediate learners, and learners of special English. Beginners need to learn the basics of English. Students who have reached an intermediate level benefit from learning general English skills. But what about students who want to learn specialist English for their work or professional life? Most students, who fit into this third group, have a clear idea about what they want to learn. A bank clerk, for example, wants to use this specialist vocabulary and technical terms of finance. But for teachers, deciding how to teach specialist English is not always so easy. For a start, the variety is enormous. Every field from airline pilots to secretaries has its own vocabulary and technical terms. Teachers also need to have an up-to-date knowledge of that specialist language, and not many teachers are exposed to working environments outside the classroom. These issues have influenced the way specialist English is taught in schools. This type of course is usually known as English for Specific Purposes or ESP and there isn't ESP courses for almost every area of professional and working life. In Britain, for example, there are courses which teach English for doctors, lawyers, reporters, travel agents and people working in the hotel industry. By far, the most popular ESP courses are for business English.

Questions 31 to 34 are based on the passage you have just heard.

31. What is the characteristic of learners of special English?
32. Who needs ESP courses most?
33. What are the most popular ESP courses in Britain?
34. What is the speaker mainly talking about?

Passage 11

The first step to stop drug abuse is knowing why people start to use drugs. The reasons people abuse drugs are as different as people are from one to another. But there seems to be one common thread: people seem to take drugs to change the way they feel. They want to feel better or feel happy or to feel nothing. Sometimes, they want to forget or to remember. People often feel better about themselves when they are under the influence of drugs. But the effects don't last long. Drugs don't solve problems. They just postpone them. No matter how far drugs may take you, it's always a round trip. After a while, people who miss drugs may feel worse about themselves, and then they may use more drugs. If someone you know is using or abusing drugs, you can help. The most important part you can play is to be there. You can let your friends know that you care. You can listen and try to solve the problem behind your friend's need to use drugs. Two people together can often solve a problem that seems too big for one person alone. Studies of heavy abusers in the United States show that they feel unloved and unwanted. They didn't have close friends to talk to. When you or your friends take the time to care for each other, you're helping to stop drugs abuse. After all, what is a friend for?

Questions 35 to 37 are based on the passage you have just heard.

35. Why do some people abuse drugs?
36. According to the passage, what is the best way to stop friends from abusing drugs?
37. What are the findings of the studies about heavy drug users?

Passage 12

Bows and arrows are one of man's oldest weapons. They gave early man an effective weapon to kill his enemies. The ordinary bow or short bow was used by nearly all early people. This bow had limited power and short range. However, man overcame these faults by learning to track his targets at a close range. The long bow was most likely discovered when someone found out that a five-foot piece of wood made a better bow than a three-foot piece. Hundreds of thousands of these bows were made and used for three hundred years. However, no one is known to survive today. We believe that a force of about one hundred pounds was needed to pull the string all the way back on a long bow. For a long time the bow was just a bent stick and string. In fact, more changes have taken place in a bow in the past 25 years than in the last 7 centuries. Today, bow is forceful. It is as exact as a gun. In addition, it requires little strength to draw the string. Modern bows also have precise aiming devices. In indoor contests, perfect scores from 40 yards are common. The invention of the bows itself ranks with discovery of fire and the wheel. It was a great-step-forward for man.

Questions 38 to 40 are based on the passage you have just heard.

38. Why did man have to track his target at a close range when using a short bow?
39. What does the passage tell us about the long bow?
40. What do we know about modern bows?

Passage 13

There was once a man in South America who had a parrot, a pet bird that could imitate human speech. The parrot was unique. There was no bird like him in the whole world. He would learn to say any word except one. He could not say the name of his native town, Ketunnel. The man did everything he could to teach the parrot to say Ketunnel, but he never succeeded. At first he was very gentle with the bird. But gradually, he lost his temper. "You stupid bird. Why can't you learn to say that one word? Say Ketunnel or I will kill you." But the parrot would not say it. Many times the man screamed, "Say Ketunel, or I'll kill you." But the bird would never repeat the name. Finally, the man gave up. He picked up the parrot and threw him into the chicken house. "You are even more stupid than the chickens." In the chicken house, there were four old chickens, waiting to be killed for Sunday's dinner. The next morning, when he went out of the chicken house, the man opened the door. He was shocked by what he saw. He could not believe his eyes and ears. On the floor lay three dead chickens. The parrot was screaming at the fourth, "Say Ketunel, or I'll kill you."

Questions 41 to 43 are based on the passage you have just heard.

41. Why did the man lose his temper?
42. Who killed the three chickens?
43. Why was the man shocked at the scene the next morning?

Passage 14

In Britain, if you are found guilty of a crime, you can be sent to prison or be fined or be ordered to do community work such as tidying public places and helping the old. You may also be sent to special centers when you learn special skills like cooking, writing and car maintenance. About 5 percent of the present population are women. Many prisons were built over one hundred years ago. But the government will have built 11 new prisons by next year. There are two sorts of prisons. The open sort and the closed sort. In the closed sort, prisoners are given very little freedom. They spend three to ten hours outside their cells when they exercise, eat, study, learn skills, watch TV and talk to other prisoners. All prisoners are expected to work. Most of them are paid for what they do, whether it is doing maintenance or cooking and cleaning. Prisoners in open prisons are locked up at night, but for the rest of the time, they are free within the prison grounds. They can exercise, have visitors, or study. And some are allowed out of the ground to study or to do community work.

Questions 44 to 46 are based on the passage you have just heard.

44. What do we know about women prisoners in Britain?
45. In what way are open prisons different from closed prisons?
46. What do we learn about prisoners in Britain?

Passage 15

London taxi drivers know the capital like the back of their hands. No matter how small or indistinct the street is, the driver will be able to get you there without any trouble. The reason London taxi drivers are so efficient is that they all have gone through a very tough training period to get special taxi driving license. During this period, which can take two to four years, the would-be taxi driver has to learn the most direct route to every single road and to every important building in London. To achieve this, most learners go around the city on small motorbikes practicing how to move to and from different points of the city. Learner taxi drivers are tested several times during the training period by government officers. The exams are terrible experience. The officers ask you, "How do you get from Birmingham palace to the Tower of London?" and you have to take them there in the direct line. When you get to the tower, they won't say, "Well done." They will quickly move on to the next question. After five or six questions, they will just say, "See you in two months' time." And then you know the exam is over. Learner drivers are not allowed to work and earn money as drivers. Therefore, many of them keep their previous jobs until they have obtained the license. The training can cost quite a lot, because learners have to pay for their own expenses on the tests and the medical exam.

Questions 47 to 50 are based on the passage you have just heard.

47. Why are London taxi drivers very efficient?
48. How long does the training period last?
49. Why does the speaker think the driving test is a terrible experience?
50. Why do learner drivers have to keep their present jobs?

短篇文章听力答案

1. C) He had his foot caught between two posts in the river.
2. A) He jumped into the river immediately.
3. D) He thanked the young man and then ran away.
4. C) Controlled drinking helps people keep their wits as they are.
5. B) Pleased.
6. A) At a conference.
7. D) To join her father on Christmas.
8. B) She survived the accident.
9. C) To avoid the strong sunlight.
10. D) They took Julia to a village by boat.

11. B) He wanted to kill time before boarding the plane.
12. D) Clothes and scientific papers.
13. C) He had taken the woman's case.
14. D) Reasons for changes in family life in Britain.
15. A) Because millions of men died in the war.
16. A) The concept to "the family" as a social unit.
17. B) Those who expected to have several children but could only have one.
18. D) Because their parents want them to grow up as fast as possible.
19. A) Two types of only children.
20. C) Their parents expect too much of them.
21. C) They gave a special dinner for him.
22. D) He was deeply touched.
23. A) Sam's wife did not think that the company was fair to Sam.
24. B) They receive little or no support from public taxes.
25. C) Private schools run a variety of programs.
26. A) The churches.
27. D) She said she was wrongly accused of stealing.
28. D) A Christmas card.
29. B) She was shut in a small room for 20 minutes.
30. C) They still suspected that she was a thief.
31. D) They know clearly what they want to learn.
32. A) Professionals.
33. B) Courses for businessmen.
34. C) English for Specific Purposes.
35. B) To feel good.
36. A) To help solve their psychological problems.
37. A) They need care and affection.
38. C) Because it did not shoot far.
39. B) It was invented after the short bow.
40. A) They are accurate and easy to pull.
41. D) Because the bird failed to say the name of the town.
42. C) The pet bird.
43. A) The bird had finally understood his threat.
44. D) They are a small portion of the prison population.
45. A) Some of their prisoners are allowed to study or work outside prisons.
46. B) Most of them get paid for their work.
47. B) Because they have received special training.
48. D) Two years or more.
49. A) Government officers are hard to please.
50. C) They cannot earn money as taxi drivers yet.